584739

CW01171473

SETTING THE WATCH

Many liberals consider CCTV surveillance in public places—particularly when it is as extensive as it is in England—to be an infringement of important privacy-based rights. An influential report by the House of Lords in 2009 also took this view. However there has been little public, or academic, discussion of the underlying principles and ethical issues. What rights of privacy or anonymity do people have when abroad in public space? What is the rationale for these rights? In what respect does CCTV surveillance compromise them? To what extent does the state's interest in crime prevention warrant encroachment upon such privacy and anonymity rights? This book offers the first extended, systematic treatment of these issues. In it, the author develops a theory concerning the rationale for the entitlement to privacy and anonymity in public space, based on notions of liberty and dignity. She examines how CCTV surveillance may compromise these rights, drawing on everyday conventions of civil inattention among people in the public domain. She also considers whether and to what extent crime-control concerns could justify overriding these entitlements. The author's conclusion is that CCTV surveillance should be appropriate only in certain restrictively defined situations. The book ends with a proposal for a scheme of CCTV surveillance that reflects this conclusion.

Studies in Penal Theory and Penal Ethics: Volume 5

Studies in Penal Theory and Penal Ethics

A Series Published for
the Centre for Penal Theory and Penal Ethics
Institute of Criminology, University of Cambridge

GENERAL EDITORS
ANDREW VON HIRSCH, ANTHONY E BOTTOMS

Ethical and Social Perspectives on Situational Crime Prevention
edited by Andrew von Hirsch, David Garland and Alison Wakefield

Restorative Justice and Criminal Justice: Competing or Reconcilable Paradigms?
edited by Andrew von Hirsch, Julian Roberts, Anthony E Bottoms, Kent Roach and Mara Schiff

Incivilities: Regulating Offensive Behaviour
edited by Andrew von Hirsch and Andrew Simester

Previous Convictions at Sentencing: Theoretical and Applied Perspectives
edited by Julian V Roberts and Andrew von Hirsch

Setting the Watch: Privacy and the Ethics of CCTV Surveillance
Beatrice von Silva-Tarouca Larsen

Setting the Watch

Privacy and the Ethics of CCTV Surveillance

Beatrice von Silva-Tarouca Larsen

·HART·
PUBLISHING

OXFORD AND PORTLAND, OREGON
2011

Published in the United Kingdom by Hart Publishing Ltd
16C Worcester Place, Oxford, OX1 2JW
Telephone: +44 (0)1865 517530
Fax: +44 (0)1865 510710
E-mail: mail@hartpub.co.uk
Website: http://www.hartpub.co.uk

Published in North America (US and Canada) by
Hart Publishing
c/o International Specialized Book Services
920 NE 58th Avenue, Suite 300
Portland, OR 97213- 3786
USA
Tel: +1 503 287 3093 or toll-free: (1) 800 944 6190
Fax: +1 503 280 8832
E-mail: orders@isbs.com
Website: http://www.isbs.com

© Beatrice von Silva-Tarouca Larsen 2011

Beatrice von Silva-Tarouca Larsen has asserted her right under the Copyright, Designs and Patents Act 1988, to be identified as the author of this work.

All rights reserved. No part of this publication may be reproduced, stored in a retrieval system, or transmitted, in any form or by any means, without the prior permission of Hart Publishing, or as expressly permitted by law or under the terms agreed with the appropriate reprographic rights organisation. Enquiries concerning reproduction which may not be covered by the above should be addressed to Hart Publishing Ltd at the address above.

British Library Cataloguing in Publication Data

Data Available

ISBN: 978-1-84946-084-2

Typeset by Columns Design Ltd, Reading
Printed and bound in Great Britain by
TJ International Ltd, Padstow, Cornwall

To my husband Jorgen and my son Nicholas

Acknowledgements

My heartfelt thanks to Andrew von Hirsch for his inspiration and support. I am also very grateful to Mary Gower, Stuart Feather, Helen Krarup, and Ann Philips at the Institute of Criminology in Cambridge, who could not have been more helpful.

Preface

The lyrics of pop songs often reflect the Zeitgeist and current preoccupations.

Some years ago, 'Hard-Fi', hailed as the 'next major British band', released the album *Stars of CCTV*. Its eponymous title song had this somewhat frantic refrain:

> Every move that I make
> gets recorded to tape
> so somebody up there
> can keep me safe.
> I'm going out tonight
> I'll get my hair just right
> I'm always looking good
> for my spot light. . . .
> a winning smile up to the gallery,
> gonna get my face on the six o'clock news.*

Closed circuit television (CCTV) surveillance has found its way into British consciousness after all, in spite of the apparent indifference citizens display in the face of the CCTV phenomenon. While not directly an ethical discourse, the song has a message: the words not only capture today's obsession with getting noticed and famous, and how unquestioningly we have bought into the promise of security; they are also telling us that we should not be fooled—being watched by millions of cameras as we go about in public does something to us and it makes us change how we behave. In spite (or because) of its upbeat mood, the song is cunningly subversive. We want to challenge the naive and gullible simpleton with the winning smile. Is it not rather grating to think that every move gets recorded on tape? I may not always want the spotlight when I go out. And anyway, who is that somebody up in the gallery, and can he really keep me safe? How is it that my face could end up on the six o'clock news? If I have not got my hair just right, that could be rather embarrassing.

In my discussion of the ethics of public CCTV surveillance, or open-street CCTV as it is often called, I shall pursue this theme and try to unpick the questions the song raises in the minds of those who listen. My focus

---

* Stars of CCTV
Words and Music by Richard Archer
© Copyright 2005 BMG Music Publishing Limited.
All Rights Reserved. International Copyright Secured.
Used by permission of Music Sales Limited.

will be on the moral reasons why we should be entitled to object to being watched by CCTV cameras and the people behind them, and how to resolve the tension between this entitlement and our interest in being kept safe from crime. This requires four layers of analysis that will be spread over four chapters. In chapter one, I shall explain why a claim to an exclusive private sphere can also be upheld in a public space. Chapter two will show how CCTV surveillance interferes with this claim to a private sphere in public. In chapter three, I shall examine the purported countervailing justification of this interference by crime prevention objectives. Based on the foregoing analysis, chapter four will set out policy principles for the regulation of public CCTV, with regard both to its implementation and execution, and provide an overview and critique of the existing regulatory framework in the UK.

Beatrice von Silva-Tarouca Larsen
May 2010

Summary Contents

Preface	ix
Contents	xiii
1 Privacy Interests in Public Space	1
2 Does Public CCTV Violate Anonymity Interests?	41
3 Crime Prevention's Possible Legitimising Role	93
4 Policy Principles and the Regulation of Public CCTV Surveillance	147
Conclusion	185
Bibliography	187
Index	197

Contents

Preface ix
Summary Contents xi
Contents xiii

1 Privacy Interests in Public Space 1

I. The Concept of Privacy 2
   A. von Hirsch's 'three circle' theory and the right to anonymity 2
   B. The ethical principles underlying privacy 5
   C. The scope of the privacy claim 10
   D. The private versus public dichotomy 12

II. Is There a Claim to Privacy in Public Space? 15
   A. The 'neutral' concept of privacy 16
   B. Private territories in a public environment 18
      1. Material and situational access barriers in a public setting 20
      2. Conventions of discretion 21
   C. Normative reasons for the protection against unwanted scrutiny in public places 22
      1. The interest in the 'presentation of self' 22
      2. The interest in anonymity 24
      3. Moral dimensions of the conventions of 'civil inattention' 25
      4. Anonymity vis-à-vis the State 29

III. The Boundaries of Access Control in Public Spaces 30
   A. Spatial boundaries 31
   B. Normative boundaries 31
      1. Criteria for determining disclosure and access entitlements 32
      2. Material expectations in public space 34
      3. Suspension of anonymity 36

IV. Is There Scope for Anonymity in Late Modern Society? 36

V. Moral Concerns Raised by the Restriction of Anonymity and the Justification of Public CCTV Surveillance 38

2 Does Public CCTV Violate Anonymity Interests? 41

I. Modalities of Public CCTV Regimes and Their Modus Operandi 42
   A. CCTV technology 42

xiv *Contents*

	1.	Placebo cameras	43
	2.	Static cameras	43
	3.	Pan, tilt and zoom (PTZ) cameras	43
	4.	Mobile cameras	44
	5.	Cameras with audio capability	44
	6.	'Talking' cameras	44
	7.	Night vision cameras	44
	8.	Cameras with recording facilities	45
	9.	Multiplex analogue tape systems	45
	10.	Digital systems	46
		(i) Facial recognition systems	47
		(ii) Radio frequency identification (RFID) tags	49
		(iii) Algorithmic monitoring	50
		(iv) Automatic number plate recognition	51
		(v) Data sharing with public sector databanks	51
B.	Who is in charge of public CCTV surveillance?		53
C.	Surveillance practices		54
	1.	Active and passive monitoring	54
	2.	Access and reviewing policies	55
	3.	Directed surveillance	56
	4.	Choice of locations	58
	5.	Surveillance techniques	58

II. Is CCTV Just Another Pair of Eyes? — 59
 A. In what way is public CCTV surveillance different from real space appraisal? — 60
 B. How intrusive is CCTV? — 62
  1. Does CCTV surveillance intrude upon the presentation of self? — 63
  2. Is virtual scrutiny less invasive than physical scrutiny? — 66
   (i) The implications of 'distanciation' — 66
   (ii) The disempowering effect of the observer's inaccessibility — 69
  3. Is CCTV surveillance non-judgemental? — 71
  4. Is CCTV surveillance 'sanitised' by the observers' professional mission? — 74
  5. How does recording affect anonymity interests? — 77
   (i) The implications of the fixing of one's picture — 77
   (ii) Does the 'disembedding' effect reduce the impact of scrutiny of recorded footage? — 79
   (iii) Exposure to an uninvited audience — 81
   (iv) Recording without reviewing — 82
 C. Does public CCTV increase the pressure to conform? — 85
  1. How much control can be exercised through CCTV surveillance? — 86

		2.	Does CCTV surveillance only restrict our options to commit crimes?	89
3	Crime Prevention's Possible Legitimising Role			93
	I.	Models for Resolving Conflicts between Privacy Interests and Crime Prevention Objectives		94
		A.	Dworkin's 'rights as trumps' conception	94
		B.	von Hirsch's approach	95
		C.	The ECHR model for resolving questions of priority between privacy and public interests	98
	II.	The Value of Anonymity		103
		A.	What constitutes the weight of a right?	103
		B.	Examples of highest-ranking rights	104
		C.	The value of free speech	105
		D.	Placing privacy in the hierarchy of rights	107
			1. The importance of the protection of intimacy	109
			2. The value of privacy of the home	110
			3. Rating anonymity in public space	111
	III.	The Importance of Public CCTV's Crime Prevention Mission		117
		A.	Whose interests are served by public CCTV?	117
		B.	What are the objectives of public CCTV and to what extent are they concerned with crime prevention?	119
		C.	What is the persuasive force of the crime prevention arguments supporting public CCTV?	120
			1. Does public CCTV respond to an urgent need for enforcement?	122
			(i) Lack of guardianship in public space	122
			(ii) Fear of crime	124
			(iii) Probable cause for suspicion that crimes will occur	127
			2. How serious are the crimes targeted by CCTV?	128
	IV.	How Effective is Public CCTV Surveillance for Combating Street Crime?		130
		A.	Findings of empirical studies	130
		B.	What are the mechanisms by which CCTV sets out to combat crime and are they likely to work?	132
			1. Active interventions in crimes in progress	134
			2. Increasing the risks of detection and punishment for offenders	134
			3. Deterrence by making detection and conviction more likely	136
			(i) Do potential offenders realise that the probability of apprehension has changed?	139

			(ii) Would the potential offender take the altered risks of punishment into account when deciding to offend?	139
			(iii) Does the potential offender believe that there is a non-negligible likelihood of being caught as a result of CCTV?	141
			(iv) Would the potential offenders who commit crimes in public be willing to alter their choices in the light of perceived changes in the likelihood of being caught as a result of CCTV?	142
	C.	General conclusions about the potential effectiveness of public CCTV for combating crime		144

4 Policy Principles and the Regulation of Public CCTV Surveillance — 147

I.	Policy Considerations for Public CCTV Surveillance			147
	A.	Interference with people who are not suspected of wrong-doing		147
	B.	Preserving anonymity in public space		149
	C.	Preventive evidence collection		152
	D.	Covert CCTV surveillance		154
	E.	Placebo surveillance		155
	F.	CCTV's role in the fight against terrorism		155
	G.	CCTV for monitoring people inside their cars?		157
	H.	CCTV for catching shoplifters?		158
II.	The Regulation of Public CCTV Surveillance			159
	A.	The implementation of public CCTV schemes		160
		1.	Selection of locations	160
		2.	Proper budgeting and funding	160
		3.	Periodic operational review	161
	B.	The execution of surveillance		162
		1.	Informing the public	162
		2.	Audio surveillance	163
		3.	Night vision cameras	163
		4.	Passive versus active monitoring schemes	164
		5.	The reviewing of recordings	165
		6.	Identification of recorded individuals	166
		7.	Safeguarding the evidential value of recordings	169
		8.	Limited storage period for recordings	170
		9.	Safeguards for ensuring fair practice	171
			(i) Record keeping	171
			(ii) Layering controls for discretion	172
			(iii) Supervision and training	172

C.	The structure of the regulatory framework dealing with public CCTV surveillance	173
D.	The regulation of public CCTV surveillance in England and Wales	175
	1. Relevant regulations	176
	2. The achievements of the existing regulation	178
	3. The shortcomings of current regulation	180

Conclusion   185
Bibliography   187
Index   197

1

Privacy Interests in Public Space

CLOSED CIRCUIT TELEVISION (CCTV) involves observing people as they go about in public spaces that are open and accessible to everyone. This situation is different from the scenario one usually associates with a claim to privacy, lacking two important features: seclusion and intimacy. The person who is abroad in the streets does not set himself apart from the public domain and is in no position to exercise control over who is to be admitted to that space. As a rule, such a person would be in pursuit of mundane business, not engaged in activities of an intimate nature.

This has not prevented those who are critical of the unrestrained proliferation of CCTV from claiming that CCTV surveillance in public amounts to a violation of privacy interests. Even the most fervent advocates of CCTV do not deny that this is conceivable, and few take the position that privacy interests simply do not exist in a public space. However, not many attempts have been made to provide an analysis of why a person should have a right not to be watched when he has willingly subjected himself to being observed by a random audience, and why he should have an interest in privacy if he is engaged only in innocuous activities.

A theoretical framework has been put forward by Andrew von Hirsch in his article 'The Ethics of Public Television Surveillance'.[1] In section I. below, I shall summarise von Hirsch's ideas, comment on them and use them as a basis for developing my own conception of privacy in public space.

---

[1] A von Hirsch, 'The Ethics of Public Television Surveillance' in A von Hirsch, D Garland and A Wakefield (eds), *Ethical and Social Perspectives on Situational Crime Prevention* (Oxford, Hart Publishing, 2000) 57.

2 Privacy Interests in Public Space

I. THE CONCEPT OF PRIVACY

A. von Hirsch's 'three circle' theory and the right to anonymity

Andrew von Hirsch argues that whereas a person who visits open, publicly accessible spaces cannot object to others seeing him and taking perfunctory notice of him, he may nevertheless claim to go about without being identified and subjected to intense and prolonged scrutiny. Unless the person provokes special attention by the way he comports himself, he has reasonable expectations to be left alone and to remain anonymous. Prevalent norms of behaviour—'anonymity conventions' to use von Hirsch's term—limit the degree of mutual observation in public to momentary and casual appraisal. Closer approaches, such as eavesdropping on other people's conversations or trying to join in, or audio/video-taping them, would be considered inappropriate.[2]

For von Hirsch, the expectation of anonymity in public spaces belongs to the realm of privacy interests. These he defines as an entitlement to non-disclosure and protection from scrutiny by unchosen others, giving a person control over whose expectations he needs to satisfy. In von Hirsch's conception, there are three circles of activity where privacy has a role to play, with a differing kind of protection afforded to each circle. The narrowest circle concerns an individual's most personal feelings, expressions and relationships, and the intimate aspects of his body.[3] von Hirsch calls for the strongest protection against involuntary disclosure for matters belonging in this circle. A person should be able to keep his intimate life to himself or reveal it only to chosen others. For von Hirsch, intimacy interests are not restricted to the home; they can also extend to the public domain—to the extent that there occurs intrusive scrutiny of others' intimate business.

von Hirsch's second circle relates to the social and working sphere. Privacy in this context gives a person a right to withhold information about his life outside his professional functions, because he should not be answerable (eg to his employer) for choices and actions that lie outside those functions. Disclosure may reasonably be demanded as far as it is germane to specific aspects of the business at hand. Thus an employer would be entitled to know when his employee wishes to take his holidays, and for how long, but not what activities he plans to undertake while away from work. von Hirsch acknowledges that the dividing line between legitimate requests for information and what should be protected against

[2] *Ibid* at 64.
[3] *Ibid* at 63ff.

disclosure may be difficult to draw, as this second circle concerns relationships with chosen associates who by the nature of the association have a legitimate interest in having some idea of the kind of person with whom they are dealing. He does not elaborate on this subject, however, as it is of no particular importance in the context of public CCTV.

The first and the second circle have in common that the information to be withheld is of a certain personal quality and meaning, which is the usual domain of privacy interests.

It is with the third circle that von Hirsch moves beyond the traditional scope of privacy, by acknowledging an entitlement to freedom from scrutiny, irrespective of the type of activity a person is pursuing. He draws this broader notion of privacy from the conception of privacy as 'control over presentation of self', which, referring to Ervin Goffman's analysis of 'The Presentation of Self in Everyday Life',[4] is concerned with protecting a person's ability to affect how he presents himself to the world. This conception of privacy was developed by Thomas Nagel, Alan Ryan, David Feldman and Ferdinand Schoeman. In this view, the existing conventions of discretion are an important way of keeping under a modicum of control to whose expectations a person needs to respond, and whose curiosity he has to satisfy. 'Anonymity conventions', which govern our behaviour in public, dictate, von Hirsch explains, that a person going about in generally accessible places may be subjected to casual scrutiny, but should otherwise be left to pursue his business. People might find his behaviour silly or irritating, but anonymity conventions demand that they leave him in peace. This, von Hirsch argues, is particularly important in public, as it is there that a person has the least control over whom he will encounter, and he should not be or feel called upon to respond to the expectations of such unchosen others, who may have different and possibly uncongenial values and attitudes. Because they are strangers, with whom the person has not undertaken any dealings of any kind, they have no entitlement to disclosure, making the assertion of access control more straightforward than in a case of activities falling within the second circle, according to von Hirsch. Only if someone draws attention to himself by manifestly aberrant behaviour may closer scrutiny occur: 'Others need not have to pretend disinterest, when the behaviour strongly would impinge on an ordinary person's attention.'[5]

The anonymity conventions of public space, von Hirsch points out, have nothing to do with the intimate or otherwise sensitive character of the activities involved. One 'should leave free from intensive scrutiny even the

---

[4] E Goffman, *The Presentation of Self in Everyday Life* (London, The Penguin Press, 1990).
[5] von Hirsch, above n 1, at 64.

most innocuous forms of activity'.[6] A person should be able to go about in public without having to be concerned about the preferences of the other people he encounters, and he should be so entitled even if he is pursuing only mundane business. The latter fact could, however, have an influence on the degree of priority to be given to anonymity interests, von Hirsch concedes, suggesting (but without developing the argument) that concerns about intimacy might be given a somewhat higher priority.[7]

By focusing the notion of privacy upon the interest in going about one's business without being scrutinised, judged or held accountable, von Hirsch's theory overcomes the problems of those privacy theorists who isolate particular activities or states deserving protection. They tend to place too much emphasis on intimacy and emotional intensity, which can restrict privacy protection to a narrow range of subject matters, or else require far-fetched arguments to bring less charged situations under its auspices.[8]

von Hirsch's approach is to demystify privacy, and his sober appraisal of the interests at stake cuts through the copious literature and the sometimes fuzzy prose used for the discussion of privacy issues. It has enabled him to expand the conception of privacy beyond the traditional realms of home and intimacy, and to bring an important part of people's lives—their comings and goings in general public space—within its scope.

This would also be useful when applying the theory to the particular issues raised by CCTV, and would help with the evaluation of which underlying notions of privacy are involved and what degree of priority ought to be given to the specific privacy interests at stake.

Privacy, according to von Hirsch, is the entitlement to non-disclosure, the protection from scrutiny by unchosen others and the control over whose expectations one has to satisfy.[9] This, however, describes only the claim, not the rationale for protection. Why should others not be able to scrutinise me at will, and why should they not confront me with their expectations? What are the common ethical principles that link anonymity with the right to privacy? Existing anonymity conventions support and shape the claim, but they do not provide the rationale for it. While I agree with von Hirsch's analysis in principle, his discussion of the concept of

---

[6] Ibid.
[7] Ibid at 67.
[8] See Innes's discussion 'Intimacy: The Core of Privacy' in J Innes, *Privacy, Intimacy and Isolation* (Oxford, Oxford University Press,1992) 74ff. Innes defines privacy as an agent's control over intimate matters, but her conception of intimate matters as 'any act, actions, or activities drawing their meaning from the agent's loving, caring, or liking', implies that any act, action or activity can potentially be intimate. Showing that certain acts are imbibed with the agent's loving, caring or liking requires her at times to resort to convoluted reasoning.
[9] von Hirsch, above n 1, at 63.

anonymity is too briefly stated and would benefit from a more fully-developed treatment. To answer the questions raised by public CCTV, I believe it is necessary to go back to the ethical principles underlying privacy, and to establish the connection between those and a claim for anonymity in public.

B. The ethical principles underlying privacy

The concept of privacy is based on the idea that an individual should be entitled to claim sovereignty over himself. Privacy as a form of 'self ownership' gives a person a say over matters that are more closely connected with him than with any other person, and are therefore first and foremost his own concern. The rationale for this allocation is the acknowledgement of the inherent value of the individual and therefore his claim to be respected. As Feinberg puts it, 'to respect a person or to think of him as possessed of human dignity simply is to recognize his capacity to assert claims'.[10] An elementary claim of an individual is that he is his 'own' person, that his well-being, feelings and choices count, and that he should be entitled to fashion a life that is worth living from his own perspective.[11] To quote Rousseau, a person needs to be on good terms with his self, for it is 'the only man one can never be separated from'.[12]

To be one's own person implies that one is in charge of matters that are closely bound up with one's identity and one's body. It also means that a person is not treated like an object by others, to examine and meddle with as they see fit. Privacy is concerned with the degree to which we can control access to ourselves, exclude others from participating in our lives and refuse to accept their attention. A person must have a say over how closely he wants to get involved with other individuals and how much of himself he wants to disclose, for making distinctions in the way we engage with others is of fundamental significance in human relations. We practise it almost from the day we are born, and it plays an important part in defining ourselves in the social environment in which we live. It is a way of

---

[10] J Feinberg, 'The Nature and Value of Rights' in J Feinberg, *Rights, justice and the bounds of liberty* (Princeton, NJ, Princeton University Press, 1980) 145.

[11] Closed institutions often deliberately deny the inmates privacy as a part of a 'degradation and mortification ritual': E Goffman, *Asylums* (Harmondsworth, Penguin Books, 1961) 24. Apart from censure for the actions people have committed, the implicit message is also that the moral authority of people who have given reason to be detained is not trustworthy, and therefore they should not have space 'to be themselves'. They must submit to supervision, to prevent them from creating further harm, and to re-education, to have their ways changed.

[12] L Damrosch, *Jean-JacquesRousseau: Restless Genius* (Boston, Mass, Houghton Mifflin, 2006) 412.

creating and expressing special links, of establishing points of reference, of finding and cultivating allies in a hostile world.[13]

> The boundaries between what we reveal and what we do not, and some control over that boundary are among the most important attributes of our humanity.[14]

Access control creates zones where a person is free from uninvited scrutiny. The control over to whose expectations one needs to respond, which is at the core of von Hirsch's privacy-based interest in anonymity, refers to the reason why we find scrutiny uncomfortable. We know that scrutiny implies judgement by those who scrutinise us, and that they will inevitably bring their own expectations into action when taking our measure. To be accessible to others means to be subjected to their judgements about whether one has fulfilled their standards (or their expectations), and to a negative verdict if one has not. It is typical of human nature and a reflection of the social dimension of human existence to be concerned about how one is perceived by others. We are not immune to what others think about us: the response we get from others plays an important role in how we define ourselves, and whether we feel worthy and adequate. A presumed negative opinion is apt to cause self-doubt and insecurity. We also worry about how we are seen by other people because their opinion can have negative consequences for us. In the competitive environment of human relations it is important to make a good impression and not be seen in a disadvantageous light which may impair our actual standing, not only among those who scrutinise us but in wider circles too, because people talk and communicate their impressions to others who have not been present.

If we can chose our audience, we can control who can judge us and whose expectations we have to fulfil. Under those conditions our status as our own moral authority is preserved: the judges have not imposed themselves; we have put them in their position by admitting them, and thus

---

[13] It may appear that many people today no longer care about boundary control, as they seem to be parading their whole lives on Facebook and Twitter. The phenomenon of on-line networking is complex, however, and one must not jump to conclusions. Celebrities may seem to divulge the most intimate secrets on Twitter, but it could just be an exercise for maintaining their popularity, and they tend to take extreme care to shield their real lives and to keep fans at a safe distance. On Facebook, people create on-line personas for virtual relationships, but nevertheless continue to exercise boundary control in the real world. Even for Facebook there are access barriers and layers of exclusivity. Moreover, the intention of Facebook communications was that they would be seen by friends only—no one wants potential employers (or parents) to see what has been posted. It is only starting to dawn on people that they cannot control the circulation and that their on-line personas may have unwanted repercussions in real life. Recruitment firms and employers regularly check those sites for information on candidates and to see how they have presented themselves. Users are now advised not to post compromising photos of themselves, complain about their bosses, make disrespectful remarks about their company, tell indiscrete stories about others or spend work time signing up new friends. Facebook also undertook to introduce measures for improving the protection of privacy.

[14] T Nagel, 'Concealment and Exposure' (1998) 27 *Philosophy and Public Affairs* 4.

have exercised our sovereignty. An audience that imposes itself denies us that sovereignty, subjecting us to the judgement of people whose opinion we have not sought and whose authority we have not accepted.

Unwanted exposure is demeaning, not only because one is treated like an object whose wishes to exclude scrutiny are disregarded, as if they did not count, but also because one is denied the opportunity 'to get one's act together' and made to give more away about oneself than intended. We keep many aspects of ourselves to ourselves and reveal ourselves selectively. If we had to show everything about ourselves to everybody, it would leave us helplessly exposed. Being able to control when and how closely we are scrutinised, and to present ourselves to others in a way with which we feel comfortable, and thereby influence how we are judged, protects us from the shame and pressures unwanted access can entail. Moreover, fear of negative judgement influences the way we comport ourselves when we are within view of other people; it is inhibiting and might sway our choices in order to ensure their approval. Access control allows us not to worry about others' preferences and feel free to follow our own inclinations, to experiment and to expand.

Some suggest that privacy's real value is not so much in its importance for human dignity but in the crucial role it plays for personal autonomy, as realms of personal space are essential for the development of authentic self-identity. The reductionist literature challenges the wisdom of invoking privacy altogether, deemed a concept lacking a distinctive moral value. Sceptics, such as JJ Thomson, argue that the discussion about privacy should be 'reduced' to a discussion of other rights, because the interests subsumed under the privacy label are not bound together by a common conceptual core and can all be explained by referring to other rights, such as liberty, property rights, the right not be harmed, etc.[15] Thomson acknowledges nevertheless a 'right over the person' in the right to privacy 'cluster', treating it as analogous to the right one has over one's property.[16] Thomson calls this right an 'un-grand' right, implying that its value lags behind the grander right to liberty. I dispute the reductionist view and believe that privacy has its own distinctive moral value as a means to protect an individual's claim to be treated with respect for his person and all aspects that make it up—his body, his emotions and his preferences. Privacy may amalgamate aspects of other normative ideas, but none of those is complex enough to cover the whole spectrum where the individual's value and personal space are at stake.

Liberty values enrich the concept of privacy, just as privacy's dignity values can enrich the concept of liberty, especially in connection with

---

[15] JJ Thomson, 'The right to privacy' in FD Schoeman (ed), *Philosophical Dimensions of Privacy: An Anthology* (Cambridge, Cambridge University Press, 1984) 286 f.
[16] *Ibid* at 280.

questions concerning the freedom of the press. Individual autonomy or 'human freedom'[17] implies that a person should be able fully to realise his potential as an individual, and to give expression to his peculiar capabilities and preferences.[18] This also refers back to personal sovereignty and the individual's intrinsic value and his entitlement to respect. By this rationale privacy and autonomy are linked.[19]

Privacy also confirms the individual's moral authority as an agent, but freedom of choice is only one aspect of privacy. When there is a straightforward interference with personal choice by way of an express directive or a prohibition, privacy and liberty arguments are bound to merge. However, the rationale for the protection against unwanted scrutiny, namely to give a person the chance to present himself and allow him to choose what aspects of himself he shares with others, is in my view intrinsically dignity-based. That fear of negative judgement should not sway his choices is a secondary concern.[20] This latter concern becomes more pressing, however, when uninvited observers are representatives of the authorities, for while there may be no straightforward interference with the choices of the observed, the need to meet the expectations of the authorities is particularly acute.

The assertion that autonomy-based privacy is a less problematical or ambiguous concept than one invoking a human dignity rationale is unfounded. Human dignity is not more difficult to delineate than autonomy or other fundamental values we acknowledge. Paul Roberts warns that the tendency in US constitutional law to use privacy as the functional equivalent of autonomy to support controversial legal entitlements, such as the rights to abortion and euthanasia, undermines its value,

---

[17] Nagel, above n 14.
[18] In a number of high-profile cases in the US that were centred on the right to keep the Government from intervening in personal decisions, American courts relied on liberty as the rationale for privacy. See, eg, *Griswold v Connecticut* 381 US 479 (1965), giving rights of access to contraception; *Roe v Wade* 410 US 113 (1973), bringing the right to have an abortion under the umbrella of constitutional privacy; *Bowers v Hardwick* 478 US 186 (1986), affording privacy protection to homosexual practices and challenging the constitutionality of state 'sodomy statutes'. In the US the attachment to the doctrine of liberty is much stronger than the attachment to a doctrine of dignity, while the European conception of privacy is dignity-based. For a comprehensive comparison of the dignity-based European approach and the liberty-based American approach to privacy, see JQ Whitman, 'The Two Western Cultures of Privacy: Dignity Versus Liberty' (2004) 113 *Yale Law Journal* 1151.
[19] The European Court of Human Rights has made explicit reference to the connection between privacy and personal autonomy, holding that respect for private life is rooted in the 'physical and moral integrity of the person'. See *X and Y v the Netherlands*, Judgement of 26 March 1985, A.091,11.
[20] von Hirsch seems to suggest that his conception of anonymity privacy is dignity-based, by indicating that notions of autonomy could provide an *alternative* rationale to anonymity conventions; see von Hirsch, above n 1, at 64, fn 8.

as there is no moral right or legal entitlement to lead an autonomous life.[21] Raz denies the equation between respect for people and respect for personal autonomy. He argues that 'not everyone has an interest in autonomy … it is a cultural value, ie of value to people living in certain societies only'[22]. Moreover, autonomy is not always an issue in connection with privacy claims. Roberts instances the person in a coma, who is incapable of autonomous action but still has a claim for privacy, based on human dignity.[23] One does not have to go to the extreme of Roberts's example to make the point. There are things about a person that are not matters of choice; they could not be changed, even if the person wanted to change them. Unwanted access would therefore not jeopardise the person's autonomy, but it would be degrading and embarrassing for him to be exposed to an uninvited audience, who can see more than he wanted to disclose, and to become the object of their curiosity and judgement.

Privacy can be a source of conscious gratification for the individual concerned, but the claim not to be accessed by others at will is independent of subjective preferences. It is founded on the entitlement to respect for his dignity that any individual should have on the basis of his humanity. Therefore, even if a person is not aware of the scrutiny, the 'objective conception of well being'[24] of individuals entails an obligation for the onlooker to restrain his curiosity. One might even argue that human dignity cannot be waived, because it is an intrinsic aspect of humanity that must be respected, irrespective of whether it is valued or rejected by the individual person. Whether a person who exposes himself voluntarily in a way that society considers violates his dignity should be prevented from doing so or protected against the consequences, is another question.[25]

The recognition in law of concerns for personal dignity and privacy is linked to how much social policy has regard for individual rights.[26] An

---

[21] P Roberts, 'Privacy, Autonomy and Criminal Justice Rights' in P Alldridge and L Brants (eds), *Personal Autonomy, the Private Sphere and the Criminal Law—A Comparative Study* (Oxford, Hart Publishing 2001) 77ff.

[22] Raz denies the equation between respect for people and respect for personal autonomy. He argues that 'not everyone has an interest in autonomy … it is a cultural value, ie of value to people living in certain societies only': J Raz, *The Morality of Freedom* (Oxford, Oxford University Press, 1986) 189, fn 1. However, every individual has an interest in being treated with respect, irrespective of the society in which he lives.

[23] Roberts, above n 21, at 58.

[24] Roberts, above n 21, at 65.

[25] In France, the attitude of the courts was that 'private life must be walled off, in the interest of individuals and of good morals', and a French court once held that therefore any sale of nude pictures, even if instigated by the person himself, had to remain effectively voidable, because the person had momentarily 'forgotten his dignity'. See Whitman, above n 18, at 1176. While this doctrine, which dates back to the 19th century, is no longer maintained by the French courts, the protection of a person's private life remains notoriously strong in France, in particular against intrusions from the press.

[26] Schoeman argues that privacy evolves only 'when there is a high degree of social and economic specialisation, when this specialisation liberates individuals from dependence on

authoritarian society with a rigid code of conduct will give the individual less space than a pluralistic secular society. A liberal democratic system attaches great importance to the individual and his entitlement to assert claims, and it is not surprising that the progress of liberalism in Western Europe, which characterised the last decades of the 20th century, has led to the introduction of a statutory right to privacy in most national codes of law.

C. The scope of the privacy claim

A privacy claim is defined by three elements, which are often intertwined and contribute to each other, enhancing the claim. One is the subject matter itself: a privacy claim involves matters that pertain to the individual person. There is no conclusive list of what these matters comprise—they extend to a person's body, his inner life and ways of expressing his individuality in all their variety. The second element is the exclusion of others. This implies a degree of exclusivity in the person's dealings with others, or withholding of information from uninvited parties. There may be a clear demarcation of the space one claims for oneself, most in evidence and unequivocal if expressed by an affirmative act of concealment or seclusion. But exclusion can also be circumstantial: as von Hirsch observes, the anonymity of a public setting allows a person reasonably to expect to be left alone, and later I shall examine how far one can take this claim of non-disclosure. Exclusivity might also be based solely on normative considerations: personal matters that have special significance for the individual should be his 'turf' and he should be entitled to have sole charge of them.

A loss of privacy occurs when others gain unwanted access to the person. Access to the person can be by different means and take various forms. There is sensory access by touching, looking and listening, and other forms of making direct contact and cognitive access through knowing something about someone. There is also access by way of interference with personal sovereignty, denying a person choices pertaining to himself and his body. Depending on the form of access sought to be prevented, we distinguish between three basic types of privacy interests:

---

any group, and where social welfare and security come to depend as much on individual initiative as on cultural rigidity.' His thesis is that the interests of individuals that are promoted in liberal societies are feasible only in 'materially secure, functionally articulated, self-consciously adaptive social structures, where a variety of alternative groups exist and a composite system of values has replaced the strictly hierarchical value system': FD Schoeman, *Privacy and Social Freedom* (Cambridge, Cambridge University Press, 1992) 115ff.

a) The interest in protection against direct scrutiny and other forms of face-to-face interaction (sensory privacy).
b) The interest in controlling information about oneself (informational privacy).
c) The interest in making decisions about oneself without the interference of others (decisional privacy).

Sensory privacy usually relates to the physical sphere, and the control of access to this sphere is privacy in its most literal conception. Gaining first-hand experience from face-to-face interaction represents a more direct and intense form of access than the acquisition of abstract information about people. The quality of knowledge one obtains from observing people's appearance and behaviour is vivid and complex. It is 'the real thing' and has greater intrusive potential than the propositional knowledge of informational privacy, which is without a sensory experience and abstract and one-dimensional in comparison.[27]

Decisional privacy is usually invoked in cases when access to a person is non-material, by way of limitation of his individual autonomy. However, as explained earlier, unwanted sensory access can also affect individual autonomy by exercising pressure on the observed to conform to the observer's expectations.

The third element of a privacy claim pertains to the normative reasons for allocating control over the person to the person himself: the function of privacy is to protect a person's dignity and moral authority, and the restriction of accessibility must be linked to that rationale. Unwanted participation of others in matters that concern us as individuals should be restricted, if it has the potential to undermine our dignity and moral autonomy and denies us the respect that is due to an individual human being. This normative element is important for determining the boundaries of the private sphere in the absence of a clear physical demarcation, and plays a decisive part in defining private preserves that are conceptual and not spatial or fixed.

Privacy protects the individual *in* society by providing personal space and thereby encouraging individuality and personal expression, and *against* society by enabling him to resist the curiosity and interference of others.[28] It shields the individual against the others, as individuals and as

---

[27] Fried talks about the modulations in the quality of the knowledge, distinguishing between general and intimate facts. See C Fried, 'Privacy (A Moral Analysis)' in Schoeman, above n 26, at 210. David Archard points to another and much stronger modulation in quality, namely between the *knowledge* of a fact about a person (cognitive access) and *witnessing* him doing something (sensory access); see D Archard, 'The Value of Privacy' in E Claes, A Duff and S Gutwirth (eds), *Privacy and the Criminal Law* (Antwerp, Intersentia, 2004) 19ff.

[28] German doctrine distinguishes between three types of private spheres: (1) *Individualsphaere* (the individual sphere), which relates to the specific characteristics of each individual,

groups, and against the State, all of whom may, in different ways, intrude upon his personal sphere for the advancement of their own individual, societal or political interests. The protection against the encroachment of the State and its authorities is as central a function of the privacy claim as the protection against unwanted access by private individuals, and, in view of the disparity of power, more urgent. Privacy as a political concern limits the control of the State over the lives of individuals. In our society, the demands for knowledge and control in order to achieve optimum public welfare often conflict with the interests in secrecy, seclusion and anonymity of the individual member of the community. A core problem for privacy doctrine and jurisprudence today is to define the limits of individual accountability to the collective, and to hold off the erosion of the private sphere through 'the rise of the social'—Hannah Arendt's appropriately ominous term for the increasing demands made in the name and purported interests of the majority—with its pervasive notion of public significance.[29]

D. The private versus public dichotomy

Privacy doctrine draws a line between the private realm and the public realm of a person's life, based on the understanding that the private realm designates the 'central redoubt where one can escape the grip of others',[30] whereas in the public realm some degree of access and participation by others must be accepted. The distinction between the private and the public realm of life is, however, far from self-evident. The terms 'public' and 'private' appear descriptive but are in fact normative. Conceptual analysis is required to fill the terms with meaning. We need to know the framework and what is being contrasted, and on what basis the contrast is being drawn. One fundamental divide between private and public is made on the basis of what is hidden or withdrawn versus what is open, revealed or accessible. Another variant is the distinction between what is individual, or pertains only to an individual, versus what is collective, or affects the interest of a collectivity. A third approach is sectoral, contrasting the notion of public direction and administration with the private sector and

---

(2) *Geheimsphaere* (the secret sphere), ie that part of life about which only those who are very close to a person can know, and (3) *Privatsphaere* (the private sphere), which refers to everything relating to an individual's life which he does not want to share unconditionally with others, and for which he should be able to exercise access control. (1) protects the individual *in* society; (2) and (3) protect him *against* society. See AH Robertson (ed), 'Privacy and Human Rights' in *International Colloquy about the European Convention on Human Rights, Brussels 1970* (Manchester, Manchester University Press, 1973) 34.

[29] H Arendt, *The Human Condition* (Chicago, Ill, University of Chicago Press, 1958) 38.
[30] Robertson, above n 28.

market economy.[31] The different dimensions of the private–public divide often overlap, and confusion can arise because of the different meanings of the terms for each such dimension. In section II, I shall show that the conception of privacy in public space combines elements of spatial, societal and sectoral dimensions.

Classic 19th-century liberalism promoted the private–public distinction to limit State power and to foster individual liberty. The idea was that those aspects of civic life that did not interfere with the political objectives of the State, and thus had no public significance but were of personal significance, should be outside the reach of the State. Such separation is not acknowledged by totalitarian or theocratic regimes: all aspects of people's lives, however personal, come under the political prerogative. However, even under liberal democratic rule, the definition of the private versus the public is a matter of continuous debate. Boundaries are often hard to draw, as Schauer has demonstrated in his examination of whether 'public figures can have private lives', and what information concerning politicians should be subject to a right of non-disclosure and what belongs in the public domain.[32] An individual rarely leads a solitary existence, and what concerns him often involves other people; and they may have an interest in knowing about such concerns and having a say in them. The political and social agenda regularly interferes with individual interests in spite of their private connotation, such as private property, personal life style choices, domestic and family matters.

Today the public realm is expanding as political objectives of the State are no longer primarily focusing on ideological and military concerns but increasingly are defined by reference to social control and community protection—against crime or health hazards, for example—and from that perspective few aspects of civic life remain that have no public significance.[33]

---

[31] But see Weintraub, who identifies four major organising types of public/private distinction: (1) the liberal-economistic model distinguishing between State administration and market economy; (2) the 'classical' approach to the public realm in terms of political community and citizenship; (3) the anthropological approach which sees the public domain as a sphere of fluid sociability defined by conventions; (4) the distinction between the family and the larger economic and political order. This list is not exhaustive; there are other versions of the dichotomy. J Weintraub, 'Varieties and Vicissitudes of Public Space' in P Kasinitz (ed), *Metropolis: Centre and Symbol of our Times* (Basingstoke, Macmillan, 1995) 29.

[32] See F Schauer, 'Can Public Figures Have Private Lives' in EF Paul, FD Miller Jr and J Paul (eds), *The Right to Privacy* (Cambridge, Press Syndicate of the University of Cambridge, 2000) 294.

[33] In the UK, new powers of entry into people's homes and private property increased from fewer than 10 in the 1950s to more than 60 in the 1990s. The laws are often vague, providing sweeping power to officials and little protection for private citizens. See H Snook, *Crossing the Threshold: 266 ways the State can enter your home* (London, Centre for Policy Studies, 2007).

Under traditional privacy doctrine, the boundaries of the home were viewed to constitute a natural divide between private and public space. Private space was inside the home, public space outside. In English law this idea was taken to its extreme, as privacy (and often also autonomy) was seen as the preserve of real estate ownership that came with the entitlement to territorial domain. Those who were not property owners had no claim, and the infringement of privacy was bound up with the violation of material property rights. Remedies were for trespass to land or personal property. The finding of the British courts that the use of tapping devices by the police to intercept a person's telephone calls was not unlawful as it did not involve physical trespass against the plaintiff's property, was only a logical, if very literal, reading of that approach.[34]

Whilst 'the prototypical private preserve is no doubt spatial and perhaps even fixed',[35] the emphasis on property ownership overlooks the fact that privacy is not purely a spatial concept, and that the idea of 'self ownership' follows a different logic from property ownership. A focus on spatial ownership would mean that although de facto one may enjoy privacy, privacy is not acknowledged as a value in its own right. As long as I can rely on material control of a certain space, I do not need to bother with the more elusive claim to sovereignty over the person. I can exclude others by virtue of physical boundaries, and people must stay off my property because of my material control, not out of respect for my dignity and personal sphere. The shortcomings of this approach become apparent when for some reason material control and access barriers fail to protect against intrusion. This is a problem today, for factual enjoyment of privacy is under threat since physical seclusion is no longer a guarantee of protection from scrutiny in an age of technical devices designed to overcome access barriers. Moreover, the new technologies make it possible to scrutinise people surreptitiously, thus depriving their targets of the opportunity to object and take countermeasures against the intrusion. In the light of these developments it has become necessary to rethink the scope of the protection of privacy, and to test the meaning and significance of privacy in various situational contexts.[36] This process also implies a re-evaluation of traditional boundaries and conceptions of public and private space.

To determine the scope of decisional privacy, it has always been necessary to use normative evaluation, for the private sphere is here not

---

[34] See *Malone v Commissioner for the Metropolitan Police* [1979] 2 All ER 620, Ch 344.
[35] Goffman, above n 4, at 29.
[36] In the field of intellectual property, technological developments have caused a similar need for re-assessment of the scope and protection of copyright. New copying technologies are increasingly threatening the rights of creators and their enjoyment of the benefits of their work, and today legislators are forever trying to catch up with the challenges of the digital age.

delimited by spatial boundaries but by the conceptual boundaries of moral autonomy which the individual should enjoy in matters that are closely bound up with his person and his life.[37] The exclusion of others is thus a normative decision.[38] But while it is widely recognised that seclusion and physical barriers have little significance in this context, the historical notion of property and material access control still lingers when it comes to delimiting sensory privacy. There seems to be some reluctance to abandon the prototypical fixed spatial preserve, and with it the (fictitious) idea of a literal distinction between public and private space, of being able to draw a clear line between the private location where one's claim to exclusivity is tangibly demarcated, and the open public space where no claim to exclusivity exists.

Nevertheless, the restriction of an entitlement to private space to domestic dwellings has already been abandoned by modern privacy doctrine for some time. Access control and protection against unwanted scrutiny are now being granted to people in various places outside their homes. They include localities that are open to the general public, such as offices, restaurants and similar venues, for it was recognised that the same normative considerations—namely human dignity, personal identity, and physical and moral integrity—that speak for access control and non-interference in a domestic setting also support an exclusive redoubt in these relatively public settings.[39] However, the claim to privacy in the street and entirely public spaces seems to represent a greater challenge.

II. IS THERE A CLAIM TO PRIVACY IN PUBLIC SPACE?

The privacy claim I am discussing is one of sensory privacy: should we be protected against unwanted scrutiny and sensory access when we venture

---

[37] The US Supreme Court has interpreted the Fourth Amendment providing freedom from search and seizures in the home as also providing freedom from interference by the State with decisions concerning a person's own body (see above n 18), by way of analogy between the intrusion into the privacy of the home and the intrusion into the privacy of the personal physical sphere.

[38] Similarly, intellectual property is not based on material control over a creative work, which is lost once a work is published, but on the allocation of exploitation rights to the creator of a work, for reasons of fairness (it is the fruit of his labour and imagination) and social utility (to encourage creativity).

[39] In *von Hannover v Germany*, 4004-VI EUR.CT.HR, the Strasbourg Court declared that there is a zone of interaction of a person with others, even in a public context, which may fall within the scope of 'private life'. In *Niemitz v Germany* (1993) 16 EHRR 97, it was held that the search of law offices had been a violation of Article 8 ECHR, arguing that the sphere of professional activities does not, in principle, fall outside the protection afforded by Article 8: 'The object of Article 8 is essentially that of protecting the individual against arbitrary interference by the public authorities. The scope of the right to respect for private life is such that it secures to the individual a sphere within which he can freely pursue the development and fulfilment of his personality.' (para 55).

abroad? It is undeniable that the streets and public places are 'public' locations in the sense that they are open to everybody, but the presumption that this rules out any form of privacy would be jumping to a conclusion without having done the conceptual work. I agree with Schauer that it is more conducive for analysis to avoid the labels 'public' and 'private' altogether. Instead, I want to explore whether there is scope for a personal sphere in public places, and a moral entitlement to its protection, grounded in the ethics of privacy. My arguments will be based on the broader conception of privacy, building on the 'Right to Anonymity' and 'Control over the Presentation of Self'.

A privacy claim, as discussed in section I.C. above, is characterised by three elements:

a) the subject matter (which concerns a person's body, feelings and manner of comportment);
b) the exclusion of others; and
c) the moral entitlement to exclude others.

The first question to investigate is whether we are dealing with subject matters of a private nature when a person is engaged in mundane pursuits that have no particular intimate significance. Is a person's personal sovereignty and dignity at stake when he performs ordinary activities and there is nothing intrinsically embarrassing about those activities? The second question is whether there is scope for access control when we are in full view and plainly accessible. Have we not relinquished that control by going out and mingling with others? How does one determine the boundaries of the private sphere in a communal space in the absence of clear spatial 'markers', ie 'signs of some kind by which the claim to a personal preserve is made visible'?[40] Lastly, I shall examine whether we have a moral entitlement to expect people to 'stay away' when we are in a public environment. Where does one draw the line between engagement and exclusion when one shares a public place with others?

A. The 'neutral' concept of privacy

There are many matters which are personal to the individual: a person's thoughts, emotions, physical appearance, body, voice, his preferences, how he expresses himself and relates to others, the way he leads his life and what has happened to him in the course of it. The spectrum is wide and reflects that the individual manifests himself in many ways and forms of expression. The question is, how widely should one draw the circle for

---

[40] E Goffman, *Relations in Public. Microstudies of the Public Order* (London, The Penguin Press, 1971) 41.

matters where a person should be entitled to take charge and to exclude others? Andrew von Hirsch distinguishes three circles of privacy, affording differing degrees of protection to different, concentric circles of activity: the inner and intimate life, the social and working life, and a person's activity in public (see section I.A. above). This distinction may be useful to delineate different types of privacy interests, but it does not define what qualifies as private subject matter. Nevertheless, it posits that privacy interests can exist in any context, since the three spheres in fact encompass the whole spectrum of a person's existence.

There is a conception of privacy I shall call the 'intimacy' conception, which requires that in order to qualify as private, the matters relating to the person need to be of an intimate physical or emotional nature. It is most in evidence in cases of decisional privacy, when the focus is on issues of personal autonomy. The entitlement to resist certain interferences with personal decisions is often based on the intimate nature of the issue and the fundamental importance the decision may have for a person. (Matters concerning family life seem to be viewed as having emotional and intimate charge as well as fundamental significance by definition). Perhaps the threshold for a claim to decisional privacy is raised so high in order to avoid creating, via the privacy argument, the general entitlement to autonomy 'through the backdoor' that alarmed Paul Roberts.[41] However, a state of physical or emotional exposure seems for many to be also a *conditio sine qua non* for an entitlement to protection against unwanted scrutiny. Thus the refusal to acknowledge privacy interests in public is often connected with the trivial nature of the activities and the lack of intimate insights gained by observers.

It is true that a person is most in need of control where issues of intensely personal significance are concerned. The closer something is bound up with one's identity, the worse one would suffer from outside interference. Similarly, the need for protection against unwanted scrutiny is greatest when a person is physically or emotionally exposed. Onlookers might see the person in an unflattering condition and tend to feel superior. Deprived of protective armour, one is vulnerable, and uninvited attention could be embarrassing and humiliating. In our cultural environment it is still the prevailing view that to be observed in a state that evokes man's animal nature (nudity, sexual intercourse, excretion) is demeaning. This also applies to situations when a person is not in a position to control himself, which is viewed as a quintessential human ability, distinguishing him from animals and the prerequisite for man's personal sovereignty. There are therefore particularly strong reasons to shield the intimate physical sphere of the body from scrutiny to protect a person's dignity.

---

[41] See above n21.

Moreover, the taboo surrounding the aspects and activities relating to this sphere has the additional function of protecting the onlooker too from exposure to the 'primitive' side of human nature, which is also assumed to be embarrassing for him as a fellow human being.

However, it is not only uninvited scrutiny of intimate aspects that is disrespectful, and personal autonomy becomes an issue not only when fundamental choices are at stake. An individual also defines himself through trivial decisions, and to do so without shame or pressure to change is not unimportant for his well-being. If self-determination is the rationale for decisional privacy, there is no logic in distinguishing categorically between important and unimportant matters as long as they relate directly to the person and his chosen self-expression. (The personal importance of the subject matter may play a decisive role for the weight of the privacy interest, however, which becomes relevant if it conflicts with others' individual or communal interests.)

There can be no doubt that when someone scrutinises my appearance, what I do and how I behave, he captures something of my person, my individual way of being, whatever I do and wherever I am. Like von Hirsch, I view the idea that a privacy claim can arise only with regard to emotionally charged, intimate or family matters as unduly narrow, and subscribe to a more 'neutral' concept of privacy. To limit individuals' prerogative of disclosure to intimate matters would deprive people of the chance to exploit the full spectrum of distinctions and variations in personal contact when relating to others, and force them into undesired closeness. Taking a neutral stance means that one does not look at the state a person is in but rather asks whether the person has been accessed. Thus one avoids both the delimitation of the private sphere based on speculations about subjective sensitivities, as well as a forced spatial concept of privacy that relegates the claim to specific locations where we are expected to be engaged in intimate business. The broader notion of privacy as 'control over the presentation of self' implies that others should have no claim to more informed knowledge about me or get more closely involved without my invitation than the circumstances dictate. Focusing on access does not mean that privacy is treated solely as a physical dimension. There is also a conceptual side to the claim to be protected against unwanted access, requiring an evaluation of the situation and the context of a person's engagement with others, and a normative assessment of whether one can reasonably expect to exclude them.

B. Private territories in a public environment

Privacy, as I have stated above, requires a degree of exclusivity and reservation in one's dealings with others. The question is whether it is possible to maintain an exclusive sphere when one is in a public place in full view of whoever else is there. Have I relinquished control over who has sensory access to me by choosing to go abroad; or how closely have I become involved with the other people, and how much knowledge are they able to claim about me?

When I step out in public, I must presume that I shall encounter other people. I have to put up with their presence as I cannot claim the space to myself, and do not know whom I will meet. Andrew von Hirsch puts special emphasis on the fact that the people one meets in public are 'unchosen' others, which, he says, makes it particularly important to determine how much they may impose their expectations on one another. I may not have chosen the individual people I meet, but I have nonetheless chosen the company of others and accepted a random audience. However, despite my unquestionable exposure—people can see me—I have not engaged unconditionally with the people I encounter, or implicitly accepted to share a great deal about myself. Although I have made myself generally accessible when I mingle with others, I retain personal preserves, which I can withhold from the others and defend against them if they overstep the boundaries.

Ervin Goffman has identified eight situational and egocentric 'territories of the self' that are not staked out geographically and fixed in place but move around with the individual.[42] In public space, those that matter most concern the 'egocentric preserve'—the physical and mental sphere that revolves around the individual: the 'personal space' that directly surrounds him; the 'use space' that he needs for his immediate instrumental needs (such as crossing the road, or moving on); 'the sheath' of skin and clothing which covers his body; 'the possessional territory' of the personal effects he carries with him; 'the information preserve' of the facts he has not disclosed; and 'the conversational preserve' or the choice of those to whom he wants to talk.

Goffman is an empiricist observing social practices, and his account of the territories of the self is descriptive without value judgement; but his account can also help to explain them in terms of their normative function. To an important degree a person is also able to exercise boundary control

---

[42] Goffman, above n 40, at 28ff. Goffman's eight 'territories of the self' comprise: (1) Personal Space: the space surrounding an individual. (2) The Stall: a well-bounded space to which individuals can lay temporary claim (seat, table). (3) Use Space: the territory around or in front of the individual claimed for instrumental needs. (4) The Turn: the order in which a claimant receives a good of some kind relative to other claimants. (5) The Sheath: the skin that covers the body and the clothes that cover the skin. (6) Possessional Territory: any set of objects that can be identified with the self and arrayed around the body (personal effects, handbags). (7) Information Preserve: the set of facts about himself to which the individual expects to control access while in the presence of others (this is the preserve which according to Goffman is traditionally treated as 'privacy'). (8) Conversational Preserve: the right of an individual to exert some control over who can summon him to talk.

through his own initiative and by taking advantage of circumstantial conditions. I shall first examine the material and situational access barriers in public space, and then analyse the significance of the social practices ensuring the enjoyment of individual exclusive preserves in public.

1. Material and situational access barriers in a public setting

Material access barriers in public space are provided by physical obstacles that prevent others from perceiving aspects of the person that are not openly displayed. A person can conceal himself under protective layers of clothing, behind sunglasses, by arranging his hair so that it hides the face, by wearing different types of head gear or face masks, or cover up completely under a burka. To prevent other people from listening in on a conversation, he can keep his voice down, or he can refuse to talk to them, to give information and to get drawn in by them. He can also take advantage of existing screening facilities and hide from view. In doing so, a person can send clear signals of demarcation to bystanders that these preserves of the self are not intended for sharing. There may not be fixed spatial boundaries, but territories of the self can nevertheless be closely guarded, requiring an act of purposeful transgression by others for gaining access to these concealed and often intimate spheres.

Circumstances such as traffic, weather, poor light and material obstacles that block the view impede scrutiny. Factual access barriers may also result from the natural limitations of sensory appraisal. People are only able to view each other from their particular position and only so long as they stay within each other's sight, or listen to a conversation only if they are within earshot. As a rule they can see who can observe them and take that into account. They can make sure not to give away too much about themselves, and look for cover. The ephemeral nature of the impression people gain of each other is an important exposure-reducing factor. The image is fleeting and cannot be re-examined. It is available only while the person to whom it relates is physically present and only to those who are co-present, ie in the same place at the same time. This limits the audience and gives one a degree of control over the type of audience one has to confront, rendering it somewhat foreseeable and manageable.

Interaction plays an important part in safeguarding the territories of the self in public. People can defend the territory of their body and the space immediately around it, ward off intruders, refuse to engage with someone and deny requests for information. If someone pesters them with more than customary curiosity, they can take steps to impose a distance by giving that person a hard stare, shooing him away, getting out of his sight or soliciting the help of others.

However, situational access barriers and personal markers indicating one's claim to certain personal preserves do not guarantee boundary protection. They can be overcome not only through technology, but also through stealth and by reckless and intrusive behaviour. Essentially, we also depend on the cooperation of the others to acknowledge and respect our territories of the self. We can expect such cooperation, because the conventions that set the code for our comportment in public stipulate discretion, distance and non-interference.

2. *Conventions of discretion*

Andrew von Hirsch calls the rules of discretion that are specific to the interaction of people in public 'Anonymity Conventions'; Goffman speaks of 'Conventions of Civil Inattention'[43]; and Nagel refers to the 'Conventions of Non-Acknowledgement'.[44] Anonymity conventions, von Hirsch explains, dictate

> that there should be only casual and momentary scrutiny, which means that the person can go about his or her business with little reference to the expectations of other observers.[45]

Ruled out are intrusive curiosity (drawing too close; following; trying to overhear a conversation), surreptitious observation (so that the observed is not taken unawares and can adjust his behaviour if he wishes) and identification requests. Closer scrutiny is permissible only when a person calls attention to himself by manifestly aberrant behaviour.

I think it is necessary to specify public space etiquette even more precisely and to give the full particulars of what is deemed intrusive. The terms 'civil inattention' or 'non-acknowledgement' better capture the spirit of the complex social ritual than 'anonymity', as it is not just a question of leaving a person unidentified by name or personal data.[46]

von Hirsch has stated the core principle for street encounters: One does not show more than a passing neutral interest in one's fellow passers-by. Other rules follow from that: One does not participate in or seek to listen to other people's conversations, nor ask personal questions and try to become familiar with them. One looks at another fleetingly and (circumstances permitting) from a reasonable distance. This way people get only a superficial impression of one another, and are not made to give away more than what they display voluntarily; no one can claim to arrive at an informed opinion about the other person. It is also considered improper to violate the factual and physical impediments a person relies on for

---

[43] E Goffmann, *Behaviour in Public Places* (New York, Free Press, 1963).
[44] Nagel, above n 14, at 7ff.
[45] von Hirsch, above n 1, at 64.
[46] To be anonymous literally means to be 'of unknown name'; the *New Oxford English Dictionary* also defines it as meaning 'impersonal and unindividuated', and I am using anonymity in this sense of the term.

guarding his personal preserves, to barge in on someone who is attempting to screen himself, or to take photos of people against their will and to use binoculars or zoom lenses. Another rule is that members of the crowd are to be treated as part of the crowd. Picking out an individual and making him the target of special attention would be rude and inappropriate. A person who goes out in public must put up with being seen, but he can reasonably expect to be left to his own devices and not be singled out or made the subject of comment. He cannot prevent people he encounters from forming a—perhaps negative—opinion about him, because it is impossible to control people's thoughts, but people are supposed to keep these opinions to themselves. It is not done to communicate one's judgement to the person concerned, or to confront him to discuss it.

I want to examine whether there is a normative entitlement underlying these social practices of discretion in public space. Why should a person's wish for exclusive territoriality in public override the wish of others to invade it?

C. Normative reasons for the protection against unwanted scrutiny in public places

1. *The interest in the 'presentation of self'*

Goffman conceived his 'Theory of the Presentation of Self' by observing that people spent much of their lives acting out different roles, showing different aspects of their 'self', depending on the particular setting ('region'), in an effort to give the appearance that their activity in the region maintained and embodied the required standards. The role is

> tailored to the requirements of the occasion ... projecting a given definition of the situation ... and fostering the understanding that a given state of affairs obtains.[47]

Role playing is not devious, observes Goffman, but a way of compartmentalising and coping with the varied expectations to which we have to respond. It would be overwhelming if we had to be everything to everybody at the same time. It is therefore important, Goffman argues, that a person should be able to determine how he presents himself to the world without being answerable to his present audience for matters that lie

---

[47] Goffman, above n 4, at 19.

outside the scope of the business at hand.[48] As von Hirsch says, 'a tolerable existence is one in which not all one's activities, even of a quite routine nature, are everyone's business'.[49]

Goffman wrote *The Presentation of Self* in the late 1950s.[50] At that time, the code of behaviour and appearance was strict, and standards were exacting. Some of the conventions of the more regimented society of previous generations were still in force. People tended to dress up when they went out, behaved formally and with restraint. Keeping up appearances is important in a society with low levels of tolerance. To be caught straying from the code would entail social disapproval, if not intervention by the authorities. In public, in particular, people had to comply with conventional standards; and if they failed, they risked being reprimanded and might even be compelled to change their behaviour.

Goffman's emphasis on the 'presentation of self' has to be understood with these consequences in mind. Most people moved in geographically limited circles, where they were known, at least by sight, to many of those they encountered, and the impression they made mattered for their standing in the community. One had to present a respectable image that showed one to be in compliance with the rules. Conventions of discretion meant that one would not be the subject to intrusive curiosity, as long as one maintained appearances. This eased the stress of conformity and gave people a fair chance to pass muster.

In the pluralistic and secular societies of today there remain few standards of appearance or rules of comportment in public. People may sport the oddest clothes, and behave in strange and uninhibited ways in the streets, without encountering much attention or disapprobation. Keeping up appearances and presenting the right image still matters within one's peer group and social circle, because one's status within that group depends on a favourable impression; but in the streets, the impression one makes is of much less consequence. For the most part, one does not know the people, may never see them again and need not care much about their opinion. The emphasis as regards an entitlement to privacy in public has shifted from the interest in controlling the presentation of self, to the interest in disappearing into the crowd and not being personally acknowledged or confronted—to the interest in anonymity.

---

[48] *Ibid*, ch 3.
[49] von Hirsch, above n 1, at 63.
[50] To set the scene for his theory, in the introduction to his book Goffman quotes at length from William Sansom's satirical novel *A Contest of Ladies*. Its hero, Preedy, is a man about town in an English seaside resort in the 1950s, whose life is composed of a series of social roles. Always looking and acting the part, Preedy's life runs smoothly, until he takes the role of 'ardent suitor' to its logical conclusion by getting married. Too late he realises that he is now forever landed with the infinitely more demanding role of 'devoted husband'.

2. The interest in anonymity

Anonymity, the unidentified and impersonal existence we mostly lead when we are in public, is a condition of modern life. It is a result of migration from small communities, whose members knew and therefore took an interest in each other, to new, bigger and more densely populated places, where people are strangers to each other. Lacking a common point of reference, and aided by the flow and volume of comings and goings, they pass through the public arena without much interaction. Encounters remain impersonal and aloof. People have come to count on the anonymity the public space has to offer, and value it, in spite of the isolation and loneliness that come in its wake. To be submerged in the collective eases the burden of individual accountability. It provides an escape from the intensely personal examination and demands to which a person may be subjected on the domestic front, and from the challenges he faces in his professional life.

In small communities, one must still expect to be recognised and acknowledged, but even people who know each other often prefer to preserve the impersonal nature of the public space and to benefit from the neutrality it affords.[51] One could argue along the lines of Goffman's 'Theory of the Presentation of Self' that the 'self' a person presents in the street is today determined by a presumption of anonymity: one engages with others on impersonal terms only and does not expect to be individually accountable. As a consequence, one can afford to take less care with appearance and be less guarded in one's behaviour. Anonymity claims more space for the individual, and relies on a higher degree of discretion than the presentation of self. The expectation that in the normal course of one's stay in public, encounters with others will remain at arm's length, incorporates elements of all three interrelated aspects of privacy, namely secrecy, solitude and the claim to receive only cursory attention.[52] This last aspect—the claim to receive only cursory attention—is a serviceable definition of anonymity on its own, but anonymity also comprises something of the other aspects. There an element of secrecy, or room for concealment, for it is implied that what is not obvious is left hidden, and of solitude, in the sense that the audience is qualified. By mingling with people in a given space one has given access to those who are co-present, but has not accepted an audience of other people elsewhere.

---

[51] In Cambridge, it used to be the unwritten rule among academics not to greet each other in the street.

[52] Ruth Gavison considers each of these elements as constituting a distinct independent form of privacy, anonymity being the claim to receive only cursory attention. However, she also states that the concept of privacy is richer than any definition centred round only one of these elements. Gavison, 'Privacy and the limits of law', in FD Schoeman (ed), Philosophical Dimensions of Privacy: An Anthology (Cambridge, Cambridge University Press, 1984)51.

3. Moral dimensions of the conventions of 'civil inattention'

Andrew von Hirsch remarks that the everyday conventions concerning anonymity in public places are supported by a moral entitlement to anonymity:

> The convention that there should only be casual and momentary scrutiny protects a person from having to respond to the unchosen audience encountered in public, some of whom may have different and uncongenial values.[53]

The interaction between conventions of anonymity and the normative justification of anonymity needs to be explored in greater depth. What role do moral considerations play in the development of convention? The question could also be reversed: What is the role of social practices in the context of the moral argument? I shall try to unpick how the two are connected.

Conventions are informal social norms that regulate various modes of interaction, especially social interaction in everyday life. Their requirements incorporate and acknowledge certain interests and values. Conventions of discretion are designed to curb curiosity and to limit people's involvement in other people's affairs. They are based on notions of civility and tact, which take into account people's feelings and pride, and the recognition that respect for the individual sometimes calls for leaving a person to his own devices and sparing him uninvited attention in order not to embarrass, importune or constrict him. This is in effect the rationale for privacy, and therefore it is fair to say that conventions of discretion respond to and endorse a moral claim to privacy. By restricting unwanted scrutiny and recognising personal preserves in public, the social rituals express an unspoken consensus in favour of privacy and its underlying values.

The rules of conventions of discretion are based on what Rawls calls 'consensus values', ie values that will be respected by diverse social groups in spite of otherwise conflicting concepts of the good. The consensus values of tolerance, respect for physical integrity and equal respect among the plurality of social groups have generated rules of fair procedure for the settling of conflicts and the acceptance of diversity in the modern pluralistic society.[54] Conventions of discretion offer pragmatic solutions for complex situations. They fill in the either too abstract or too personal notions of respect, dignity and autonomy, and make privacy a workable concept in everyday life.[55] The yardstick for what represents an attack on

---

[53] von Hirsch, above n 1, at 63f.
[54] See J Rawls, 'The idea of overlapping consensus' (1987) 7 *Oxford Journal of Legal Studies* 1ff.
[55] It is up to legal doctrine to translate civility rules into workable concepts in a legal context.

dignity cannot depend on personal sensitivity. Each individual has his own code of honour and his personal sensitivities where he can be easily wounded. One person may feel embarrassed when someone listens in when he sings in the bathroom, but does not mind being seen in the nude; whilst another is quite happy to discuss his innermost emotions, but wants to keep a low profile on a 'bad hair' day. Rules for social relations do not respond to idiosyncratic needs but are made for identifiable groups of people with standard requirements. Conventions of discretion reinforce certain cultural taboos, by responding to beliefs that certain aspects of human life should not be publicly exposed—with the corresponding dictate not to look at them. This helps to ensure that those 'backstage' areas in fact stay removed from the public eye.[56] The degree to which discretion is practised reflects the moral and political climate of a society. The fact that today we can count on such a high level of inattention in public, is an expression of the liberal and secular character of modernity and the prevailing endorsement of individual well-being and personal autonomy. The regulatory power of conventions is derived not only from the shared values, but also from the shared interest of the group in adhering to the rules which benefit all.

As an integral part of social practice, 'civil inattention' has contributed to the creation of a conceptual personal space without physical seclusion. It is interesting to note that conventions of discretion only really take effect when there are no physical access barriers, or when those fail to protect. When a person is physically secluded, his inaccessibility is primarily due to territorial sovereignty. When I lock the door to my apartment, others can get to me only by forcibly intruding, and they leave me in peace largely because gaining entry would require a major effort and entail risks of retaliation. I enjoy privacy as a result of my entry control, not because of the consideration of others. Conventions of discretion, however, allow me privacy when I do not have that degree of control over my environment but depend on the cooperation of others for my personal sphere. Conventions institutionalise this cooperation through the 'mutual protective devices'[57] of rituals of polite distance.

The concept of exclusive preserves in spaces that are accessible to others is not new, and appears to have been feasible and compatible with the common use of those spaces. In the past this may have been for many the only way of enjoying privacy, since until fairly recently few could claim an exclusive space of their own and life took place in communal settings. For many this continues to be the reality. Conventions of discretion create invisible barriers and personal preserves, even while one is surrounded by

---

[56] This idea is further developed by Schoeman, above n 26, at 119.
[57] A Giddens, *The Consequences of Modernity* (Cambridge, Polity Press, 1990) 83.

other people. Protection from scrutiny thus extends not only to what cannot be seen, but also to what 'should not be seen' out of respect for the individual. The exclusion of others is due not to physical obstacles but to a normative stance, which allocates personal territoriality to me and dictates to those around me to back away from it, because that preserve is central 'to my subjective sense of selfhood, my ego and the part of me with which I identify my positive feelings'.[58]

Goffman's 'territories of the self' that a person carries with him can all be linked to this rationale. Preserving the territories of the self is a condition for maintaining one's dignity and physical well-being when one is amongst people. 'Personal space' makes room for my physical presence, protects me from feeling encroached upon and allows me to be comfortable. Even more important is that people stay away from 'the sheath' which covers my body. What happens to my body and its immediate surroundings is foremost my concern, because I am the one who feels it and suffers from its consequences, and it is my 'self' that is on display. The closer to the skin the intrusion gets, the more it violates my self-ownership. It is also prone to embarrass me and make me fearful of what people might think about me. 'Possessional territories' that are 'identified with me and arrayed around my body',[59] like my handbag or briefcase, are really an extension of my personal space and part of me, and therefore I should control access to them. 'Use space' acknowledges my entitlement as an individual who counts, to get my share of the space available to everyone, and to use it for the instrumental needs that correspond to the general purpose.[60] 'Information' and 'conversational preserves' permit us to determine how we relate to others and how much we want to open ourselves up to them. Having a say over how closely we get involved with others is at the core of our interest in privacy, and counts in particular when we share space with a random group we did not choose or do not know.

Conventions of discretion protect the individual in public locations from the humiliation, embarrassment, inconvenience or unpleasantness of unwanted access. All rules of public space discretion go back to this rationale. One should not stare at a person, even if he is in full view,

---

[58] Goffman, above n 40, at 60.
[59] *Ibid* at 38.
[60] The remaining two of Goffman's eight territories of the self, 'The Stall' (a seat or table, or other well-bounded space to which one can lay a temporary claim) and 'The Turn' (the claim to receive goods in a certain order), also incorporate the basic idea of human dignity in the sense that an individual should be treated as someone who counts and who can make claims. If I occupy or reserve a place that is at the public's disposal, others should take note of my presence and not act as if I were not there or had no claim to it. Similarly, I should be served when it is my turn, for to pass me over would be like treating me as if I did not exist or had a lesser right to be served than others.

because this might embarrass him and amounts to treating him as an exhibit. Fleeting appraisal means that people receive only a superficial impression and not much substance by which to judge each other. A passing glance merely skims the surface of a person without threatening his dignity and turning him into the spectator's object. The rule of non-confrontation is a protection against insults and pressure to conform. Strangers, to whom one owns no personal consideration or allegiance, have no right to impose their standards and expectations, and should not tell me to my face whether I suit their preferences. Without communication and confrontation, I would not become aware of an unwelcome judgement; and even if I did sense it, I can ignore it as long as I am not personally addressed. Moreover, the embarrassment experienced in any circumstances when one is confronted with a judgement about oneself (even if it is positive) would be acerbated by the fact that there is an—often large—audience to witness it. To be singled out and addressed would not only mean being made answerable *in front of* an audience, but would also involve the audience as judges and make one answerable *to* an audience. The need for protection against the pressures to conform is particularly urgent in public places, considering the exposed position of an individual when he is outnumbered by potentially hostile strangers. Public space etiquette helps one to stand one's ground, for the veto of close scrutiny and uninvited approaches means that there is less reason to be concerned about their judgement.

Apart from promoting intrinsic values, conventions usually also have a pragmatic regulatory function.[61] Civil inattention is prescribed not only to protect the dignity and autonomy of the individual, but at the same time to diffuse potentially explosive encounters of people of different cultures and clashing convictions massing in limited space. A code of discretion reduces friction. Problems arise when people take too much interest in each other: they become insistent and personal, start to find fault, criticise, offend and take offence. This provokes aggression and recriminations. If a code of discretion did not exist, people would not simply tolerate intrusive behaviour; they would take protective measures of their own, perhaps to the point of physically preventing others from crossing over into their

---

[61] The Cambridge greeting code referred to in n 50 above provides a solution to the problem posed by the high number of academics circulating in a small area. If the social graces had to be observed at every encounter, too little time might be left for research. New rituals of discretion constantly develop as new social scenarios present themselves. A more recent example is a practice that has evolved following the introduction of credit card security codes, requiring the customer to tap in his secret personal number into a terminal held out by the cashier. After verifying that the card is suitable, the salesperson demonstratively turns his back to indicate his discretion, and remains in that position until the customer has finished entering his code.

preserves. Anonymity conventions promote a harmonious solution. They neutralise the atmosphere in public and create the distance that is essential for peaceful coexistence.

The basic rules for discretion have remained fairly constant over the years: one should not spy on people, or eavesdrop on their conversation; one should respect someone's signals of demarcation and not use tricks to overcome their access barriers; one should not physically importunate someone; and one should not embarrass people by staring at them. However, we cannot rely on social conventions alone to provide the just measure of discretion required to preserve human dignity and individual autonomy, and the fact that discretion is not much practised by a society does not annul the normative reasons for protecting privacy and anonymity interests. But it says something about the moral code of the society, and the value it attributes to the individual, if those entitlements are not endorsed. In an authoritarian society, for example, the thriving of individuality is not a salient concern, and direct or indirect pressure to conform is exercised readily, especially when behavioural standards are broken publicly. It would be seen as an act of defiance that might have a corrupting effect on general morals if it went unchallenged. Even in a liberal society, deviations from norms that might be acceptable in private are less likely to be tolerated if a public display is made of them.[62]

4. *Anonymity vis-à-vis the State*

Conventions, it should be noted, are a form of civil self-regulation: they are mutual protective devices that derive their binding power from the shared interests and the relative equality of those who engage with each other. This creates a 'give and take' balance, which allows for flexibility suited to dealing with complex and varying situations. 'Civil inattention' is a fitting expression for the civilian practice of discretion, civility being a virtue among fellow members of society but not a concept one would use in connection with the exercise of State power. The territories of the self, the rules of discretion and their rationale are valid, however, whether one deals with members of the public or representatives of the authorities. Boundary control against the intrusion of the State is as much needed in the public arena as it is in secluded places, especially as in public one is not screened off and out of sight but easily accessible. Anonymity is the antidote against

---

[62] Gay lovers who are openly affectionate in public still risk harassment. Although homosexuality is no longer unlawful in the West, some parts of society continue to consider homosexuality morally wrong. The slapping of children, although against the law in some countries, may be tolerated if it happens at home (as long as there are no signs of excessive abuse), but if it occurs in a public locations, bystanders or the police might interfere.

the controlling powers of the State. The practice of 'non-acknowledgement', which like 'civil inattention' means 'leaving a great range of potentially disruptive material unacknowledged and therefore out of play',[63] is the mark of a liberal regime. However, one cannot rely on social rituals to enforce anonymity and 'non-acknowledgement' claims against the State. Conventions do not bind the authorities. There is no mutuality of interests, and the civilian sanctions of disapprobation, reprimands and other forms of pressure, that members of the public can visit upon each other for breaches of social protocol, have little bite when applied against the State. Boundary control vis-à-vis the State needs special protection through institutional guarantees, but conventions of discretion can provide the model for the authorities concerning how to deal with people in public and how to manage

> the distinction between foreground and background, between what invites attention and a collective response and what remains individual and what may be ignored.[64]

III. THE BOUNDARIES OF ACCESS CONTROL IN PUBLIC SPACES

A general feature of privacy interests that do not pertain to a fixed enclosed space is their circumstantial variability. The boundaries of access control can be situational and temporary. They may be the result of factual restrictions, or they may be dictated by certain legitimate expectations of the other users of the space. If privacy is 'the set of conditions where people are relatively free of obligations to those outside their immediate circle',[65] privacy in public operates under a somewhat different set of conditions. The more we interact with others, the less we can claim freedom from obligations. Those with whom one 'co-mingles' in the street are not part of one's 'inner circle', but they nevertheless are within the circle of one's immediate surroundings, and that may entail certain responsibilities towards them. There are also spatial boundaries limiting the territories of the self in public. I shall first discuss the spatial boundaries and then examine the normative boundaries, and the extent to which legitimate expectations of other users may trump anonymity interests.

---

[63] Nagel, above n 14, at 6.
[64] *Ibid* at 8.
[65] D Feldman, 'Privacy-related Rights and their Social Value' in P Birks (ed), *Privacy and Loyalty* (Oxford, Clarendon Press, 1997) 26.

A. Spatial boundaries

The boundaries of the territories of the self depend on external factors—Goffman lists population density, location, type of social occasion as examples[66]—and keep shifting according to the circumstances at hand. While the principle of entitlement to a personal preserve in public is a moral, not a spatial, issue, what may be a question of 'feet or inches' is its realistic range. Anonymity conventions aim to mitigate the impact of one's exposure in public, but they cannot impose unreasonable restrictions. There are factual limitations to the amount of physical personal territory available in public, affecting particularly the claims that have a strong spatial aspect, like the claim to personal space around a person and 'use space' for one's instrumental needs. Physical encroachments, often quite intimate ones, occur invariably when space is scarce (eg in the Underground at rush hour). What makes them neutral from a privacy perspective, and distinguishes them from wilful intrusion, is that getting close to the other person is due to external circumstances; because it is not a chosen intrusion, it connotes no disrespect, even though the closeness may be unpleasant and embarrassing.[67]

Spatial restrictions do not annul the control over other territories of the self, such as the objects one carries around, or the informational and conversational preserve, although in given circumstances concessions may have to be made with respect to each of them too. Certain behavioural restraints of anonymity conventions, however—namely, that you do not stare or express your opinion about people—come into their own in situations of enforced closeness, and their observance is particularly commended.

B. Normative boundaries

The question of the normative boundaries of our exclusive personal spheres arises whenever our activities bring us into contact with other people. When do matters that relate to ourselves—our physical and mental identity—cease to be only our own concern, and when does 'our business' becomes also the business of other people such that we may no longer exclude them? Boundaries may be dictated by certain legitimate expectations of the other users of the space which might entitle them to check and judge those they encounter as to whether they have fulfilled them.

---

[66] Goffman, above n 40, at 31.
[67] However, if people take advantage of the enforced proximity to obtain even more intimate contact, say by 'feeling up' their neighbour, they do act wilfully and disrespectfully, and thereby violate privacy interests.

Moreover, situations might occur during a person's stay in the public arena, when it would not be wrong for the other individuals, or the State, to intrude on his territory, and their right to disclosure could trump his interest in anonymity.

1. Criteria for determining disclosure and access entitlements

In his analysis of the second circle of privacy interests, the social and working life, von Hirsch suggests that disclosure of information may reasonably be demanded for aspects germane to the business at hand.[68] This makes sense for the following reasons: In my working life, the audience I have chosen are those whom I encounter in the course of my work and who are affected by my work. By offering my labour and skills, I have implicitly agreed to expose myself to their judgement. My employers and clients have a right to expect that my work is up to standard, and to obtain information as to whether I possess the necessary competence. This does not mean they must know and judge everything to do with me. There are large parts of my life that have nothing to do with my professional performance and therefore should be off limits. In a professional context, the type of audience I have chosen is one for my professional performance, but I have not asked them to judge my other qualities as a human being, and my personal profile and history that are unrelated to my work do not concern them as long as those are of no consequence to them within the given context.

This statement sounds reasonable enough, but it glosses over some questions. Schauer goes to great length in analysing the conceptual and normative dimensions of the public's interest in the revelation of facts about government employees and people seeking public office.[69] How far should the right to disclosure be stretched? Schauer's distinction between materiality issues and relevance issues is pertinent, and not just in respect of candidates for public office. Material information, Schauer explains, concerns the qualities and qualifications necessary to perform a job. The question of materiality implies an analysis of what the job actually *is*, and which qualities or qualifications are material to perform it. Employers (and the public) have a justified interest in disclosure of material qualifications and qualities, Schauer holds; but he acknowledges that there may be differences of opinion as to what qualities are material for a job, and even more so for holding a particular public office.[70] Extending the claim for

---

[68] von Hirsch, above n 1, at 63.
[69] Schauer, above n 32, at 293.
[70] A distinction may have to be made between *direct* materiality and *collateral* materiality, and a more complicated moral analysis is needed to decide if an employer should be entitled to information about issues that are *collaterally* material for the employment. For example,

information to relevant facts penetrates much deeper into personal territory. It means asking what other traits may be causally or indicatively relevant to determining whether people have the material qualifications required for the job, and expecting to be told whether the candidate has these traits or not.[71] Considering that people have wide-ranging conceptions as to what traits are causally relevant to determining ability for a job, relevance issues are open to personal and potentially arbitrary judgement. Schauer argues convincingly that in a voting context, a right to know whether a candidate possesses certain traits that are relevant in the eyes of certain voters might be morally defensible.[72] However, these arguments are specific to the democratic entitlement of voters to indulge their preferences, and do not apply in a standard employment situation. Privacy protection against unwanted disclosure of personal information in the professional sphere could largely be eroded if employers could demand to know about personal traits or habits of a candidate that in their eyes are relevant to determining whether he has the material qualification. The extreme scrutiny of their private lives that political candidates have to endure in the name of voters' 'right to know' gives one an idea of where this might lead.

The criteria for disclosure entitlements developed by von Hirsch and Schauer are applicable not only to informational privacy. Their model has general merits for the task of defining the boundaries of privacy when people enter into transactions and relations with each other, as they do when they share the public space. The question whether and to what extent access for others is material (I prefer this term to the more inclusive 'germane', which is closer to 'relevant') for the shared business at hand, is more to the point than the standard distinction of privacy doctrine between 'self' and 'other-regarding' conduct. The concept of 'other-regarding' conduct has to be treated with caution, not only because of its elasticity, in which it is comparable to 'relevant', but also because it shifts the focus to the concerns of the community without asking how important those concerns might be.

von Hirsch opines that while in the second circle it may be difficult to resolve what information should or should not be protected from disclosure, the entitlement of non-disclosure is more straightforward in third-circle relationships between people in public space:

---

should it be legitimate to enquire about candidates' exercise regime to assess their likely state of health, since this could affect the company's insurance premium? I think not, because the question intrudes far into personal terrain, has nothing remotely to do with the actual performance of the job, and the employer's interest in keeping the insurance premium low is not as important as the employees' interest in being free from pressure to exercise.

[71] Schauer, above n 32, at 300.
[72] *Ibid* at 308ff.

> The second circle concerns relationships with chosen working and social associates who have certain legitimate matters to transact with the person involved ... whereas the third circle concerns *strangers*—those with whom the person has not undertaken dealings of any kind.[73]

This statement is not entirely accurate. The people I encounter in the street may be strangers, but since I share a space with them, I have in fact undertaken certain dealings with them, and this should entitle them to have certain legitimate expectations concerning me. This means that my claim of non-disclosure is no longer as simple as von Hirsch suggests and that the scope of access entitlements of others has to be determined. The decisive criterion is again, I believe, materiality: I have to submit to scrutiny and judgement as to whether I fulfil expectations pertaining to aspects that are 'material to the business at hand'. In the following section I shall examine what that implies and how these expectations may affect anonymity.

2. Material expectations in public space

In public space the 'business at hand' is the safe accommodation of many people in the same place and their simultaneous use of the available space. Strangers or not, what people in the street can legitimately expect from each other—and material to the business of sharing public space—is that those who use it do not threaten and harm others; material also is that they do not claim too much of the shared space for themselves, and thereby obtrude on the personal preserves of others and their instrumental needs.[74] The question is how much scrutiny is necessary to ascertain whether the people around us fulfil the material qualifications? Obtrusive behaviour is self-evident and impossible to miss. Reassuring oneself of a person's 'lack of hostile intent' towards others, to use Giddens's term,[75] according to common social practice takes no more than a passing glance, and must not jeopardise anonymity. The assumption implied in that rule is that hostile intent can be spotted relatively easily and instantly. We know, however, that people's outward appearance alone is not an entirely reliable indicator of their intentions. The rule really means that unless a person has manifested hostile intent, by way of threat or initiation of harmful acts, he is presumed to be harmless and will not be subjected to closer investigation.

---

[73] von Hirsch, above n 1 at 63f.
[74] Goffman distinguishes between two types of territorial offence: *intrusion*, where one person encroaches on another's preserve and thereby functions as an impediment to the other's claim; and *obtrusion*, where a person makes over-extensive claims to personal space, causing others to feel that they themselves could be seen as functioning intrusively, even though they believe this is not the case; Goffman, above n 40, at 50.
[75] Giddens, above n 57, at 81.

It takes a considerable leap of faith to practise anonymity. As Giddens observes, 'civil inattention is a fundamental aspect of trust relations'.[76] People are given the benefit of the doubt that they fulfil material expectations and qualify as 'safe' users of public space. Only if they do something obviously threatening will they lose the trust and have to reckon with focused scrutiny. To wait for the manifestation of hostile intent means taking a risk; by then harm may already have been caused, or it may be too late to stop people in their tracks.[77] Trust plays an important part too in this respect: trust in civic self-reliance, trust that the other bystanders lend support, trust that the threatened harm is of a kind that can be thwarted or which does not cause irreversible damage, trust that the offender is impressionable and that he can be overcome by a common effort.[78] Even if community cooperation is not organised and members of the community no longer accept an obligation for the good behaviour of each other,[79] ordinary citizens have always played an important part in maintaining public order.[80]

There may be circumstances in which the basis for trust is lacking: if a street is deserted, there is little prospect of community solidarity and one has to be more circumspect. In a lonely encounter, the interest lies in anticipating events, for if the other person has hostile intentions, one's only chance to avoid harm could be to take flight, and the sooner one realises this, the greater the chance to escape. Instead of waiting for evidence of harmful intentions, it is advisable to look out for evidence of traits that might be indicative of dangerousness. This brings relevance issues into play; but broadening the scope for reassurance does not have to affect anonymity, as long as one does not go about it in an intrusive manner. Social practice does not permit this, for moral reasons (if there is no show of hostility, people are entitled to anonymity) as well as pragmatic reasons (close scrutiny and the implied suspicion is offensive and might provoke a fight). Anonymity conventions show how to go about checking without intruding, not only for individuals, but also for the authorities. Pragmatic reasons may not be pertinent when the authorities do the policing, for people have to defer to the powers of the State, but this does not confer an

---

[76] Ibid at 88.
[77] Obtrusive behaviour does not cause the same problems, as it is usually an ongoing process, which can be corrected by challenging the person to give up his excessive demands.
[78] All of this is somehow summed up in the classic appeal to bystanders to 'stop thief'!
[79] The medieval institution of 'frankpledge' (a Saxon term), a form of private policing organised by the community, relied on the principle that all members of a community accepted an obligation for the good behaviour of each other and contributed to maintaining order. See TA Critchley, *A History of Police in England and Wales*, (London, Constable, 1978) 34.
[80] See J Shapland and J Vagg, *Policing by the Public* (New York, Routledge, 1988). Activities include challenges to suspicious individuals and low-level sanctions, such as blocking obstructively parked cars.

36 Privacy Interests in Public Space

entitlement on the authorities to intrude on people in public. The normative boundaries are also binding for the State, but a formal mechanism is needed to warrant that the State adheres to them.

3. Suspension of anonymity

In the face of dangerous events such as crimes, accidents or disasters threatening a public location, or in the wake of such events, it becomes material for everyone's safety to identify the cause and source of the danger, to prevent the escalation of damage and to mitigate the effects. Anyone visiting public places, as I have contended above, incurs a degree of responsibility for the safety of the place. This responsibility evidently implies that one must abstain from harmful behaviour, but it also means that people can be expected to cooperate with efforts to avert harm when the shared space is being threatened by extraordinary and imminent dangerous events. In those circumstances common sense dictates civil *attention* rather than *inattention*, and the claim to anonymity recedes, for to bring the situation under control, closer scrutiny and supervision of those present, and restraints on personal autonomy, may be required.[81]

IV. IS THERE SCOPE FOR ANONYMITY IN LATE MODERN SOCIETY?

We associate the entitlement to anonymity, and the social practices that ensure it, with modernity and the liberalism, individualism and personal freedom that have characterised this period. Over the last decade a process of re-evaluation of political and social credos has been taking place, which has also affected the attitude to anonymity. It is now increasingly questioned whether the claim to anonymity can still be defended under present social conditions, or whether it has been exploited and taken too far.

Communitarians claim that the liberal emphasis on individual autonomy and privacy interests disregards the responsibilities individuals owe to the community.[82] The streets are viewed as a quintessential part of 'the social',

---

[81] Under Art 13, § III, of the German *Grundgesetz*, the authorities are permitted to intrude into people's homes without a special mandate (*Ermaechtigungsgesetz*), if it is to prevent obvious present and serious dangers to the community and individual lives (such as when there is a fire). The idea behind that exception is that the guidance of the law can be waived if a situation is manifestly dangerous, and if anyone can see the need and justification for an intrusion. See BGH Neue Juristische Wochenschrift (NJW) 1991, 2651, and comments by K Amelung, 'Zur strafprozessualen Verwertbarkeit von Videoaufzeichnungen ohne spezialgesetzliche Ermaechtigung—BGH, NJW 1991, 2651' (1993) 3 *Juristische Schulung* 196.

[82] See, eg, M Sandel, *Liberalism and the Limits of Justice* (Cambridge, Cambridge University Press, 1998) and A MacIntyre, *Whose Justice? Which Rationality?* (London, Duckworth, 1988). *Cf* Duff, whose liberal communitarianism seeks to combine 'normative

the sphere where people are accountable to the community and where the need for management and control ought to curtail anonymity considerations.

For many persons, the public space has come to represent a hostile environment that inspires fear and insecurity. A common theme today is that the idea that the public peace of cities can be kept primarily by 'an intricate almost unconscious network of voluntary controls and standards among the people themselves ... and enforced by the people'[83] is not valid anymore. Voluntary standards of civility are no longer the norm, and the old informal rituals of enforcement no longer work, it is argued. Moreover, where once it was necessary to carve out a space for the individual in public, individuals have now extended their territorial demands in public beyond their due, treating the public space as their private space. Absorbed in their own world they encroach on the space of others, who do not dare to fight back. There is a feeling that people have resorted to excessive discretion to shield themselves against aggressive invasive and obtrusive behaviour (and involuntary voyeurism and eavesdropping), and fearful of negative reactions they are no longer prepared to defend public order.

The increase of street crime has also prompted doubts whether the implicit trust in people's harmlessness which has formed the basis of anonymity conventions is still warranted. Inattention is dangerous in urban environments nowadays, the reasoning goes, and waiting for the manifestations of hostile intent would be to leave it too late to prevent harm. A passing glance is no longer sufficient to ascertain that our material expectations in public are fulfilled, for in our informal, pluralistic society appearances convey no distinct message or quick clues about people's intentions.[84] In pre-modern times it was in fact easier to make assumptions based on appearance, for looks, dress and manners gave away a person's background and status. Strangers stood out; and as they could not be gauged so readily and, being outsiders, could not be presumed to endorse the same values or feel solidarity with the community, they were consequently scrutinised more closely. Today distinctions are blurred and it is much more difficult to judge a person from the way he looks. The youngsters wearing hoods and chains and other 'tough' attire are unlikely to be all juvenile delinquents; but some might be, and people are scared.[85]

---

individualism with a communitarian metaphysics': RA Duff, *Punishment, Communication and Community* (Oxford, Oxford University Press, 2001) ch 2.

[83] Jane Jacobs quoted in S Cohen, *Visions of Social Control: Crime, Punishment and Classification* (Cambridge, Polity Press, 1985) 217, fn 42.

[84] How is one supposed to check people for absence of hostile intent when they wear burkas and face masks?

[85] 'Topman', a high-street clothing brand for young men, once described its new look for the season as modelled after a teenager 'looking for something for his first court case', while House of Fraser has called a clothing line 'Criminal'. When not in uniform, Etonians are hard

38 *Privacy Interests in Public Space*

The Labour Government had been advocating severe cuts in personal liberties and a return to regulations, discipline and supervision to fight street crime and anti-social behaviour. The 1998 Crime and Disorder Act made community safety a core issue of government policy, expanding the powers of the authorities and the police for dealing with public order issues. Since then, further barriers were removed in the 2002 Review of the Act, and the Home Office was continually advocating adding more powers, implying greater restrictions for civil liberties.[86] The balance between rights and responsibilities has to be readdressed and the public arena reclaimed for the community, and if that comes at the expense of personal space and anonymity, so be it, has been the slogan of politicians.[87] Anonymity plays into the hands of those with hostile intentions, it is claimed, and contributes to the shortfall in guardianship and protection from harm affecting the public space today. One of the solutions promoted for effectuating the control and management of communal life in the streets is CCTV surveillance in public space, with official 'experts' acting as the new guardians, taking over the checking of people for the absence of harmful intentions. This pro-active and more thorough way of monitoring is predicted to achieve substantial improvements in security in the streets. The expected increased likelihood of apprehension and punishment due to CCTV is also presumed to act as a deterrent for potential offenders.

V. MORAL CONCERNS RAISED BY THE RESTRICTION OF ANONYMITY AND THE JUSTIFICATION OF PUBLIC CCTV SURVEILLANCE

While the detail of the arguments of the communitarian critique will not be dealt with here, I want to make two points against the communitarian approach. First, if one holds that the community has claims over individuals, one would need an account of what principal claims the community should have. Without such an account of what types of claims the community has against the individual, it is not possible to gauge to what end and in what way the State may properly interfere with the lives of

---

to distinguish from the boys of the notorious Windsor council estates; whereas the thief who in a clever manoeuvre stole my handbag and those of several other clients from under the table in a coffee shop, looked a picture of respectability, as one could see later on CCTV. To avoid suspicion, pickpockets and con men have always tended to dress well, hence the expression 'Dapper Dan'.

[86] Among others, proposals included short-term holding facilities in shopping malls and high streets, and the lowering of the threshold for taking fingerprints and for the identification of people accused of non-recordable offences. See Home Office Consultation Paper, March 2007.

[87] See Tony Blair's speech, 'Re-balancing of the criminal justice system', 18 June 2002, at <http:// www.pm.gov.uk/output/Page 5359.asp>.

individuals. If a theory about the community's claims is put forward, the basis of this theory needs to be explained. It might be argued that the demands made by the community are ultimately based on individual well-being. It then remains to be explained why and to what extent that would be the case. However, if individual well-being is the ultimate criterion, the concept of the community, as representing separate distinctive values, is misleading. This approach might also encourage ascribing the community's intrusions to individual interests, when in reality they are not. If, on the other hand, the explanation is that the community has a higher value than its constituent individuals, this ultimately signifies that individuals are there to serve the community.

Liberalism's emphasis on personal well-being and on the individual's entitlement to choose his own version of the good life has been criticised by some communitarians as being 'atomistic'. MacIntyre and Sandel, prominent representatives of communitarianism, argue that such a view ignores the individual's embeddedness in the community and his commitments to others. This view seems mistaken. It is *because* people are not separate, and must deal with each other and with the community, that the community is capable of exercising so much pressure on them. The individual thus needs rights against the community and needs the constraints liberalism has to offer. Any approach holding that collective interests are foundational, deriving from the importance of the community itself, can result in the individual being sacrificed to the interest of the many.[88] There is no doubt that a variety of collective interests are important for people's well-being. But the community is composed of individual people, and if one subscribes to the values of autonomy, human dignity, equality and individual thriving, these values should provide the ultimate justification for the obligations imposed on the members of the political community, not some ulterior claim of the community in its own right.

The central question is then whether the communal interest in being protected against crime and disorder in the streets should override the individual's entitlement to anonymity. The supporters of public CCTV justify it by positing that the interest in the safe use of public space overrides the interest in anonymity. The issue is too complex to allow such a categorical statement to go unchallenged. The most repressive regimes (the former German Democratic Republic and North Korea come to mind) have a tendency to claim that their denial of civil liberties is only for the better protection and security of their citizens. To determine priority questions between public and private interests, the competing interests

---

[88] See von Hirsch and Ashworth's critique of Duff's communitarian justification for long-term confinement of dangerous offenders, beyond the term of punishment deserved by the seriousness of the committed offences, A von Hirsch and A Ashworth, *Proportionate Sentencing—Exploring the Principles* (Oxford, Oxford University Press, 2005) 105ff.

have to weighed, criteria must be established to measure their importance, and the dynamics of their relationship need to be examined. However, the first step is to examine whether public CCTV has the potential to interfere with the anonymity interests at all, or whether it is, as its advocates purport, just 'another pair of eyes'.

2

Does Public CCTV Violate Anonymity Interests?

PUBLIC, OR 'OPEN-street', CCTV refers to CCTV surveillance regimes set up by the local authorities with a view to improving the safety of the public space. Under the 'Crime Reduction Programme CCTV Initiative' introduced by the Labour Government in 1999, nearly five million CCTV cameras have been installed, and ever-more powerful surveillance technologies have been developed and introduced with the backing of the Home Office.[1]

Closed circuit television surveillance, a recurring argument goes, does not interfere with anonymity. It is merely 'another pair of eyes', replicating the passing glance by which we reassure ourselves in the street, but invading the territories of the self even less, as virtual scrutiny via cameras does not encroach on a person in any physical way. This statement sounds superficially plausible, but it does not do justice to the capabilities of CCTV cameras and their operators, and fails to examine the intrusive potential of virtual scrutiny: what does it really mean for the observed person, and how might he be affected by it? It should not be overlooked that public CCTV surveillance replaces informal social rituals practised by civilians with formal supervision by officials who have access to the State's monopoly over the legitimate use of force. This changes the terms of relations between observers and observed. Whereas individuals interact with each other on an equal footing and share a mutual interest in anonymity, the authorities have no such interests, and because of their differential powers, they can skew norms of discretion and intimidate civilians without fear of countervailing social pressure.

---

[1] The first round of the CCTV initiative was launched in May 1999. It provided funding for new and extended CCTV schemes, especially for housing areas, public car parks, and town and city centres. In the second round, running until 2002, there was additional emphasis on schemes to help reduce the fear of crime in rural areas, small shopping centres and transport links. Local business and communities were encouraged to set up joint public CCTV partnership schemes. In the third round, the Home Office continued to encourage and co-fund the expansion and updating of local CCTV operations.

42 Does Public CCTV Violate Anonymity Interests?

In this chapter, I shall explore whether the observation of people through cameras, the recording of their images on film by or on behalf of the authorities, and the reviewing of these recordings, interfere with the anonymity they should be entitled to expect when about in public space. To judge the impact of CCTV surveillance, one has to take into account that public CCTV is actually a very diverse phenomenon, with regard both to its technical capabilities and to the organisational and operational set-up. These factors influence how closely a person can be watched, who his audience is, and what might ensue from the observation. I therefore start by examining the technological and operational options of public CCTV regimes, and what they imply for the person in the street. This will be followed by a comparison between direct face-to-face appraisal and virtual scrutiny by cameras, and an analysis of the intrusive potential of public CCTV surveillance.

I. MODALITIES OF PUBLIC CCTV REGIMES AND THEIR MODUS OPERANDI

A. CCTV technology

In recent years, there has been a rapid process of refinement and development of surveillance technologies designed to optimise the yield of information obtained by CCTV cameras. Closed circuit television technology determines the sensory quality of the cameras and vision-enhancing devices, the systems for recording, storing and distribution of information, as well as the means for processing intelligence. At its more sophisticated level, CCTV technology allows a keenness of perception and insight which by far exceeds the capabilities of natural vision. We are used to thinking of CCTV images as grainy black and white, but today pictures are in digital and high-resolution colour. Infra-red and heat-sensitive cameras can see in the dark, and might have a reach of several miles. Microwave cameras can spot objects underneath a person's clothes. Digital image processing improves picture quality by enlargement, and by increasing brightness and definition. Biometric methods and dynamic systems are being tested that will enable computers to check crowds for the presence of particular individuals (biometric face recognition systems). To ease the burden of live monitoring, programmes are under development for the automatic recognition of 'suspicious' behaviour, allowing for a 'robotisation' of surveillance. Images produced by CCTV can be processed by using algorithmic software and linked to databanks holding personal data, adding a new dimension to the visual information collected and enhancing its value.

Many of the new technologies are still in an experimental stage and not yet fully reliable. The cost of the equipment and the commitment required for making effective use of the technological capabilities will hamper the implementation and slow down any large-scale replacement of the more basic existing installations. Multifunctional systems at the high end of the spectrum are, for some time to come, likely to be reserved for selective operations. The following paragraphs give an overview of the technologies currently available or in state of development, starting with the most elementary options.

1. Placebo cameras

Local authorities are known to have installed 'dummy' cameras. No images are relayed or recorded, and no one is watching. The mere presence of cameras is claimed to act as a deterrent, although there is no evidence to support this claim over a longer period.[2]

2. Static cameras

A camera surveys an area from one fixed angle and displays the consecutive images on a monitor for surveillance personnel to watch simultaneously (in 'real time'), or records the images for later review. Static cameras capture only the particular aspect of a location that is within their field of vision, not what lies beyond. Much of what is going on therefore escapes them, and it is easy to avoid being caught on camera. In the United Kingdom a considerable number of these basic CCTV cameras are still in operation.

3. Pan, tilt and zoom (PTZ) cameras

High-performance cameras include 'pan' (moving the cameras from right to left through 360°), 'tilt' (moving the cameras up or down through 270°) and 'zoom' (lenses permitting a closer view) capabilities. Such PTZ cameras can follow people and vehicles, and take close-up views. A good quality zoom lens allows the observer to identify someone at a distance of 150 meters and to read the menu in the hands of a person sitting in an outdoor café, even the text message on his mobile phone.

The later generation of CCTV cameras is usually equipped with PTZ technology. To date the functions still have to be initiated (with the push of a button) by surveillance personnel, watching events live. However, as part of the drive for automated (and therefore less costly) surveillance, 'intelligent' cameras are being developed that would dispense with the need for

---

[2] The conditions for successful deterrence will be discussed below in ch 3, section IV.B.3.

human input by using algorithmic monitoring programs, telling the cameras to focus automatically on suspicious incidents. This technology will be discussed at 10.(iii) below.

4. Mobile cameras

In addition to the cameras that are a permanent fixture for monitoring a particular place, security forces are using mobile cameras installed on top of vehicles, but also in helicopters and aeroplanes, that can be taken to varying locations for temporary surveillance. In cooperation with the police, defence companies are developing military surveillance methods for extensive civilian security operations in the UK: the project involves using unmanned aerial vehicles (UAVs) to cover large areas and to monitor the surveillance feed from CCTV cameras.[3]

5. Cameras with audio capability

These are cameras equipped with powerful microphones that can pick up conversations. They are not well suited to the noise levels of city centres and high density environments where CCTV cameras are installed as a rule, and are not employed for standard public CCTV surveillance.

6. 'Talking' cameras

The latest novelty in CCTV technology in the UK is the 'talking' camera. Loudspeakers are fitted to a camera, through which operators can communicate directly with the people in the street. After trials in Middlesborough, where the scheme has been used to stop vandals and tell people to pick up their rubbish, the Home Office provided £500,000 in grants to adapt cameras in further 20 locations. John Reed, the Home Secretary at the time, declared that the scheme was proven to work and that the communities sharing the grant would feel the benefits.[4]

7. Night vision cameras

Various technologies are used to create light sources in the dark that are invisible to the human eye but can be picked up by night vision cameras and processed to produce discernible images. Infra-red equipment adds light, heat sensors react to the heat energy emanating from the body,

---

[3] See 'CCTV in the Sky: police plan to use military-style spy drones', *Guardian*, 23 January 2010.
[4] The then Home Secretary also announced that competitions would be held at schools in many of the areas for children to become 'the voice' of CCTV cameras. See <http://politics.guardian.co.uk/homeaffairs/story/0,2049786,00.html>.

transforming it into images, and there are cameras which emanate electro-magnetic microwave signals and depict the reflections they receive on a monitor. Microwaves can penetrate non-conductive substances, and make it possible to see through most materials and detect what is hidden underneath a person's clothes, and even to look into his body. 'Passive millimetre wave technology' is being explored for scanning the area between skin and clothes for the detection of weapons and drugs.[5]

There is no official information as to the state of implementation of night-vision and microwave technology in connection with public CCTV schemes in England, as disclosure of its use is not obligatory. It is often hinted that the police and the secret services have set up a highly sophisticated CCTV system including microwave and night-vision facilities in connection with the Congestion Charge System for Central London, and microwave cameras are already in use for airport security checking. The Data Protection Act 1998 and the Information Commissioner's Code of Practice for CCTV contain no restrictions regarding night vision cameras; on the contrary, the latter explicitly encourages the use of infra-red equipment in poorly-lit areas. There is no reference to microwave technology.

8. Cameras with recording facilities

Not all CCTV schemes use real-time live monitoring. Surveillance personnel may be present for only a number of hours each day, or cameras may not be manned at all and merely record events automatically for later perusal. By recording events on tape or digital carrier a permanent record is created, and the fixed images can be reviewed at any time and by anyone who has or has been granted access to the stored tapes. Cameras either record automatically and continuously, or 'on-demand' when the recording button is activated. On-demand recording to date requires human input, but the 'intelligent' cameras using algorithmic monitoring programs (see 3. above and 10.(iii) below) will trigger the recording mechanism automatically.

9. Multiplex analogue tape systems

An area is often surveyed from different angles by several cameras. Images are recorded on multiplex tape systems with the capacity to store frames

---

[5] These technologies are being researched by the United States Defense Department's 'Human ID at a Distance' Project; more information can be obtained at <http//: www.darpa.mil iao/HID.hrm>.

from up to 16 cameras on one tape. Surveillance personnel can watch the frames on multi-screen installations and thereby supervise what is going on in a relatively large area.

Multiplex analogue tape systems record frames from different cameras sequentially, rather than recording frames of images from one camera continuously. However, rather than using 25 frames per second from one camera, only a fraction of the frames recorded by each camera is used; the rest is deleted. The more cameras stored on a multiplex system, the more information discarded. In a five-camera system this could be as much as 80 per cent of the information available from each camera.[6] For this reason the record created by the system does not provide a complete picture of the event, and it is sometimes impossible to locate the frame capturing the exact moment of an incident needed for proof in court.

10. Digital systems

The future belongs to digital cameras, electronic recording and storing of images on computers.[7] Digital systems are able to capture and record a much larger number of frames per image and produce a more complete record than analogue systems.

The drawback of digitisation is the ease of data manipulation. Once a digital image that has been modified is copied, all traces of the manipulation are eliminated. There will be no evidence on the copy of any break in the underlying continuity and no loss of quality in the copy, which would make it possible to distinguish the copy from the original of an analogue recording. The difficulty of identifying the original master and excluding the possibility that an image has been manipulated can affect the evidential value of digital CCTV footage. Nevertheless, the superior capabilities of digital technology have made it the technology of choice, and the UK Government set funds aside for upgrading existing systems from analogue to digital.

Digital recordings create databases that can be selectively retrieved and organised. Digital images may be accessed via the Internet from anywhere, allowing for information-sharing systems. The images from one location may be viewed simultaneously, or time-delayed on connected monitors in other places and by people who have no connection with the events. The coupling of digital images to algorithmic software opens up entirely new ways for monitoring and classifying images. Closed circuit television

---

[6] M Constant and P Turnbull, *The Principles and Practice of CCTV* (Hertfordshire, Paramount Publishing, 1994) 133f.
[7] For an overview of the capabilities of digital systems, see C Norris, 'From Personal to Digital. CCTV, the panoptikon, and the technological mediation of suspicion and social control' in D Lyon (ed), *From Surveillance as Social Sorting. Privacy, Risk and Digital Discrimination* (London, Rutledge, 2003) 292.

databases can be processed, using data mining and pattern recognition software, and they can be shared and linked with other computers and databases containing 'positive' and 'nominative' (ie personally identifying) data about people. Combined with face or biometric recognition programs (see (i) below), this could revolutionise the process of identification. Several international programmes are dedicated to the research and development of digital systems' potential for investigative purposes.[8]

The following applications of digital technology and algorithmic processing are already in use or currently being tested.

(i) Facial recognition systems

Facial recognition technology utilises computerised pattern-matching technology. It scans people's faces and compares them against an existing database of facial images in order to find a match. Video cameras with facial recognition capabilities ('facecams' or 'smart' CCTV) permit the screening of people recorded by CCTV cameras against a watch-list to detect whether a known suspect is among them.[9] Smart CCTV could also be used for enforcing curfews and exclusion orders. The first public installation of a facial recognition system in the UK occurred in the London Borough of Newham. In cooperation with the software manufacturers Visionics, the Newham authorities installed the UK-developed 'Mandrake' facial recognition system, which is linked to a database containing the faces of approximately 100 suspects. It means that people in the area will be routinely scanned and have their faces matched against the database. The claim is that the suspects can be electronically recognised in the crowd when they visit the area, although there is insufficient evidence to support this claim.[10] Facial recognition technology is also employed at airports for tracing known terrorist suspects. The Central London Congestion Charge Scheme allegedly uses smart CCTV, with security cameras zooming in not only on the licence plates of the cars, but also on the faces of drivers entering into the Congestion Charge zone. The images are said to be immediately cross-referenced to an intelligence and police database of criminals and terror suspects for matching, with the help of facial recognition software.

Facial recognition systems lend themselves to the identification of any person captured on CCTV—a criminal record is not a prerequisite for being subjected to the process. Faces can be matched against passport and driving licence files and similar types of nominative data banks. Millions of

---

[8] *Ibid*, at 268ff.
[9] The use of 'facecams' to search for wanted criminals among the public at the American Super Bowl XXXV in June 2001 caused much controversy in the US.
[10] 'A Cautionary Tale for a New Age of Surveillance', *New York Times*, 7 October 2002.

people have enrolled in schemes connecting indexical personal data about them, such as their names and addresses, with their likeness and unique biometric features.[11] Face recognition is, however, hampered by the complexity of the data involved. As well as needing to define what makes faces different enough for a computer to distinguish individuals, a reliable system would have to overcome differences between the appearance of a person on the image taken by CCTV and the image against which this is to be matched. The 'Face It' software engine, the most sophisticated type of facial recognition technology, works by analysing up to 80 facial building elements, which are then encoded into a mathematical formula called 'faceprint' that is unique to a person's face. Once a faceprint has been made, it can be processed at much greater speed than facial images.[12] Whilst an electronic faceprint is said to be unaffected by changes in lighting, facial angle, expression, hairstyle or facial hair, mere digitised facial images are not. Matching can effectively be jeopardised by simple alterations to the appearance, sunglasses or obstacles preventing a full frontal view. This might be counteracted by using a biometric recognition method, which concentrates on those unchangeable features, such as fingerprints, the iris or the geometry of hands and veins, but in spite of improved camera technology, such details are not always clear on CCTV recordings.[13] Computers have no problems finding people's eyes on a picture, but cannot yet scan the irises of a person in motion from afar.[14]

Experts concur that in an ideal biometric authentication system, neither the 'false accept' nor the 'false reject' rate should exceed 0.1 per cent. (A 'false accept' error occurs when the system incorrectly declares a successful match between the input pattern and a pattern in the database that does not really match it. In a 'false reject' error, the system declares a failed match, even though the data match.) In evaluations conducted in the US by the National Institute of Standards and Technology, error rates for all biometric systems exceeded this level.[15] It might still take some years

---

[11] In future a European passport will hold two biometric chips: a facial scan and a fingerprint. A passport encoding facial features is already required for entry into the US as a visitor.

[12] For an overview of facial recognition technology, see P Brey, 'Ethical Aspects of Facial Recognition Systems in Public Places' (2004) 2(2) *Journal of Information, Communication and Ethics in Society* 98. The 'Face It' system has been used in Newham and Birmingham, and in Tampa, Florida ('the Ybor City Scheme').

[13] A team at Maryland University is aiming to invent a system whereby a facial image can be matched to a person's 'gait DNA', an individual code created for the way a person walks. See BBC News, 15 September 2007, <http://news.bbc.co.uk/2/hi/programmes/from_our_own_correspondent/6995061>.

[14] For an account of biometric recognition methods and the problems involved, see B Wirtz, 'Biometrische Verfahren. Ueberblick, Evaluierung und aktuelle Themen' (1999) 23 *Datenschutz und Datensicherheit* 129.

[15] AK Jain and S Pankanti, 'Beyond Fingerprinting' (2008) 299(3) *Scientific American*, Special Issue: 'Will Technology Kill Privacy' 57.

before biometric technology permits fully reliable, automated, immediate face-matching in video surveillance. Nevertheless, already at this stage, biometric recognition systems can be enlisted to assist with the identification of people recorded on public CCTV and locate where they live.

(ii)   Radio frequency identification (RFID) tags

Radio frequency identification tags are powerful tracking devices that are imbedded in a growing number of identity documents, driving licences, transit and toll passes, public transport cards (eg the 'oyster card' for London's transport network), phones and credit cards. Each card incorporates a microchip, encoded with a unique identification number. Tags can be read by a reader device: the radio frequency is picked up by an antenna connected to the chip, causing it to emit the ID Number. Passive tags depend on a reader to initiate communication and supply power. Active tags, such as toll passes, can initiate communication with a reader or another tag. Passive tags can be read from as far away as 30 feet, active tags from 300 feet. The code is matched with a detailed list of personal information, kept in a central database.[16] The ID number can thus serve as a lead to reveal the carrier's identity. For example, as the holder of an American RFID-enhanced driver's licence reaches the border control station in certain US states, the ID number has already been fed into a Homeland Security database and the driver's photograph and other personal details are displayed on the border control official's screen.

These RFID tags are also embedded in a growing number of consumer items, like another type of bar code. This could permit manufacturers to track individuals, to identify them via their credit card details and to use the information for targeted direct marketing—a method already used for location-based marketing via mobile phones. People are often unaware not only of the risks they incur by carrying RFID tags, but even of the fact that tags have been embedded in the items at all, and that they could thus be tracked without their knowledge or consent. (One can of course be tracked anywhere if one carries a mobile phone that is switched on, but at least one can switch it off, or leave it at home.) The European Commission has acknowledged that the technology might have serious implications for privacy, but has so far declined to regulate it.

Using RFID codes might be a more effective and reliable way of identifying people than biometric authentication systems (see (i) above). By equipping CCTV cameras with a reader device, they could pick up the RFID codes embedded in items people carry around, allowing surveillance

---

[16]   For an overview of the capabilities of RFID tags, their growing significance and the resulting dangers for privacy, see K Albrecht, 'RFID Tag—You're it', *Scientific American, Special Issue*, above n 15, at 48.

personnel to access the associated data and thereby identify the tag holder.[17] Even though most RFID tags comply with the industry standard known as ISO 14443, providing a certain degree of protection against unauthorised access, it cannot be difficult for the authorities to overcome the protective encryption. Tags that are designed for maximum ease of readability, such as the enhanced US driver's licence, would reveal the information immediately to any compatible reader.

(iii)   Algorithmic monitoring

Algorithmic monitoring is based on the idea that specific body language is indicative of certain harmful intent, and that by translating that language into algorithms, it can become electronically identifiable.[18] Cameras equipped with 'discriminator algorithms', using motion detection facilities enabling them to recognise suspicious body dynamics and changes in the environment, could then replace and/or complement human monitoring. This is seen as a major resource for combating terrorism and crime. The European Commission is sponsoring a 'Face and Gesture Recognition Working Group', and research is being carried out at Leeds and Reading Universities, to devise video sensors that are programmed not only to detect potentially criminal behaviour, but also to operate a PTZ mechanism (see 3. above). Cameras would automatically focus on individuals displaying suspicious movements, and even unmanned cameras could thus provide close-up recordings.

According to a spokesman for the London Tube, a system of 'intelligent' CCTV was tried at Liverpool Street station, but had to be abandoned because it generated too many false alarms.[19] A simpler version of smart cameras, capable of distinguishing between moving people and motionless packages, is being tested on the New York subway for the detection of explosives. This seems a more feasible undertaking than the problematic task of determining and identifying what qualifies as 'suspicious' behaviour.

---

[17] Albrecht tells of a practice in an English amusement park that illustrates RFID's tracking potential. On entering Alton Towers, 'each visitor is offered an RFID wristband encoded with a unique ID number. A network of RFID readers placed strategically throughout the park detects each wristband and triggers nearby video cameras. Candid footage of each individual is stored in a file labelled with the wristband ID number, then made available to the customer on a keepsake DVD at the end of the day' (*ibid* at 52).

[18] A specific pattern has also been identified for recognising people intent on committing suicide by throwing themselves in front of incoming Underground trains.

[19] See ''Smart' CCTV could fight terrorist threat in stations', *The Times*, 15 November 2005.

The title of an article on smart cameras, 'Warning ... Strange Behaviour', hints at the ethical problems concerned with this technology.[20] Nevertheless, it is expected in CCTV user circles that intelligent cameras will become the norm in the next decade. A new device, nicknamed 'the Bug', is said to have been launched in Britain. It consists of a ring of eight cameras scanning in all directions, using artificial intelligence for detecting whether anybody is walking or loitering in a way that marks them out from the crowd. If the conclusion is that a person is behaving suspiciously, a ninth camera then zooms in to follow the person. Still, whether 'intelligent' cameras will ever be accurate enough to replace human monitoring, especially in crowded locations, remains to be seen.

(iv) Automatic number plate recognition

Automatic number plate recognition (ANPR) systems have been in use for some time in combination with roadside traffic cameras monitoring adherence to speed limits. The ANPR works by linking the recording of the licence plates of cars exceeding a speed limit with the central car registration data bank. The owner of the car can thus be identified, and a fine is sent to him via an automated process. The police are using ANPR not just to enforce speed limits, but also to detect stolen cars and to target uninsured drivers. Traffic cameras are therefore linked not only to the central car registration files, but also to the police national database of stolen cars and the DVLA database of uninsured cars. Vehicles that are not registered or not taxed are identified by having their number plates automatically cross-checked with a list of vehicles without a valid MOT certificate.[21]

As well as recording car licence plates, roadside cameras take photographs of the drivers. Since the picture quality has greatly improved due to digital technology, the police are increasingly relying on these images to identify and fine motorists who wear no seatbelts, use handheld mobile phones or otherwise engage in distracting activities while driving.

(v) Data sharing with public sector databanks

Ever-growing numbers of data banks and electronic registers are being set up, holding personal information on every aspect of our lives. In the UK, the average adult is said to be registered on more than 700 databases.[22]

---

[20] See *New Scientist*, 11 December 1999, 25.
[21] See 'Spy cameras to spot drivers' every move', *The Times*, 13 November 2005.
[22] See 'Surveillance Britain', *The Times Magazine*, 17 April 2010.

Database State, a report published by The Joseph Rowntree Reform Trust, lists 46 new public sector database projects, including, to name just the most relevant:

a) the National Identity Register, which will store biometric information linked toID cards. (This is now obsolete, as the ID cards project has been dropped.)
b) 'Work and Pensions Data Sharing', one of Europe's largest databases, which is to hold 85 million records, based on national insurance numbers;
c) the NHS detailed care record, which comprises GP and hospital records as well as comments by care providers;
d) 'ONSET', a record of which children are likely to become criminals (triggered by referrals to youth offending teams);
e) the 'Common Assessment Framework', which shares sensitive information on children with welfare needs;
f) 'E- borders', which will record journeys in and out of the country, and retain records for 10 years; and
g) the Schengen Information System, a European police database that lists suspects, people to be denied entry to Europe and people to be kept under surveillance.

The Drivers' Licence Register and the ANPR System (see (iv) above) are also relevant data sources.[23]

Only six of the 46 systems examined in the Report get a 'green light' for being effective, necessary and proportional, and with proper legal barriers in place against privacy intrusions. Others are considered to be almost certainly illegal under human rights or data protection laws.[24] There are hardly any constraints on the provision or sharing of sensitive personal data. Closed circuit television databases (ie the digital recordings of public CCTV cameras) could become part of the pool of data and information that is shared across traditional provider and departmental boundaries. In the UK, nearly 800 public bodies—comprising security services, police and local councils, tax authorities and NHS trusts—can claim to be in some way concerned with crime prevention and can therefore request to view

---

[23] R Anderson, I Brown, T Dowty *et al*, *Database State* (York, The Joseph Rowntree Reform Trust, 2009). The Trust promotes political reform, constitutional change and social justice.
[24] *Ibid* at 4ff.

CCTV footage, just as they would be entitled to have access to the national DNA database, and make requests to tap phone calls and monitor e-mails.[25]

B. Who is in charge of public CCTV surveillance?

Public CCTV falls under the aegis of local authorities and the police. A local authority may run the operation itself, from a control room located in a central position such as the town hall, or put the police in charge of monitoring the cameras, in which case the screens would be situated in a police station. The task of running surveillance operations is also frequently contracted out to private security firms. Under the 'Multi Agency Crime Prevention Partnerships', promoted by the UK Government to spread the cost of public CCTV, operations are set up as joint ventures between public authorities and private local enterprises. Retailers and the catering trade, in particular, have a vested interest in ensuring that their customers feel safe, and are therefore often prepared to co-fund the surveillance activities in their area. Such partnerships encourage greater communication and liaison between the private and the public sector, and give the private partners a say in the running of the scheme.

The cost of establishing a good quality CCTV scheme could amount to half a million pounds, and nearly the same amount might be incurred in annual running costs.[26] Formerly, local CCTV schemes used to be stand-alone operations, and camera operators worked from control rooms in proximity to the areas they surveyed. However, many local authorities cannot afford many hours of professional monitoring. Pooling resources and sharing costs for technology and manpower with other communities might be the answer. There is a trend to move away from localised operations, and to set up multiple monitoring stations, servicing several systems in different locations from one central point, which can be far from the areas which are being monitored.

---

[25] The Report of the Interception of Communications Commissioner for 2008 revealed that an average of nearly 1,000 requests a day are made for 'communications data'. See 'Our state collects more data than the Stasi ever did. We need to fight back', *Guardian*, 31 January 2008.
[26] See G Wade, 'Funding CCTV: The Story So Far' (2000) 7(2) *CCTV Today* 28ff.

C. Surveillance practices

1. Active and passive monitoring

There are two distinct strategies for public CCTV: active monitoring in real time (also referred to as 'live' surveillance); and passive monitoring by way of recording and time-delayed review of events. In the case of live surveillance, cameras are manned by surveillance personnel who monitor the ongoing events on the screens. It usually implies (and only then does it make sense) that surveillance personnel have a link to the police. If the operator believes that an incident in the street calls for a police intervention on the ground, he will ask for dispatch forces to be sent to the scene of the incident. Often operators are also in contact with store detectives and other private security personnel in charge of monitoring 'mass private space', and may assist them in keeping track of people and point the police in their direction.[27]

Today, active monitoring is usually combined with recording. When cameras are manned, there are two alternative systems for recording:

a) the cameras are programmed to record everything within their view automatically (the prevailing system in England); or
b) the recording mechanism is activated by surveillance personnel when they deem that a situation warrants the preserving of evidence of events (the general practice in Germany).

Passive monitoring schemes record everything on tape or digital carriers for time-delayed review. Surveillance operations using unmanned cameras are not set up for direct intervention with ongoing events. The objective here is to collect evidence for investigative and forensic use.

Surveillance schemes using digital recording devices have to be registered under the Data Protection Act 1998. This is a formality—the Act allows the acquisition of data by way of making CCTV recordings as long as the administration of the recordings is in accordance with data protection principles.[28]

---

[27] Mass private space constitutes facilities owned by private organisations that offer themselves as being generally available for public use without restriction of specific purpose (such as shopping malls, leisure complexes and transportation terminals). For a discussion of surveillance in mass private properties see A Wakefield, 'Situational Crime Prevention in Mass Private Property' in A von Hirsch, D Garland and A Wakefield (eds), *Ethical and Social Perspectives on Situational Crime Prevention* (Oxford, Hart Publishing, 2000).

[28] See ch 4, section II.D.2. and 3.

Modalities of Public CCTV Regimes and Their Modus Operandi 55

2. *Access and reviewing policies*

Policies vary from operation to operation. Under the most conscientious CCTV regimes, such as Cambridge City Council's, the only people admitted to the control room are surveillance personnel on duty. The police are excluded unless expressly invited to assist operators in a particular situation, or if permission has been granted following a formal request by the police to watch events live. Tapes are stored, but not reviewed, unless a crime has been reported to the police. An official request has to be made by a police superintendent, indicating the suspected crime in question, its time and location. Recorded footage may be accessed only by enforcement personnel dealing with the crime, and only the passages relating to the incident under investigation are made available for review. Unclaimed recordings are destroyed unseen after one month.[29]

In other regimes, practices are often more relaxed. There may be unmonitored comings and goings to and from the control room of colleagues working in other departments, and even outsiders are sometimes admitted. In an experiment, residents of an East London housing estate will be able to watch live CCTV footage from the communal areas of the estate on a giant public plasma screen, and, for a small fee, on their own TVs too via a broadband connection.[30] When the police are in charge of CCTV, control rooms are usually readily accessible to all staff. Operations run by the private sector tend to give the police free access, to involve them and get their cooperation for dispatch missions. A high intervention rate confirms the worth of the operation to the council and the local enterprises who co-fund the running costs and on whom the continuation of the scheme may depend.[31]

There are often no conditions attached to the reviewing of recorded footage; it can be reviewed freely and in its entirety by surveillance and law enforcement personnel. Considering the amount of accumulated material, it is unlikely that all tapes will be reviewed as a matter of routine[32]; but it may mean that surveillance personnel, police and authorities pore over

---

[29] At one point the UK Government wanted to enforce a minimum storage period for recordings of six months, but the recommendation of the Code of Practice for the Use of CCTV Surveillance issued by the Data Protection Commissioner in 2000 is to keep the footage 'no longer than necessary'. For public CCTV crime prevention schemes, a 30-day storage period is considered acceptable.

[30] The experiment is piloted by the Shoreditch Trust, an East London regeneration agency, which also subsidises the cost of the broadband connection to private homes.

[31] Not surprisingly, the liaison with police dispatch forces seems to work best when the police are in charge of the CCTV operation, and requests for interventions are most likely to be complied with if they come from an operator who is part of a police team.

[32] The author was told that for the London Borough of Kensington and Chelsea the police have a formal agreement with the council allowing them to review all footage, but that effectively only recordings from high-crime zones (Notting Hill, Portobello, Earl's Court) are monitored regularly.

stretches of footage in minute detail, especially under passive monitoring regimes. There is a much wider scope for scrutiny when recorded footage is examined in order to uncover unspecified criminal activity (so-called 'fishing expeditions') than when particular sections are reviewed to investigate a concrete incident.

Third-party use and disposal of recordings to the media are further matters for concern, especially in the UK. Before the Information Commissioner's Code of Practice for the Use of Closed Circuit Television came into force in July 2000, which limits the disposal of public CCTV footage to third parties, those in charge of CCTV could decide what to do with the tapes. Projects to outlaw the use of CCTV footage for entertainment purposes were never carried out. Although third-party use was discouraged by Home Office Guidelines, this policy was not actively enforced and sanctions for non-compliance had little bite. Tapes were liberally passed on or sold to television stations for news reporting, 'candid camera' and 'crime watch' programmes. The use of CCTV footage by the media remains a troubling grey area. Also, it is still possible that CCTV intelligence might be made available as evidence in civil litigation, such as insurance claims, divorce proceedings or employment disputes.

There is little transparency concerning the exploitation of the intelligence obtained through public CCTV by the authorities themselves. The data protection principle of purpose specification, whereby information must not be used for purposes other than those declared at the time of data collection, is only vaguely restricting. 'Crime prevention', as the official designated purpose for collecting information, can be stretched to cover a wide range of potential applications and interested parties. (See above, section I.A.10.(v).) The speculation surrounding the extent of intelligence gathering and processing under the aegis of the 'Ring of Steel' initiative in Central London exemplifies the degree of uncertainty: Are the pictures linked to data banks for identification? Are they passed on to other government agencies? Is there a file of regular visitors? Is it used for ethnic profiling? These questions highlight the fact that the public are not fully informed about the Government's agenda regarding the use of CCTV intelligence and what goes on behind the scenes.

3. Directed surveillance

In the UK, section 26 of the Regulation of Investigatory Powers Act (RIPA) 2000 permits three types of covert surveillance, provided that surveillance is necessary and proportionate:

a) 'directed';
b) 'intrusive'; or
c) 'covert human intelligence source' (CHIS).

The last type of covert surveillance refers to undercover police officers or informants and is of no relevance to CCTV surveillance.

'Intrusive' surveillance is defined as covert surveillance carried out in relation to anything taking place on residential premises or in any private vehicle. Provided that cameras do not overlook private residences, CCTV surveillance in public space does not qualify as intrusive surveillance. Great care has to be taken to position cameras, especially those equipped with PTZ technology, in such a way that they cannot overlook private gardens or doorsteps, or see through the windows of people's homes.

'Directed' surveillance is covert but not intrusive surveillance that targets a particular person while he is in public space. It can involve 'tailing' someone and photographing or recording him. Public CCTV schemes are being used for 'directed' surveillance. Even if the public is alerted to the presence of cameras, this would qualify as a covert operation as the designated person would be unaware of being targeted. Originally intended for anti-terrorist investigations, directed surveillance can be used for reasons including 'the purpose of preventing and detecting crime'(RIPA 2000, s 26(2)). It requires only internal authorisation by a designated person who believes it is necessary and proportionate. Even the British public, usually so complacent about public CCTV, were shocked when it transpired recently that local councils had been employing it liberally for directed surveillance too. Operators of CCTV cameras had been ordered to spy on individuals for trivial reasons, such as investigating if they were cheating over school catchment rules, dumping rubbish or letting their dogs foul the street. Following a public outcry, the Home Secretary announced that stricter conditions would be imposed and that junior council officials would lose the authority to order directed surveillance.[33] However, it is doubtful that the goalposts will be moved far enough. According to the then Minister for Policing,

> there is no doubt that a wide range of public authorities need to be able to authorise surveillance under RIPA in order to protect us from those who would do harm.[34]

Benefit fraud teams, child maintenance investigators and many other public authorities are able to order directed surveillance.

My analysis concerns the standard type of public CCTV surveillance, which is overt, and I shall not discuss directed surveillance in detail. However, the recent revelations about council practices highlight the dangerous potential of public CCTV and how easy it is for the authorities to abuse it for unwarranted intrusions into anonymity.

---

[33] See 'Thousands spied on by councils but few prosecuted', *Guardian*, 24 May 2010.
[34] See 'Code of practice to limit power of councils to snoop on public', *Guardian*, 5 November 2009.

4. Choice of locations

England is singular as regards the pervasiveness of public CCTV. More than four million video cameras monitor streets, parks and council estates, and often cover large areas within a town. The cameras installed across London's Underground will increase in number from 6,000 to 12,000 over the next few years, and Britain's top traffic policeman, the head of roads policing at the Association of Chief Police Officers ('ACPO'), went on record with plans to install roadside spy cameras with ANPR 'every 400 yards along the motorway'.[35] No other European country has a surveillance network of comparable ambit. France, following closest after England, has far fewer cameras, and stricter regulations. In Germany, CCTV is used only selectively, for specific areas that have been identified as centres of criminal activity ('hotspots of crime'), leaving the public domain predominantly free of cameras.[36] In the UK, no particular conditions are attached to the implementation of public CCTV, other than that it should serve general crime prevention purposes. Local authorities have discretion as to the necessity of a scheme, and the location and number of cameras. The proliferation of CCTV surveillance in public in the UK has been driven by political motives, as central government and local authorities were keen to demonstrate that they were taking a pro-active stance in promoting public order and easing fear of crime.

5. Surveillance techniques

The intensity of scrutiny imposed by CCTV depends not only on surveillance technology, but also on the techniques employed by those monitoring the cameras. Fair-practice guidelines for surveillance personnel usually advise that people's privacy must be respected, but what this implies is not fully explained. Mostly, the operator on the job is left to judge for himself whether it is appropriate to concentrate on a particular person, to follow him and to use the zoom facility for getting a closer view. Even if an operator adheres to the principle that people should be scrutinised only when there are reasons to suspect criminal activity, the standards of 'reasonable suspicion' allow for discretion and are influenced by subjective judgement and attitude. Moreover, the remit of CCTV in the UK goes

---

[35] See 'Spy cameras to spot drivers' every move', *Sunday Times*, 13 November 2005.

[36] In 2001 there were only 14 public CCTV schemes in all of Germany, but there has been a push for expansion in recent years; see M Gras, *Kriminalpraevention durch Videoueberwachung* (Baden Baden, Nomos Verlagsgesellschaft, 2002) 263ff. The standards vary for the selection of sites for surveillance. Some of the federal states impose stringent conditions regarding the level of crime and risk assessment; in others, the police have a wide margin of discretion for choosing a location. For an overview of the regulation of CCTV surveillance under the federal states' laws, see D Buellesfeld, *Polizeiliche Videoueberwachung oeffentlicher Strassen und Plaetze zur Kriminalitaetsvorsorge* (Stuttgart, Boorberg, 2002) 151ff.

beyond crime prevention, extending to public propriety, giving a wide scope for scrutiny. People might also be picked out because risks may be attributed to them based on their appearance. Type-casting is difficult to avoid, given the number of people to monitor and the fact that in judging a situation, surveillance personnel have to rely exclusively on virtual impression and visual clues. Visual scrutiny is their only means of assessment; they have no background knowledge about the people, and cannot draw upon the complex signals received from face-to-face contacts. A lack of standardised training and lax supervision fosters a *laissez-faire* climate that could be conducive to arbitrary scrutiny and invasive practices.[37]

II. IS CCTV JUST ANOTHER PAIR OF EYES?

Privacy-based opposition to CCTV surveillance tends to be concerned primarily with the recording of events, not live surveillance.[38] Live CCTV surveillance is often considered the equivalent of real space appraisal. A CCTV camera, it is argued, only represents 'another pair of eyes', and the person in the street is subjected to no more intense scrutiny than is customary among persons in public space. His anonymity is not infringed, for his identity is notrevealed; the observer in the control room only sees the obvious and absorbs information that is in the public domain. All that is expected from the person in the street is that he abstain from committing crimes and public order offences. This, the argument goes on, mirrors the expectations users of public space are entitled to hold as regards each other and does not curtail any legitimate options. Anonymity does not entitle anyone to commit crimes.

It is the recording of events that is generally seen as posing a threat to privacy interests. However, there is usually no objection in principle to recording as such. The use of the footage is perceived as the problem. In the UK, this is assumed to be an issue of data protection, which can be resolved by registration of the CCTV scheme with the Information

---

[37] Norris and Armstrong describe the practices of camera operators under three different public CCTV schemes under the heading 'Watching the Watchers' in C Norris and G Armstrong, *The Maximum Surveillance Society: The Rise of CCTV* (Oxford, Berg,1999) 91ff.

[38] Even under German and French law, where the recording of a person's image is considered to violate the basic right of self-determination, less issue was taken with live surveillance. Only recently has criticism also been directed at live surveillance, based on its 'big brother' effect and on data protection concerns. For a review of the discussion in Germany see V Goetz, 'Oeffentliche Videoueberwachung im Kontext der praeventiven Polizeiarbeit' in JM Jehle and M Gras (eds), *Oeffentliche Videoueberwachung, oder Little Brothers are Watching You: A European Comparison* (Goettingen, Universitaet Goettingen, 2003) 110; <http://www.jura.uni-goettingen.de/privat/j-m.jehle/videoueberwachung>.

Commissioner and adherence to the provisions in his Code of Practice for the Use and Distribution of CCTV Recordings.

I think this approach is too simplistic and does not explore sufficiently the intrusive potential of CCTV. In what follows I shall compare the effects of real-space appraisal and CCTV surveillance, and show that virtual scrutiny by means of cameras and the making of recordings of people as they go about in public space can interfere with anonymity expectations. The analysis will take into account that CCTV surveillance is a diverse phenomenon, and will evaluate the invasive potential of the various regimes.

A. In what way is public CCTV surveillance different from real space appraisal?

The exposure a person has accepted when abroad in the public domain qualifies his privacy claim. He can no longer expect to avoid scrutiny and judgement, but his accessibility is limited and under the proviso of anonymity. It is useful to recall what anonymity implies for encounters among members of the public in real space.

In public an individual can expect:

a) to be subjected to reflexive casual face-to-face appraisal by people who are co-present;
b) to be able to interact with his observers and use signals of demarcation;
c) not to be picked out of the crowd or to be confronted with people's judgement about him;
d) to be under no obligation to please those he encounters and to fulfil their personal expectations, other than those concerned with the communal use and safety of the common space;
e) to limit his visibility by counting on factual barriers;
f) to leave only a transitory impression;
g) to keep his name and personal data unknown by those who do not know him already.

By contrast, when one is scrutinised by CCTV cameras:

a) there is no face-to-face contact between the observer and the observed. The observer does not see the physical person but his image that the cameras transmit onto a screen. Due to this 'distanciation', the observed is spared the physical inconvenience that accompanies close scrutiny;
b) the scrutiny is not casual, it is purposeful and systematic;
c) vision-enhancing technologies make it possible to take a closer look at

people than with the naked eye. Physical barriers do not always afford protection, as they may be overcome by technological means, and cameras view the events from a vantage point above the obstacles blocking the view at ground level;

d) monitoring is not reflexive. The observer sees the people in the street, yet he remains invisible to them. This 'one-way mirror' effect favours the observer: he alone is free to scrutinise unimpeded; those observed cannot scrutinise him or fend him off. Moreover, the observed have no effective warning that they are being scrutinised, permitting them to adjust their behaviour. This limits their chances of concealment. Even when CCTV is advertised, cameras are out of sight and easy to forget. The person in the street never knows if and when an operator is looking at him, and it is hard always to be on guard;

e) direct communication or interaction between observer and observed is not possible. The observer cannot take action with immediate effect on the observed: the latter's progress is not affected by the scrutiny and he remains integrated in the general flow. He has no way of gauging what impression he has made on the observer. However, dispatch facilities provide the observer with the option to act through intermediaries who, at his instigation, are able to pick a person out from the crowd and communicate to him (implicitly or explicitly) how he has been judged by the observer. If cameras are not manned and surveillance only takes the form of delayed reviewing of recorded footage, the distanciation between the observer and the observed becomes more pronounced. They are separated by time and space, which renders any form of interaction and communication between the observer and the observed, even through intermediaries, improbable or at least more difficult;

f) observer and observed are not on equal footing. The observed is a civilian without official status or power, whereas the observer represents the authorities, partaking in the formal, organised exercise of power. By being able to call on the police, he has access to the State's monopoly on the legitimate use of force, and can visit unpleasant consequences upon the observed if he disapproves of his comportment;

g) when events are recorded, a person's impression is no longer fleeting. The fixing of his image allows unlimited reviewing by anyone at any time. It also permits technical manipulation to enhance the revealing quality of the image and, in the case of digital recordings, electronic processing to exploit their informational value further.

B. How intrusive is CCTV?

As we have seen, there are fundamental differences between being appraised by others whom one encounters in the street and being scrutinised via cameras live, or studied on film by invisible observers. Closed circuit television imposes a *sui generis* type of scrutiny which may have *sui generis* implications for anonymity. The rules that are valid for physical encounters are not directly applicable to virtual access. The unnoticed appraisal, the artificial eye, the remoteness of the observers and the special powers they can call upon—characteristic features of public CCTV surveillance—could render it at the same time more and less intrusive. Less, because the scrutiny by cameras takes place at arm's length, and more because CCTV technology bestows powers of vision that people in real space do not possess. More also because the expectations of an audience representing the authorities may weigh more heavily on the person in the street than those of an audience composed primarily of equals.

To judge whether public CCTV infringes anonymity expectations, one has to go back to the characteristics and rationale of the entitlement to anonymity. The entitlement to anonymity is concerned with the protection of a person against unwanted access when he is in public. To preserve his dignity and his autonomy, a person must not be treated like an object for others to scrutinise and judge at will; he must be able to exercise control over the presentation of self and to defend the 'territories of the self' that are central to his sense of his own worth and his claim to a space for himself.

The first question to ask, therefore, is whether CCTV surveillance deprives or restricts a person's control over how accessible he wants to be. Can the observer behind CCTV cameras see more than those people encountered face to face, and in what sense might he interfere with the way a person wants to present himself in public?

The second issue is whether virtual scrutiny has the capacity to violate a person's dignity. The observed is not physically beset by it, usually remains unaware of how he is judged and is not picked out of the crowd. It is said that he is neither shamed nor blamed. Since everyone is subjected to CCTV surveillance, not just those suspected of criminal activity, it does not imply a negative distinction. Add to this the fact that the person remains unidentified and one might wonder whether CCTV scrutiny is not so de-personalised that a person's dignity as an individual remains intact. After all, the observer is not out to judge the people in the street on personal merits. His interest lies in enforcing the law, and pertains to the situation rather than the individual.

The third question to examine is whether CCTV surveillance imposes demands that go beyond the legitimate social restrictions in public space. The proposition is that CCTV does not confront the person in the street with undue expectations, for the scrutiny only serves to establish absence of hostile intent. The expectation that a person does not threaten or harm others is material to the sharing of public space, and a person abroad has to submit to be judged by these criteria. Against the argument, that conformity with criminal laws is all that is expected by surveillance personnel, stands the accusation that CCTV is conditioning us to habituated anticipatory overall conformity, working so insidiously that none of us can remain immune, and that it extends Bentham's Panopticon[39] across the entire social fabric.

1. Does CCTV surveillance intrude upon the presentation of self?

Closed circuit television cameras scan people, their looks, their actions and whereabouts, all of which qualify as matters pertaining to the individual person. As long as cameras can make out individuals, and not just the movement of the crowd, there should be no question that private subject matter can be at stake.

A privacy claim requires a degree of exclusivity and reservation. I explained earlier that there are many things about a person one encounters in the street that are not immediately obvious to everyone, and by a combination of conventions of discretion, factual barriers and interaction, a person is able to withhold these aspects from others and they remain in his exclusive domain. Anonymity claims pertain to controlling access to this private territory. There is no exclusivity, however, about aspects that are in full view, and one cannot claim to control access to what is obvious. This subject matter has entered the public domain and has lost the quality of secrecy.

Archard disputes that privacy interests are violated, for he considers that what is perceived through the cameras is 'non-restricted' personal information because it is on view for everyone else to see.[40] But I dispute that an observer behind CCTV cameras sees no more than what meets the eye of those we encounter in the street. The observer benefits from a prime position and panoramic views, and has no other business to distract him. In virtue of the cameras' capabilities, his gaze is more intrusive and, unlike real-space appraisal, is not casual but purposeful and systematic. Public

---

[39] 'Bentham's Panopticon' was a concept for a prison designed by the English philosopher Jeremy Bentham in the first half of the 19th century. It had a centralised watch tower from which all prison cells could be overlooked by a supervisor. Although the supervisor would have been able to concentrate on only a few cells at a time, prisoners would always have to reckon with their being under observation, for they would never know when it was not their turn.
[40] D Archard, 'The Value of Privacy' in E Claes, RA Duff and S Gutwirth (eds), *Privacy and the Criminal Law* (Antwerp, Intersentia, 2006) 13 at 25.

CCTV surveillance can access 'restricted' personal information that is not in the public domain. To quote an operator:

> you notice things other people don't. People just lead their lives going from A to B. They don't see what happens in between.[41]

From his bird's eye view the observer can overcome obstructions that mar a person's sight on the ground, making it difficult to hide from his gaze. He therefore has the chance to focus on a person in the street more intensely than people who take the measure of each other in passing.

The revelatory quality of CCTV depends on the quality of the pictures the cameras transmit. Basic sweeping camera systems without PTZ facilities may only show the movements of the crowd and produce blurred images of individuals. In that case even the privileged position of the observer does not provide him with better insights. Footage filmed by that type of camera would also be of poor quality, although more information can usually be extracted from recordings by enlarging the pictures or otherwise enhancing their quality and by rerunning the scenes. Digital PTZ cameras, however, show people in graphic detail. Vision-enhancing technologies make it possible to take a closer look than with the naked eye. Before long we may also see a proliferation of night vision cameras which see in the dark, of heat sensitive instruments, which make things visible that are covered up, and of electronic monitoring devices, interpreting our gestures and anticipating our actions.

The observer behind the camera is favoured by the 'one-way mirror' effect, which allows him to pore over a person's activity without giving the target the chance to respond. The CCTV operator can pick a person out and spy on him at his leisure as no passer-by would be able to do unchallenged. The camera can linger on physical details, witness emotional responses and detect features that are not obvious to others—matters the person in the street could reasonably have expected to be able to withhold from those he encounters in public space. Surveillance via CCTV has been aptly described

> as a means to transforming into a front region the various largely unseen activities previously taking place backstage on the city streets.[42]

One of the basic rules of discretion, which has remained constant throughout many changes of conventions, has always been that spying on people is objectionable. A spy uses stealth, trying to catch a person out when he is not prepared, and takes advantage of the unsuspecting and therefore defenceless target. Spying involves an imposition of uninvited scrutiny, be it

---

[41] 'Pan, tilt, zoom', *The Observer Magazine*, 2 April 2006, 28.
[42] RP Jones, *Modern Penality and Social Theory* (Cambridge, Institute of Criminology, 2000) 195.

by someone the person would not have admitted, or at a time he would prefer not to be seen, or at closer quarters than he would have conceded voluntarily.

Even when CCTV is advertised, it always operates with an element of secrecy. Cameras are inanimate objects (which makes one forget about the humans behind them), they are usually placed above one's field of vision and are likely to be ignored in a way a person who is present is not. It is the people who are co-present and the events at hand that absorb our concentration in public space. We may be vaguely aware that cameras have been installed, but not in a way that properly informs our imagination. The unobtrusiveness of CCTV surveillance can easily lull us into a false sense that there is no other audience than the people we see. We tend to forget about the observers behind the camera and do not prepare for their scrutiny; we may, therefore, fail to prevent them from obtaining knowledge about us we would rather not share. Yet, of all possible audiences, keeping up appearances in front of CCTV operators would be particularly advisable, considering their mission and powers.[43]

It is true that images alone do not yield information about names and identity. To deny that there may be an interference with anonymity interests, though, merely because CCTV surveillance as such does not deprive a person of his incognito identity, would not do justice to the more complex idea of anonymity, developed in the previous chapter. Anonymity and the claim to control the 'presentation of self' have a wider scope than just being able to withhold one's identity. Nevertheless, CCTV can make inroads even into anonymity *sensu stricto*. While a person may not be identified by name, regular visitors of the surveyed space become known to the operators and identifiable by appearance and habits, especially if they are distinctive in one way or the other. This lays the groundwork for tracing the individual's identity without too much investigative effort. Personally identifiable information can also be obtained with the help of face recognition technologies, and through the linking of recordings to positive and nominative data.

---

[43] When Robert Peel introduced patrolling policemen ('Peelers' or 'Bobbies' as they were called) in 1829, the officers were required to wear their uniforms both on and off duty, to alert people to their presence and to avoid the impression that secret government agents were spying on the population. See *The Bobby—Icons of England*, at <http://www.icons.org.uk/theicons/collection/the-bobby/features/changing-uniform>.

2. Is virtual scrutiny less invasive than physical scrutiny?

(i) The implications of 'distanciation'

When a person is observed through CCTV cameras and when footage of him is reviewed, there is no direct contact between him and the observer. The observer looks at a picture of the person, not at the person himself. Since privacy is about access control, the manner by which a person is accessed is a central criterion for determining the degree of invasion he suffers as a result of the unwanted approach.

David Archard differentiates between sensory and cognitive access.[44] He is right to value the quality of 'sensory knowledge' (when one sees/ witnesses someone) more highly than that of 'propositional knowledge' (when one knows something about someone). Looking at someone involves a more direct and intense experience of the other person, and therefore potentially is more intrusive. The thought of having an unwanted witness while one is engaged in certain activities is embarrassing and inhibiting; one may be less troubled by someone having propositional knowledge, not acquired through direct perception of one's actions.[45]

There is no doubt, however, that live CCTV surveillance is a form of direct perception. Although there are modulations in the quality of knowledge gained because such surveillance lacks some of the sensory elements intrinsic to physical appraisal, it is a first-hand experience of the 'real thing', not a mere account of it. The operator of the camera is a direct, contemporaneous witness. Nevertheless, the sensory access is mediated by technology. The 'one-way mirror' functions at the same time as a glass wall which distances the observer from the observed. The operator can look on, but he cannot act. Moreover, the physical remoteness and the invisibility of the observer cannot be entirely insignificant as regards the intrusiveness of his gaze. The virtual appraisal by remote observers is bound to affect a person differently from the face-to-face confrontation with a co-present spectator. The absence of direct personal interactions reduces the discomfort of being scrutinised. I explained earlier that an important function of anonymity conventions in real space is to restrain the overt manifestation of interest in bystanders and to prevent people from expressing their opinion about those whom they encounter. In the case of virtual scrutiny no such contact takes place. To be scanned by disembodied media has no immediate material effect, and is therefore less

---

[44] See above n40 at 19f.
[45] The difference becomes apparent when comparing the sensory experience (cognitive knowledge) of watching one's parents having sex (which would be upsetting for both parties) with the propositional knowledge that one's parents are likely to have sex (which is an abstract fact, not a personal experience, leaving the parents' personal sphere unviolated).

uncomfortable than being eyed up by someone who is physically present and who might smack his lips, gloat or express his appreciation (or disapproval) in other ways. The robust manual frisking employed by some airport security controllers doubtless creates greater unease than being scanned by cameras.

A person's physical progress in public space and his integration into the general crowd are not impaired by CCTV. Often he is oblivious of being watched; and even if he were aware of the cameras, he would not be able to tell for certain when they focus on him. Nobody physically forces himself on that person and he does not have to fend off importunate curiosity. Focusing the zoom on someone is not comparable to moving in on someone in real space, because the targeted person can continue on his way unhindered. In terms of the 'territories of the self' (see chapter one, section II.B.), he retains full control over the 'use space', his 'possessional territory' and the 'conversational preserve'. He is not bothered or embarrassed in front of others by the attention, nor singled out and called to justify himself in the same way as he would be by the insistence of a curious individual, or the inquiries of a suspicious policeman in a real-space scenario. People tend to be less inhibited when they cannot see the person who looks at them and cannot gauge his reactions, even if they know that someone is watching them.[46] An invisible observer is less troublesome, because we are spared any indication of how we are perceived by him.

One reason why we need privacy is our preoccupation with the impression we make on others. It tends to deflate us if the feedback we get is negative or different from what we expect. In real space, where we are up against our audience, the convention of inattention and the de facto fleetingness of the encounter spare us some of the discomfort of unwelcome reactions. However, the distance we claim is fictional, to a degree, when we face each other. We might pretend lack of interest, but as long as people are within our field of vision, our antennae are alert for signals indicating their opinion about us; and our self-confidence is on precarious grounds as we watch out for their reaction. If the person looking at me is not physically present, those signals do not come through. Surveillance personnel remain anonymous throughout. Observer and observed are unlikely ever knowingly to meet. The person in the street is therefore

---

[46] In *An Audience with Kylie* (ITV Network, London, 22 September 2001), Kylie Minogue recounted that when she was filming what was to become her most famous video clip, featuring her song 'Spinning Around', showing her wearing the notorious golden micro hot pants (recently on show at the Victoria and Albert Museum), she banned everyone with the exception of one cameraman from the set, because she was too embarrassed to be seen in such a revealing garment. She was obviously not embarrassed, however, by the thought that millions would see her gyrating suggestively on MTV and other music channels, where the clip was on heavy rotation for many months.

spared the shameful prospect of having to confront the uninvited witness who has seen too much, made all the more embarrassing by both parties being aware of it. Even when a police officer is dispatched, facing him is not quite the same as facing the observer himself, for the policeman's knowledge is propositional, and therefore of less intrusive quality. This makes it easier for the observed to distance himself from the alleged events, to deny the accuracy of the imparted information and generally to save face.

People may be less bothered by virtual scrutiny than by physical scrutiny, but they still have to submit to an intrusion into their egocentric preserves. The observer behind a CCTV camera can move into the personal space, the physical and mental sphere that revolves around the individual, look underneath his sheath and tease out information. His may not be a physical presence, but he is a presence nevertheless, who appraises and judges, and who has to be reckoned with. Although little research has been done on the effect of cameras on those who fall routinely beneath their gaze, it is unlikely that the awareness of being observed has no effect on our sense of self and is without psychological impact. We are conditioned to take into account how the world reacts to us, and we cannot help being concerned about the impression we make, even if we do not see the reaction of others. People react differently to virtual scrutiny—some play to the hidden audience (the 'Stars of CCTV' of Hard-Fi's song, quoted in the Preface to this book), others prefer to appear as inconspicuous as possible to avoid attention, but I posit that hardly anyone is entirely immune against becoming self-conscious when he is aware that someone is looking at him. One is being judged, after all, and somehow, consciously or involuntarily, prepares for it, even if one pretends to be unfazed.

It is true that there is no communication and confrontation between the observer and the observed, and the unknown opinions and reactions of absent observers are less unsettling or hurtful than manifest reactions in person.[47] This does not mean, however, that the interest in controlling access cannot be infringed without the person knowing of the violation of his space. The concept of privacy to which I subscribe is essentially dignity-based. The rationale of privacy is to spare a person the indignity of being scrutinised and subjected to judgement when he is not prepared for it. Becoming the unwilling object of an uninvited observer is an affront which is not conditional upon subjective awareness of that fact. A human being has—for reasons suggested in chapter one—an intrinsic claim to be

---

[47] Hence the German saying: '*was ich nicht weiss, macht mich nicht heiss*' (what I don't know does not make me get hot under the collar).

treated with respect, which can be infringed even if the individual has no knowledge of it, or no wish to enforce his claim.[48]

Another question is whether autonomy can be affected if a person is unaware of being watched. However, this cannot be an argument in defence of covert surveillance. Covert surveillance and not informing people when they are scrutinised is more disrespectful than overt CCTV. Overt surveillance at least acknowledges that a person is entitled to know what is happening to him, and gives him a chance to assert some control. The assumption that covert surveillance does not impinge on autonomy is wrong in any case: the mere existence of secret surveillance activities, which are not disclosed to the people who are being watched, is a challenge to autonomy. The possibility of covert surveillance can create a permanent state of insecurity and thus exercises pressure to conform, even when an individual might not be certain when and if he has actually been targeted. Knowing it might happen, but not knowing when, means one can never relax one's guard. The European Court of Human Rights held that secret monitoring of mail and telephones affected not only the actual victims, but all users of the postal and telecommunications services too, even if they had not been bugged. They could claim victim status, for the effect of secrecy would be that intrusions would become unchallengeable and privacy protection might be reduced to a nullity.[49]

One should also not forget that CCTV surveillance does not have only virtual effects. Dispatch facilities mean that communication and confrontation can take place by way of intermediaries. The observer may not be visible himself, and he may not be able to interact directly, but he can mobilise the police to act on his behalf, and therefore cannot be treated as someone of no consequence.

(ii) The disempowering effect of the observer's inaccessibility

Surveillance by CCTV empowers the observer and disempowers the person in the street. Even though a virtual observer's options for action are restricted, his inaccessibility gives him the upper hand over the observed. The CCTV operator can unilaterally determine the timing, length and intensity of his scrutiny. The person in the street has to submit to his gaze and to his agenda. In the English film 'Red Road', by the Oscar-winning director Andrea Arnold, audiences can experience for themselves what it is like to watch people's lives on a bank of screens, and are able to get an

---

[48] Paul Roberts's earlier quoted example of the person in a coma (see ch 1, text to n 22) illustrates not only that privacy claims may be independent of autonomy and grounded solely in dignity, but also the objective nature of a dignity claim.
[49] See *Klass and others v Federal Republic of Germany* (1979–80) 2 EHRR 214, paras 34ff.

inkling of the empowering effect this has.[50] On the ground, people can control access to themselves, and defend their territories of the self by interacting with those who threaten to invade it. The virtual observer is immune against such defensive measures: while he can assume an active role, the observed is confined to passivity. All the observed can do is avoid places under surveillance, which is not always an option. David Bond, an Englishman who wanted to find out if, in surveillance Britain, it is possible to vanish, counted no fewer than 200 CCTV cameras within 100 yards of his home.[51]

The observer's inaccessibility allows him to disregard the conventions of discretion. Conventions regulate behaviour on the basis of general compliance, but apart from a mutual interest in their observance, it also needs mutual controls, group pressure and assertiveness to enforce them. For the authorities, conventions may also incorporate certain moral obligations for their dealings with citizens, but they do not have the same binding force as for civilians. There is no mutuality of interests, and enforcement is hampered by the disparity of power. However, conventions are weak regulators when overstepping them is feasible without the intruder being answerable. With CCTV surveillance, the authorities can act behind the scenes, and the complex and skilled management of interaction, which is the basis of civil inattention and which the police are also, as a rule, advised to observe, is not required. There is no need to tread carefully or to justify their interest to their target or to the people around him, for the intrusion goes unnoticed and the observed cannot defend his space. Even statutory constraints might be disregarded, without anyone noticing or being able to object. Access control is seriously impaired by this disparity of power, and the entitlement to be treated with respect is endangered. One is relegated to the role of an unwitting object whose feelings and preferences need not be taken into account, for the authorities to scrutinise as they see fit.

The relation between the observer and the observed is skewed in another respect. Not only has one the advantage of gaining unwanted access to the other, but he also has the added advantage of not having to disclose

---

[50] The 'surveillance thriller', released in 2006, tells the story of Jacky, a CCTV operator who covers a tough Glasgow housing estate and one day sees a man who belongs to her past appear on the screen. She starts to track him obsessively, using her position to pursue her personal design.

[51] 'Surveillance Britain', *The Times Magazine*, 17 April 2010. See also 'Erasing David', David Bond's film about his journey, released in British cinemas in April 2010. Tips on how to 'live off-grid', ie how to sidestep CCTV cameras, and the official and commercial tracking, collection, processing and exchange of data, can be found in N Rosen, *How to live off-grid. Journeys outside the system* (London, Doubleday, 2007). To retain a level of anonymity, we are advised, amongst other things, to cover our heads, use tinted car windows to keep our faces off camera and to install an infra-red light bulb above car licence plates in order to dazzle speed cameras, preventing them from reading the numbers.

anything about himself. When each party is both observer and observed, the indignities of exposure are more evenly distributed. There is no such parity between the operator of a CCTV camera and the person in the street. The situation favours the operator: only he examines and judges according to his standards. The impact of his scrutiny is not neutralised by what I described earlier as 'the equalising effect of the mutual process of self disclosure' that occurs during face-to-face encounters, for the operator does not have to reciprocate the insights he obtains and submit to the scrutiny and judgement of the person in the street.

3. Is CCTV surveillance non-judgemental?

A prime concern of contemporary public policy is to manage the risks resulting from living in densely-populated, freely-accessible spaces, where people of differing beliefs and varying personal agendas mass together. There is a widespread assumption that informal social control mechanisms are overtaxed by these situations, and that new strategies for the protection of the public space have to be devised. A shift has taken place, from individualistic offender-orientated policies, which are thought by many to have failed and to be unsuitable for use on the large scale, to a new version of crime prevention, addressing no longer individuals but factors and criminogenic situations. The strategy of situational crime prevention (SCP) involves

> the management, design or manipulation of the immediate environment ... so as to reduce the opportunities for crime and to increase its risks.[52]

Measures involving SCP, it is claimed, do not target individuals but diffuse conditions that are conducive to crime.[53] Instead of a moral appeal, the idea is to 'design out' crime by using 'target hardening' measures and devices that make the commission of crimes more difficult. Several authors have pointed out the detachment from individual focus of security strategies that emphasise the control of entire groups and categories.[54]

Surveillance via CCTV is often defended as a policy that takes a technocratic approach, intent on target hardening, opportunity reduction and event anticipation. The observer checks out the situation for risk

---

[52] M Felson and RV Clarke, 'The ethics of situational crime prevention' in G Newman, RV Clarke and SG Shoham (eds), *Rational Choice and Situational Crime Prevention: Theoretical Foundations* (Aldershot, Ashgate,1997) 197.

[53] RV Clarke and P Mayhew (eds), *Designing out Crime* (London, HMSO, 1980).

[54] Eg S Cohen, *Visions of Social Control: Crime, Punishment and Classification* (Cambridge, Polity Press, 1985) 140; AE Bottoms, 'Crime prevention facing the 1990s' (1990) 1(1) *Policing and Society* 3; R Castel, 'From Dangerousness to Risk' in G Burchell, C Gordon and P Miller (eds), *The Foucault Effect: Studies in Governmentality* (Chicago, Ill, University of Chicago Press, 1991).

factors, and makes an attempt at actuarial prediction, based on externalities, but does not judge or blame individuals, who in any event are unknown to the observer and remain anonymous. There is no longer a relation of immediacy with a subject, 'because there is no longer a subject', as Robert Castel puts it.[55] While a stop-and-search action would be directed against a specific person, implying that there are reasons to connect him with criminal activity,[56] CCTV cameras draw within their ambit all persons present without making such implicit allegations about them. Suspicion expresses a negative judgement, suggesting that the person who is subjected to a search procedure is less trustworthy and in this respect different from (inferior to) those who are not searched. Appraisal that is not selective but indiscriminate, it is argued, is not judgemental. It suggests no personal reproach and involves no comparative degradation.

I think that this argument is flawed, being based on three misconceptions requiring correction:

a) CCTV is not an impersonal device that impacts only on the environment.
b) The assessment of risk factors may be based on externalities, but if those are associated with an individual it amounts to a personal judgement.
c) Even if CCTV were impartial, which it is not, this does not stop unwanted scrutiny from violating anonymity interests.

These statements contain a more accurate assessment of the way public CCTV surveillance works, for the following reasons. First, 'target hardening' devices, such as locks or barriers, are typically self-contained; it is this quality that makes them neutral from a rights perspective. They interfere only with would-be thieves, who are acting on the intention to steal, but a thief who is prevented from stealing by a lock cannot claim to be thwarted as regards an entitlement. On the other hand, CCTV impacts not just on

---

[55] Castel, above n 53, at 288.
[56] Under English law, as a rule a pedestrian may not be stopped by the police unless there are reasonable grounds for suspicion that that person is carrying stolen goods or a weapon, or is about to commit, or is suspected of having committed, an offence (Police and Criminal Evidence Act (PACE) 1984, ss 2 and 3, Code A). However, in the following circumstance people may be stopped without there being reasonable grounds for suspicion: for the purpose of combating terrorism (Terrorism Act 2000, s 44); to prevent violence between armed gangs in public (Criminal Justice and Public Order Act, s 60); and when trying to catch fleeing offenders (PACE 1984, s 4). Under the Road Traffic Act 1988, s 163, a vehicle on the road may be stopped for any purpose connected with a constable's duties, without the need for reasonable suspicion that the driver has committed an offence. See D Feldman, *Civil Liberties and Human Rights in England and Wales* (Oxford, Oxford University Press 2002) 172ff.

actual or would-be offenders but on everyone.[57] Although one might say that the vetting of people in public space via CCTV is a form of 'target hardening', making it more difficult for actual or would-be offenders to get away with street crimes without being detected, the technicist label cannot hide that those who are examined are being judged as to whether they are 'safe'. Measures like security checks, physical or virtual, are centred on the person. They are normative, with actors and intentions guiding their application, and have human personal consequences.

Secondly, risk assessment is probabilistic and requires the classification of events and individuals. Since surveillance personnel have to base their assessment on visual impressions, they must judge by externalities and often rely on predictive factors. To manage the flood of visual information, actuarial practices are employed which imply stereotyping and social sorting. Surveillance works on the basis of the identification of certain wrongs, which are then tied to particular people, as Bottoms and Wiles point out. A person who displays certain characteristics, or acts in a certain way, is considered to represent a risk. Once designated as a risk, the person qualifies for closer monitoring.[58] Pretending that qualifying people according to predictive factors does not imply judgement is disingenuous. The point of reference may be externalities, but by linking these externalities to wrong-doing and 'tying' them to individuals, their moral personality is put into question. When prevention strategies are dominated by risk assessment, it is a small step from being considered a risk factor to being considered dangerous, because 'what risk presumes is precisely danger'.[59]

Thirdly, the fact that others are also subjected to scrutiny, and that one is not openly blamed or treated with suspicion, may spare one the embarrassment and feeling of inferiority one might experience when singled out by a stop-and-search order; but even if one's status among the people in the street is not affected by CCTV surveillance, one's status in the eyes of the observer behind the camera is at stake, and this might entail unpleasant consequences.

In any event, the claim that CCTV surveillance is impartial and that everyone is subjected to the same degree of scrutiny is a fiction.[60] Public CCTV may be indiscriminate, in that everybody is affected by it, but not

---

[57] For the distinction between the impact of SCP measures on actual, would-be and potential offenders, see RA Duff and SE Marshall, 'Benefits, Burdens and Responsibilities: Some Ethical Dimensions of Situational Crime Prevention' in von Hirsch *et al*, above n 27, at 28.

[58] AE Bottoms and P Wiles, 'Understanding Crime Prevention in Late Modern Society' in T Bennet (ed), *Preventing Crime and Disorder* (Cambridge, Institute of Criminology, 1995) 12.

[59] A Giddens, *The Consequences of Modernity* (Cambridge, Polity Press, 1990) 34.

[60] An example of (relatively) indiscriminate scrutiny would be the routine body and hand luggage checks all passengers have to undergo before boarding a plane. In contrast, customs controls are neither impartial nor random. As one can observe time and again, people from

everybody is equally affected, for surveillance personnel often revert to type-casting and regularly single out specific individuals or groups. Technology such as PTZ and the various methods for enhancing the picture quality of recordings, the rerunning of particular scenes and the creation of stills are designed to that end. Persons may be marked for tracking solely on the basis of race, sex or other characteristics. The observers tend to concentrate on demographic categories of persons who are statistically defined as high crime-risk groups (eg young black males) or who are generally perceived as trouble-makers (teenagers), or on unpleasant sights for customers (beggars, drunks and the homeless), making the marginalised members of society the preferred subjects of surveillance.[61]

People who are targeted by surveillance personnel are 'picked out' from the crowd. As long as they are not confronted by the police, nobody in real space becomes aware of this selection and they are spared the shame of being made answerable in front of everyone. But, as I have explained before, a virtual act can also express disrespect. And is it not even more offensive if one's integrity is questioned as a matter of categorical suspicion against one's kind, without any further substantiation?

4. Is CCTV surveillance 'sanitised' by the observers' professional mission?

Surveillance personnel are part of a range of professionals who by virtue of their work are in a position to scrutinise people and to access privileged information about them. Sometimes the professionals carrying out these tasks are chosen by those affected themselves, eg doctors or priests; at other times they are imposed by official order, eg policemen and security officers. Surveillance personnel fall into the latter group.

There is a fundamental difference between scrutiny carried out by witnesses of one's choice and imposed observation, even if in both cases the appraisal is carried out by professionals and for professional motives. Chosen professionals can rely on consent to the invasion of privacy their examination entails, provided they stay within the agreed brief. Imposed professionals, such as surveillance personnel, have not been authorised by the people whom they scrutinise.

---

certain ethnic or social groups, or of a certain appearance (beards, long hair), are the ones who are always asked to open their suitcases. The choice is based on their qualification as risk factors.

[61] According to research conducted by Norris and Armstrong, *The Maximum Surveillance Society*, above n 37, at 150, 34% of people were surveyed for no obvious reasons, merely on the basis of belonging to a particular social group. Young black men were systematically and disproportionately targeted. This is not surprising, as it is well documented that black people are stopped and searched up to 10 times more often than white people. See Statistics on Race and the Criminal Justice System – 2005 (Home Office Publication 2006) www.homeoffice.gov.uk/rds/indexhtm .

Nonetheless, a professional relationship is a somewhat sanitised relationship, because it is focused on a confined issue, and personal preferences and emotions are supposed to be filtered out. This may to a limited extent neutralise the invasive character of the scrutiny, even if the scrutiny is imposed and not chosen. A professional approach suggests objective criteria and personal detachment, as opposed to the wide-ranging expectations and subjective judgement inherent in scrutiny by a private individual. The professional observer, provided he acts ethically, checks out the 'case', approaching it with professional integrity and disregarding those aspects which are outside his brief. If the appraisal is impersonal, its undermining effect on the target's dignity is somewhat mitigated, allowing the person on the receiving end also mentally to take a step back and be matter of fact about the examination without being offended.

There is another aspect to professional scrutiny which reduces its impact on privacy: scrutiny is unsettling not only because of worries about one's status vis-à-vis the actual witness, but also because of the snowball effect of gossip, expanding the circle of those 'in the know'. As regards insights gained in a professional capacity, however, there is usually a requirement of confidentiality, stipulated by statute or code of practice, with varying levels of sanctions in case of breach, depending on the sensitivity of the information. One can thus to some degree be assured that the information obtained by the observer is not circulated outside the professional sphere and cannot taint one's reputation in the general course of one's life.[62]

Surveillance by CCTV shares some of the characteristics of a sanitised intrusion. Camera operators are not on a private assignment; they are professionals, working on behalf of public institutions, for a circumscribed purpose and not to satisfy their personal curiosity. There is, however, no guarantee of their neutrality and their maintenance of confidentiality. The abuse of position is an inherent problem in any profession with access to privileged information. In the case of CCTV, it is exacerbated by several factors. For example:

a) the professional criteria for surveillance are notoriously lax;
b) operators are recruited from all walks of life, receive only cursory training and often operate under the aegis of private, commercially-orientated enterprises which are not subject to strict regulations; and
c) operators' statement of mission is vague, leaving much room for personal attitude and subjectivity.[63]

---

[62] The neutral ground and the implied damage limitation often inspire people to open up to professional interlocutors, volunteering to share the most intimate knowledge about themselves, even if it is irrelevant for the consultation at hand.

[63] For an account of the social structuring of CCTV operators and how they operate, see Norris and Armstrong, above n 37, at 102ff.

Benjamin Goold rightly suggests that if the person in the street were able to form some reliable belief about who is behind the camera, it would help him to feel more comfortable in the presence of CCTV. This, I believe, is not so much a question of knowing the name and identity of the operator, but of confidence

> that the only person to look at me is a well trained camera operator bound by a set of clear ethical and legal guidelines and not a voyeuristic pervert and ten of his friends who have just dropped into the control room for an afternoon of entertainment.[64]

That confidence is hard to come by. The level of professionalism of surveillance personnel, their commitment to secrecy and the integrity of the system depend to a great extent on the rules adopted and imposed by the individual surveillance regime. Variations in quality of execution can be significant.

However, even if those issues were addressed by a general regulatory framework, and minimum training requirements could ensure more consistent standards, the fact remains that the person in the street cannot choose his examiner. With professionals of one's choice one can select those in whose expertise and reliability one believes and whose personality and views are sympathetic, but one does not have that comfort with surveillance personnel who are imposed by others. Moreover, the problem of the unobservable observer, to use Goold's phrase, means that there are no 'face work commitments', as Giddens calls the trust relationship one can form through face-to-face contact.[65] If we can observe the professional while he carries out his assignment, we can reassure ourselves that he acts as a good-faith professional and keeps within his brief. Closed circuit television not only gives us no choice as to who carries out the job (we might prefer a liberal operator who understands and approves of the concept of anonymity to one with low tolerance and little regard for privacy), but also no control over its execution. This is particularly discomfiting given the power bestowed on the operator by his official position, his vantage point, the technology put at his disposal and the fact that those he targets are largely at his mercy.

In any event, although professional execution may protect us from spiteful appraisal and the extra insult that this inflicts, it does not sanitise CCTV scrutiny to such an extent that it annuls the degrading potential of the act. The anonymity interest pertains not only to protection against scrutiny by people with unsavoury agendas; the claim pertains to the protection of one's personal preserves which one holds against any

---

[64] B Goold, 'Privacy Rights and Public Spaces: CCTV and the Problem of the "Unobservable Observer"', *Criminal Justice Ethics*, Winter/Spring 2000, 24.
[65] Giddens, above n 58, at 80.

outsider. Whoever invades the territories of the self of another without permission is using another individual for his ulterior purposes, discounting that person's preferences about how much he wants to disclose of himself. Denying a person a say in this matter amounts to denying that person's claim to dignity and respect, irrespective of the motives of the intruder. Some of the unsettling aspects of public CCTV relate, however, expressly to its mission: surveillance personnel represent the authorities. Unlike professionals of one's own choice, who, one can assume, act in one's own purported interest, and to whose gaze one can therefore submit comfortably, such trust cannot be placed in those professionals imposed by the authorities. Their brief is the *bonum commune*, which may not infrequently be at odds with the interests of individuals; and in the course of carrying out their professional duties, operators are likely to place legitimate personal interests of individuals second or even, in cases of conflict or doubt, sacrifice them to majority interests.

5. *How does recording affect anonymity interests?*

(i) The implications of the fixing of one's picture

The Data Protection Act 1998 regulates the use of CCTV recordings in accordance with data protection principles. However, to use de Hert and Gutwirt's terminology,[66] data protection laws are a tool for 'transparency' which promote meaningful public accountability, but they do not prohibit the acquisition of data and therefore are not effective 'opacity' tools which bar access to the information altogether. As long as the public is properly informed, the use of data in the name of public safety is permissible. In my view, recording does not raise questions of data administration alone; the acquisition of the data, through the fixing of ephemeral events, is itself problematic.

The fleetingness of the encounter in real space imposes natural limits to the degree and intensity of the scrutiny to which one has to submit in public. Onlookers receive a cursory impression; they cannot hold on to the image. This changes when events are recorded and the image of the person is preserved permanently. Making a recording renders the person more exposed to scrutiny, for it is now possible, for anyone at any time, to revisit events and to subject the person's appearance and behaviour to repeated, focused and critical analysis. An ephemeral impression fades: you can correct the image you project as you go along, and replace a silly expression with a dignified one; you can also pretend something never

---

[66] P de Hert and S Gutwirt, 'Privacy, data protection and law enforcement. Opacity of the individual and transparency of power' in Claes *et al*, above n 39, at 76.

happened. If you are captured on film, however, your image is no longer a work in progress and you cannot count on the obliterating effect of passing time. Others do not have to rely on hearsay, there is now tangible proof. If a person is accused of something, it is no longer a case of his statement against somebody else's: the recording of a person can be used as evidence against him.

Not much of the person's presentation of self may survive if image analysis is carried sufficiently far. Pictures can be manipulated and enhanced, which tends to create distortions: what seemed perfectly innocuous to the passer-by, may now be made to appear grotesque or threatening. Repeated replay makes even the most dignified gestures look ridiculous. A person is more exposed to criticism, because people can now study him intensely and claim to arrive at an informed opinion about him, whereas passing encounters in the street do not give away much on which to base a judgement. When a person goes out, he does not expect to be scrutinised in such detail, and does not prepare for that kind of attention. When his image is frozen, replayed and studied, aspects of his looks and acts will be detected which would have escaped the attention of those around him, who would have seen the scene only once and *en passant*.

Recording also threatens anonymity by facilitating identification. The whole point of recording is to catch out offenders by preserving evidence of their actions, and finding them with the help of their recorded likenesses. Surveillance via CCTV provides investigators with pictures of those who are wanted for questioning, which can be shown around and broadcast on television. The chances of tracing suspects are enhanced in a way not possible when relying on descriptions or 'identikit' reconstructions.

Another option which becomes available only as a result of recording is the use of facial recognition software and electronic processes for matching CCTV images with personal data taken from various sources. Matching the images to a database containing pictures of known and suspected criminals may not endanger the anonymity of ordinary citizens, but this can change if general databases of positive and nominative information (ID card or driving licence files) are used. As Haggerty and Ericson remark, 'the possibility for disappearance has narrowed for everyone'.[67]

---

[67] KD Haggerty and RV Ericson, 'The surveillance assemblage' (2000) 51(4) *British Journal of Sociology* 605. The Bush administration's programme for monitoring illegal immigrants from Latin America gives a foretaste of things to come. The company Choice Point (which notably helped George W Bush to win the election in 2000 by revising the Florida electoral registration list) is reported to have acquired on behalf of the Government, personal data—including date and place of birth, sex, parentage, physical description (photos), marital status, passport numbers and registered profession—from Mexico's entire list of voters, and similar files from several other Latin American countries. See 'How US paid for secret files on foreign citizens', *Guardian*, 5 May 2003.

As mentioned at II B 1 above, I disagree with David Archard, who posits that CCTV cameras only capture information that is generally available, and that it is therefore not objectionable for the authorities to record and store that information.[68] It is true that the other people in the street see what is recorded, but the information about a person's appearance and actions in public is available only as an ephemeral impression to those who are co-present, not as a transferable commodity, and many aspects become apparent only when the person can be studied via a permanent record. The State may know the names and addresses of citizens, and have propositional knowledge of what goes on in the streets, but recording overcomes the inherent restrictions which limit sensory first-hand knowledge about people and their actions in public, providing more complex and expandable information than is generally available.

(ii) Does the 'disembedding' effect reduce the impact of scrutiny of recorded footage?

Giddens's term 'disembedding' means the

> lifting out ... of social relations ... from local contexts of interaction and their restructuring across indefinite spans of time-space.[69]

This is exactly what happens when recordings of events are reviewed retroactively out of the context of their occurrence, by people other than those who were present at the time. With CCTV, the scrutiny is always virtual, whether operators watch transmissions on screens contemporaneously with the events, or examine recorded footage at a later stage. The observer looks at the image of the person, not the physical person; but, as stated before, he nevertheless obtains a direct sensory impression of that person. This is still true when footage is reviewed retroactively. Although the person becomes 'data', these are not actuarial abstract data but a personal representation of the data subject himself.

The time delay may not change the immediacy of the perception, but does it not, nevertheless, somewhat blur the boundaries between sensory and cognitive access?

What are the implications for the relationship between the observer and the observed, when the image is lifted out of its time and space context, and disembedded, as it is now possible? Does it alter the quality of knowledge? Does the distanciation between observer and observed not become more pronounced, and is the observed not less affected by the

---

[68] See Archard, above n40.
[69] Giddens, above n 58, at 21.

scrutiny? Or does the permanence of the image, its availability and processibility make up for the distanciation and result in an even greater intrusion?

As Giddens observes, the disembedding effect alters the very tissue of spatial experience,

> conjoining proximity and distance ... and creating a complex relation between familiarity and estrangement in ways that have few close parallels in prior ages ...[70]

Recorded surveillance is a fitting example of this phenomenon. The observer has unprecedented opportunities for proximity and familiarity, but is at the same time more cut off from the observed. The quality of knowledge—sensory and cognitive—is enhanced by the fixation, but its intrusive capacity is also neutralised by the spatial and temporal estrangement. Live surveillance and the knowledge that I am watched as I go about my business can make me self-conscious. Also, the expectations of my observer weigh more heavily on me when I know that he (or someone else, at his instigation) could come after me, if I fail to get his approval. When recordings are reviewed *post factum*, the scrutiny becomes a remote and an abstract possibility, and it is a human tendency to discount uncertain future events. In the mind of the observed, the observer becomes more peripheral. If there is a delay between a person's performance and its review, it means that he does not have an audience while he is in the middle of things; and if a potential reviewer were later to disapprove, the person will have moved on and be out of his way long since.

However, the person in the street would have to be certain that the cameras he encounters belong to a passive monitoring scheme. This information is usually withheld from the public, for to ease fears of crime and to promote a deterrent effect, the authorities have an interest in creating the impression that there might be guardians behind the cameras.

In any event, even if the recording of events for retroactive review causes little spontaneous discomfort, its effect on privacy remains significant. An important function of privacy is giving us control over the context in which we are seen. The context determines the criteria by which we are judged. Within a given situation we can gauge what is expected from us and perform within those parameters. If our performance is taken out of context, there will be other types of observers with differing expectations. We may be judged by criteria for which we were not prepared, risking disapproval and negative consequences from unforeseeable quarters. The fixing of one's image takes away control over how and to whom one is presented. The picture becomes a commodity in the hands of others, giving

---

[70] *Ibid* at 140.

them the freedom to access the captured person in a variety of ways. The fact that the people who are recorded by CCTV usually do not know what happens to the footage (who sees the images, what are the conditions for reviewing them, how are they processed, what information is extracted) highlights that although they are the 'data subjects', they are the objects of the process, and their wishes and preferences carry little weight.

(iii)   Exposure to an uninvited audience

A person who ventures abroad cannot choose who else may visit public places. In the streets, one is presented with a—potentially vast—random selection of people who have equal entitlement to be there. Nevertheless, the audience one encounters is limited, in the sense that it is only composed of people who are 'co- present'. The fact that one can be seen only by people who are in the same place at the same time as oneself, enables one to exercise some control over one's exposure. One can avoid certain people by choosing times and locations where they are unlikely to be around, or one can gauge who else is there and duck, find a dark corner or keep a low profile, if necessary. Such precautions are ineffectual when the audience defies delimitation by time and location and is brought in at a later stage, when it is too late to adjust to its presence.

A connection of simultaneity and location is maintained when surveillance personnel are following the events live from monitors in a control room in the vicinity. Even if they are not exactly in the same place, one could say that their presence at the outlook post is in essence coterminous in space and time. When control rooms are removed from the surveyed areas, the operators watching the events live are spatially distant, but still coterminous and contextually connected with the people they observe.

No such connection is required when recordings are used. The information contained in the pictures is available to any reviewer of the recordings, at any time. Once the digital format is established, anyone connected to the system is technically able to access the footage recorded by public CCTV cameras anywhere in the world. Thus, nobody could ever be sure who might be watching, how many observers there are, and for what precise purpose (crime prevention is an elastic concept). This is in my opinion the most significant difference between being seen by people in the street and being recorded by CCTV cameras, and it has a significant impact on anonymity. Not only might the person captured on the film be subjected to more acute scrutiny but, without consultation or a chance for him to object, unforeseeable audiences might be given sensory access to him and be able to see what he looked like, what he was doing and what company he kept. Anonymity and the presentation of self are further threatened, because with the introduction of new audiences comes a greater risk that information might reach unwanted circles, and that there might be people among them who can identify the person in the picture. It could change the nature of the role that person had conceived for himself, for instead of playing the part of an anonymous passer-by, he might be judged on personal merits, or in a different context. Looks and actions which were of no relevance in anonymous encounters, might be picked up by those other audiences because for some reason they are of relevance to them. They see the individual and burden him with subjective expectations that are more challenging than the expectations of those who are co- present, who need to reassure themselves only that his intent is not hostile.

(iv)   Recording without reviewing

Not all footage recorded by CCTV cameras is reviewed. Anonymity is not actually infringed, strictly speaking, until a human being looks at the recorded images. Does that mean that recording as such is not objectionable, as long as recordings are not reviewed? In its logical conclusion this would leave the authorities free to record everything that goes on in public as a means of preventiveevidence collection. Footage would be available and reviewing justifiable, when needed for a criminal investigation.

I posit that recording as such is not innocuous, for it lays the groundwork for infringement of anonymity. Making a recording of a person creates something akin to a file about him. Permitting the authorities to accumulate and store such files, and making them their exclusive custodians, involves a considerable risk that the authorities may tap into that source, for the State has a vested interest in exploiting the sources of knowledge at its disposal. Recording is the first step towards depriving a person of access control, which may entail further invasions of anonymity that the person on the recording is not capable of preventing. In German constitutional law, the concept that endangering basic rights can itself amount to a violation (*Grundrechtsgefaehrdung*) is established doctrine. Thus, according to prevailing legal opinion, the *making* of a photograph already constitutes an infringement to the right to one's own image, although the law talks about *circulation* (*verbreiten*).[71] The argument is that once the image of a person has been fixed, the person has reason to fear that it might be used to invade his privacy.[72] The right to one's own

---

[71] The argument that private individuals should already have a claim against a newspaper for the possession of photos taken without their consent, not only for the publishing of such photos, is based on similar grounds.

[72] When the German National Census was challenged at the German Constitutional Court because of the wide scope of the questionnaire that had to be completed, the German Government defended itself with the argument that Germany as a democratic 'Rechtsstaat' would never condone any use of the information that violated constitutional entitlements. To demonstrate the imponderable risks of preventive data collection (*Datenspeicherung auf Vorrat*), the plaintiffs' representatives related in the oral discussion with the judges what had

image should therefore include the right to decide if one's image may be recorded, in order to spare the person such concerns.[73] Many German authors go even further, saying that live surveillance qualifies as an infringement of the right to one's image if operators have the option to activate a recording mechanism, which is seen as posing an imminent and inevitable risk to the right.[74]

The political supporters of CCTV in the UK like to claim, however, that no such fears are warranted in England, and that the ready acceptance of public CCTV surveillance by the population can be attributed to trust in the system. Human rights organisations have in fact had difficulties in mobilising any opposition among the public to the proliferation of cameras.[75] I suspect ignorance and wishful thinking, not trust, to be the reason for the popular support for CCTV surveillance. The general public has not quite woken up to the potential dangers of CCTV. To merit the label trust, assumptions need not be fully informed; the lack of full information is in fact the prime condition of requirements for trust.[76] However, to engender trust that is not blind but well-merited and therefore sustainable, the belief in a system ought to be anchored in technical, organisational or procedural safeguards for its trustworthiness, and also in personal experience acquired through interaction with the system. Giddens observes that

> all disembedded mechanisms ( ) depend on trust ... vested in (their) abstract capacities' ... but 'trust mechanisms 'are also bound up with the activities of those who are within the abstract systems(...).[77]

To generate continuing trustworthiness in a faceless system, a 're-embedding' of social relations is required. Re-embedding occurs at 'access points', where transactions between abstract systems and lay individuals take place and the latter have a chance to verify that a given system and the people within deliver what they promise, and adhere to the rules.[78] For

---

happened in The Netherlands in 1939: at a census conducted by the Dutch Government some time before the German invasion, citizens were asked, among other things, to indicate their religion. When the Nazis invaded Holland, they were able to round up the Jewish population within a few days, simply by going back to those records.

[73] K Amelung, 'Zur Behandlung des Rechts am eigenen Bild', *Neue Juristische Wochenzeitschrift*, (1980) 1560.
[74] For a discussion of the relevant German literature, see Goetz, above n 38, at 109ff.
[75] According to Simon Davis, the Director of Liberty, opposition from the public had been confined to fringe groups (200 people joined an organised strike against Brighton's CCTV scheme in 1997, and Somerset farmers threatened to use guns to destroy CCTV cameras if they were set up), and it was more concerned with the replacement of police forces by cameras, or environmental issues, than infringement of privacy; see SG Davis, 'CCTV: a new battleground for privacy' in Norris and Armstrong, above n 37, at 243.
[76] Giddens, above n 58, at 33.
[77] *Ibid* at 26 and 87.
[78] *Ibid* at 87ff.

example, cashing a cheque would be an access point and a way for lay persons to confirm their trust in the banking system.

There are few such access points between the people working inside CCTV surveillance and lay individuals that would allow the person in the street to reassure himself that his anonymity is safeguarded. Surveillance personnel are 'backstage experts' who can avoid face-work commitments altogether, due to the nature of their work. The 'frontstage experts', ie the police, government and criminal justice personnel with whom there may be access points, are not necessarily aware of what happens backstage, and also have an interest in covering up failures and unfair procedures of the system. It is difficult for outsiders to verify the experts' reassuring pronouncements. The moments when insiders of the system and 'civilians' outside do connect for real, take place when police are dispatched or follow up on an incident that has been captured on CCTV. However, the re-embedding of social relations in those cases would confirm the lay individuals' concerns about their anonymity rather than sustain their trust that it is preserved. For while these encounters may be reassuring with regard to the crime prevention capabilities of the system, they also demonstrate its anonymity-infringing capabilities. After all, the reason why access points occur between insiders and outsiders is because CCTV has put the police on the track of civilians.

The reviewing and disposal of recorded material may be restricted through regulations and codes of professional ethics with legal sanctions to back them. However, these systems are not fail-safe. The enforcement of the rules is under the control of agencies and people who are part of the surveillance operation. Assurances about the enforcement of good standards, fair practice and restraint cannot obscure the fact that the public cannot influence the execution or judge the working of the control mechanisms for themselves. In the absence of personal re-embedding mechanisms, the reliability of the system could be sustained by improving external accountability. What is needed are technical and organisational control systems that are open for inspection by impartial outsiders. To date such systems have not been implemented sufficiently. In chapter four I shall examine what the options are in this respect. However, functioning control mechanisms notwithstanding, a substantial risk for anonymity remains an integral feature of the recording and retention of images. Making the reviewing of public CCTV footage conditional upon a reported crime, restricts the exposure, but the increasing criminalisation of actions based on public order considerations provides wide scope for the reviewing of footage. Moreover, the audience could be vast, given the growing number of governmental and non-governmental bodies entitled to access official data banks.

C. Does public CCTV increase the pressure to conform?

Pressure to conform curtails a person's autonomy by making him comply with someone else's expectations of what he should do, instead of leaving him to follow his own choices. There are direct and indirect ways of applying pressure. The pressure to conform resulting from unwanted scrutiny is achieved by using fear of adverse judgement. In order to avoid a negative verdict and the risk of ensuing unpleasant consequences, the person who thinks he might be watched cooperates—consciously or unconsciously—by behaving in a way that he believes would find favour with the observer.

In Bentham's Panopticon, prisoners were to be observed from a central watch tower, with the aim of making delinquents pliable, and thus susceptible to discipline and correction, by leading them to believe that they were under permanent observation.[79] Critical discussion of CCTV surveillance has concentrated on its 'Panopticon' effect. More has been written about the constraints of liberty and autonomy as a result of CCTV than about dignity issues, just as the privacy discussion has for some time been dominated by autonomy-based arguments. One reason for this could be that by focusing on questions of autonomy, it is possible to disregard the question whether seclusion is a condition of a claim to be protected against scrutiny. One can arrive at the conclusion that CCTV creates pressures to conform, even if the information gained by the observer is not secret or private. It is not even necessary to subscribe to the idea of privacy and anonymity at all. Surveillance via CCTV could be treated as a straightforward liberty issue, without a detour via privacy, as the reductionist writers would advocate.

Under my conception, CCTV violates the intrinsically dignity-based entitlement to anonymity by interfering with control over the presentation of self. That it might also affect personal autonomy is a secondary concern which, if confirmed, would aggravate CCTV's intrusive potential but is not a *conditio sine qua non*. However, whether one treats the choice-affecting potential of surveillance as a liberty or as a dignity issue, the pivotal question is whether public CCTV regimes are at all capable of inflicting pressure on the person in the street, and making him forgo legitimate options.

There are several aspects to that question. The first to explore is the degree of control and power to impose sanctions the State is actually able to exercise through CCTV surveillance. There is no denying that public CCTV surveillance is conceived as an instrument of social control. Its objective is to discourage people from committing crimes in public space,

---

[79] See above, n 39.

by holding out the threat of discovery and punishment. However, does CCTV provide the authorities with direct control and influence, or is their control and power effectively diminished by the distanciation between the observer and the person in the street? Does the member of the public experience the effects of surveillance sufficiently for it to register as pressure, or is its mark so negligible that it fails to diminish his choices of behaviour in any significant way? The previous analysis has shown that there is a difference in the intrusive quality of live and recorded surveillance; there may also be a variance in their coercive potential, which needs to be examined.

1. How much control can be exercised through CCTV surveillance?

Barbara Hudson divides contemporary penal and public safety policies into 'risk management strategies ... that ... leave the possibility of choice of good deeds and bad deeds', and 'risk control strategies ... that ... remove the possibility of choice by removing the possibility of action'.[80] She names as examples of risk control strategies curfew or exclusion from certain venues, where the removal of choice is obvious and immediate.[81]

Surveillance by means of CCTV is not of that calibre. It does not remove choice altogether but sets out to influence it. Surveillance is a tool governments employ for steering people to do what is wanted from them.[82] The prospect of the State finding out whether its rules are obeyed and the implicit threat of sanctions can be intimidating, making people easier to regiment. Public CCTV has been called a 'dispersed form of disciplinary power'.[83] The label is apposite because of the barrier separating the authorities from the people in the street. Surveillance personnel can supervise the activities of persons on the ground, but they do not control them. A policeman on the beat can take immediate disciplinary action; surveillance personnel must look on. Dispatch facilities may remedy that, but having to call on intermediaries and depend on their cooperation significantly dilutes the operators' power and the impact of their actions. Under passive and time-delayed monitoring schemes, it becomes even more difficult for the authorities to assert control, and their power to impose sanctions is even more diffuse.

---

[80] B Hudson, *Justice in the Risk Society* (London, SAGE, 2003) 75.
[81] For a discussion of the liberty issues arising with respect to exclusion strategies, see A von Hirsch and C Shearing, 'Exclusion from Public Space' in von Hirsch *et al*, above n 27, at 84.
[82] Surveillance belongs to Foucault's tactics of 'governmentality', namely 'the ensemble of institutions, procedures, analyses and reflections that allow the exercise of (nation state) power': M Foucault, *Discipline and Punish* (London, Penguin Books, 1991) 102.
[83] Jones, above n 49, at 198.

In 1999, Norris and Armstrong argued that the disciplinary potential of CCTV was held back by three factors:

a) the restricted environment where monitoring takes place, permitting those with non-conformist tendencies to shift the time and place of their activities beyond the camera's gaze;
b) the limited ability to mobilise a rapid response to monitored non-compliance;
c) the absence of the ability routinely to link a person's image to his database record, which defeats the identification of and the taking of disciplinary action against the perpetrator.[84]

While this was accurate then, the picture has changed in the intervening years, and CCTV's capabilities continue to evolve. The environment where monitoring takes place is no longer so restricted, at least in the UK, stretching over wide areas of public space, with most people having no option to avoid surveillance. Moreover, the Home Office's Second CCTV Initiative put great emphasis on the improvement of dispatch facilities, and much progress has been achieved in the development of face recognition programmes and other forms of electronic processing of personal data. With these changes the authorities have gained greater powers of enforcement, and public CCTV surveillance, from being primarily used for arm's-length monitoring, could become an effective instrument for targeted interference and sanctions. From being a 'soft' method of steering, CCTV surveillance could turn into a 'hard' one. Surveillance has been an integral part of repressive regimes in recent history, serving as an effective means for detecting and extirpating dissidence, as well as for enforcing a ruthless law and order regime. Surveillance is also a typical tool of a regime which is not secure in its legitimacy, and therefore cannot rely on citizens' loyalty. It banks on their fear of being caught, instead of their allegiance, and achieves compliance with repressive laws, not through moral endorsement—which it cannot expect—but through intimidation (behaviour is constantly monitored) and coercion (disobedience is detected and followed by sanctions).

Pressure to conform is experienced not only when the person is actually punished or reprimanded. It is the subjective belief of the potential offender in the increased likelihood of his being caught, not the objective fact, that has been found to be instrumental in achieving a deterrent effect.[85] How else could one explain the claim that placebo cameras have sometimes been successful in bringing down crime figures, at least in the short term?

---

[84] Norris and Armstrong, above n 37, at 92.
[85] See below, ch 3, section IV.B.3.

Surveillance regimes, past and present, typically pretend greater powers of detection and certainty of sanctions than really exist. Bentham's Panopticon itself was conceived as a deceptive form of control, the omnipresence of the inspector a fiction, achieved by architectural tricks.[86] Under communist and fascist regimes, vast archives of accumulated information were never exploited, and the authorities knew much less than people presumed. The fear of spies and possible reprisals, not just actual reprisals, made people toe the party line. Instilling uncertainty and fear of sanctions is an effective way of cowing people and promoting obedience. The gaze of the authorities alone can cause people pre-emptively to sacrifice the freedom to be and act as they would wish: the fact that Big Brother is watching spells potential trouble and exerts pressure to please the observer.

There are good reasons for the person in the street to be concerned about how he is perceived by CCTV operators and law enforcement personnel reviewing the footage, given that the purpose of their examination is to establish whether he is not breaking the law. Does this not imply, in a way, that one is *not* presumed innocent and that the burden of proof has shifted? The inaccessibility of the observer behind a camera means that one cannot take reassurance from checking his response and approval. In our relations with people in authority this is an important mechanism, alleviating the chill their presence is apt to cause, and giving one leave to carry on. If a policeman shows no interest, one can take that as implicit approval. The reaction of surveillance personnel cannot be gauged, however, therefore the uncertainty remains and it is better to be on guard.

In a liberal political environment, people used to enjoy relative freedom from supervision by the State. Systematic observation was associated only with a criminal conviction and penal sanctions, which could range from monitoring a person's movements[87] to nearly uninterrupted scrutiny in case of a custodial sentence. With CCTV, to be monitored by the State has become a feature of life for any citizen, without qualification. Other forms of official scrutiny are not undertaken on that scale. They tend to be localised procedures, usually of short duration and for a specific purpose. Physical searches are more intimate and disagreeable than virtual scrutiny, but they consist of a one-off interference; airport security checks are predictable, limited in scope, and quickly over and done with (although both the scope and the duration are constantly expanded). Surveillance by

---

[86] Making the presence or absence of the inspector unverifiable by the prisoner dispensed with the need for the prisoner to be observed. What mattered was that the prisoner could never rely on not being observed.

[87] A person on parole may be ordered to hand in his passport, to report to his parole officer on a regular basis or, increasingly, to wear a tag.

CCTV may continue over many hours, yielding wide-ranging information about a person of greater complexity than a search would produce. If policemen were to become pervasive fixtures on our daily routes, or if the large contingents of police deployed for a specific occasion stayed put after the event, objections would doubtless be raised and the agenda for such exceptional vigilance justly questioned. The presence of cameras is not perceived as acutely, and any repressive effect is slow to register.

Notwithstanding the populist euphemism that CCTV is 'just another pair of eyes', CCTV surveillance is not the equivalent of the mutual checking process that takes place in public. It is not community self-control but the control of communities by the State. With the authorities, the playing field is not level. Against the members of the community and their ideas of how one should behave, one can stand one's ground. One can answer back and respond to their pressure with like means. It is unwise to be as assertive against the authorities. We are conditioned to defer to them, for often their disapproval, even when unfounded, has, if not serious consequences, at least unpleasant repercussions. Given their disciplinary powers, one cannot afford to disregard the expectations of representatives of the State, and when we become the target of official interest we tend to be conscious of the need to make a good impression.

2. *Does CCTV surveillance only restrict our options to commit crimes?*

A frequent statement in defence of public CCTV is that all that is expected from the people in the street is that they abstain from criminal activities. Committing crimes is not a legitimate option, the argument goes, so asking people to conform to this expectation is not curtailing their options; the pressure to conform ends there, and people need not feel inhibited in other respects. If it was so harmless, one might ask, then why not extend the monitoring to people's homes, where committing crimes is not a legitimate option either. The slogan that law-abiding citizens have nothing to fear from public CCTV has a false ring to it, and is in fact disingenuous. The truth is that observation also constrains our legitimate options, for even if only certain types of behaviour are vetoed, the onlooker becomes witness to our comportment in general, including aspects which, although not unlawful, we may prefer not share with outsiders. To avoid this, we edit out what might be viewed as strange, ridiculous or objectionable. This is a result of unwanted scrutiny per se and is not dependent on sanctions, confrontation or identification. Unwanted observability is apt to shame a person and thereby stifle all manner of harmless, personal expression, especially if there is also the risk of being judged out of context, which one cannot exclude if recordings are made.

Moreover, the expectations of the observers behind public CCTV cameras are not so predictable as to give people in the street a clear brief of what is and what is not permissible. Even if one does not engage in criminal acts, one cannot be sure to escape from scrutiny, nor from unpleasant consequences. From the perspective of one who looks out for crimes, each act might take on a special significance. Events are more easily misjudged when viewed through cameras, for the mood and the dynamics of a situation are not always captured. What if, for example, someone misinterprets my motives, when I am just being affectionate with my child? Risk management is speculative and allows for a smaller margin of tolerance. There is no waiting for the manifestation of actual danger—any variation from the norm becomes a reason for suspicion. Operators of CCTV monitoring a public car park in Germany were instructed that seeing someone walking between cars without apparent purpose was enough reason to suspect him of a criminal offence and to train the zoom on him.[88]

In an English context, in particular, the argument that people who do not commit crime need not fear CCTV is intrinsically problematic. A substantial portion of the criminal law consists of open norms of highly undefined character. The police have a wide margin of discretion to interfere and broad investigative powers, not just limited to criminal activity. Surveillance by CCTV is employed to tackle a wide spectrum of undesirable conduct, including 'anti-social behaviour'.[89] The mission also extends to alleviating fear of crime and to general public order issues, which further blurs the boundaries. Conformity is often a question of standards and judgement. Moreover, the prevention of crime as a statement of mission does not restrict the scope of public CCTV to offences falling within the range of 'street crime'—behaviour that affects the safety of the public space. Other types of crime can also be targeted. Closed circuit television cameras are already employed to combat traffic offences and defaulters of the congestion charge, and could be used for spotting and pursuing illegal immigrants, moonlighters, benefit defrauders, tax evaders, persons who are cruel to animals, truants, drunkards and many others.

---

[88] See E Toepfer, L Hempel and H Cameron, 'Watching the Bear. Networks and Islands of Visual Surveillance in Berlin', *urbaneye* Working Paper No 8 (Berlin, Berlin Institute of Social Research, 2003) 18.

[89] Anti-social behaviour orders (ASBOs) may be obtained in an attempt to prevent 'conduct that causes or is likely to cause harassment, alarm or distress'(Crime and Disorder Act 1998, s 1; Anti-social Behaviour Act 2003). Two-step Prohibition Orders (TSPOs), ie ASBOs proscribing certain behaviour, backed up by criminal sanctions in case of contravention, effectively delegate powers of criminalisation to lower-level administrative officials. Constitutional and other rule of law constraints that govern the legitimate criminal prohibition of behaviour, including proportionality, limitation to wrongful conduct, generality and deliberation by a representative authority, can thus be avoided. For an in-depth debate of the moral problematic of criminalisation via TSPOs, see AP Simister and A von Hirsch, 'Regulating Offensive Conduct through Two Step Prohibitions' in *Penalising Offensive Behaviour* (Oxford, Hart Publishing, 2006).

Recently CCTV figured ominously in an aggressive radio campaign, to 'close in on benefit thieves'.[90] The previous Labour Government introduced a great number of new criminal offences and the definition of defiance has gained wider scope. Already, as Barbara Hudson remarks, 'the distinction between illegal and unpleasant behaviour, crime and nuisance, delinquency and disorderliness is being eroded'.[91] Excessive concern with security has promoted punitiveness and lower tolerance.

Public CCTV is locked into the penal and public safety policies of the political system, providing a ready tool for an aggressive defence strategy. Systematic surveillance, effective monitoring, dispatch and data processing capabilities, coupled with an extended public order brief and an increased use of sanctions could quickly transform a CCTV camera into a spy and a very threatening presence. From risk management, public CCTV could metamorphose into risk control strategy. When the impact of a measure is such that options of undesirable behaviour are practically ruled out, what is applied is not pressure but compulsion to conform. If the surveillance society were to take that turn, liberty considerations might take over from dignity as the prime concern. The moral objection against the violation of anonymity would then arguably no longer be primarily directed against the unwanted invasion of personal preserves, with autonomy as a secondary concern, but centre on the violation of freedom through interference by the State.

It is still early days to draw definite conclusions about public CCTV surveillance. To date, one can only speculate about the severity of the possible consequences of systematic violation of anonymity. The retrenchment of anonymity brought about by surveillance and data processing technologies is a recent development that has not yet reached its full potential. The effects of pressures resulting from fear of scrutiny have not been documented; they are gradual, and may not even have become apparent. Artists and writers, who are credited with having more acute antennas for societal change and how it infiltrates our conscious and subconscious awareness, increasingly feature CCTV surveillance and its surreptitious impact on people's minds and behaviour in their works.[92] David Lyon, the author of several critical analyses on CCTV, paints an

---

[90] Several times a day the music used to stop on the radio and a threatening voice announced: 'We are closing in on benefit thieves—by hidden cameras and by mobile surveillance. And when we get you, you will receive a criminal record, perhaps even a prison sentence.' There was no explanation on whose behalf the ominous message was delivered. Who are the 'we'—CCTV operators, the police, the Government, the secret service?
[91] Hudson, above n 79, at 69.
[92] To name but a few recent examples: the novel *Surveillance*, by Jonathan Raban (London, Picador, 2006), describes what happens to the interpersonal relations of his protagonists, as they are caught up in an America obsessed with intelligence gathering; Catherine O'Flynn writes about the effects CCTV has on a young woman working under the permanent gaze of CCTV cameras in a shopping mall, and on the camera operator himself, in

alarming picture of a society in which privacy and liberty interests are under siege.[93] His opinion reflects the concerns of this author and others quoted here, who have analysed the phenomenon.[94]

---

her novel *What was Lost* (Birmingham, Tindal Street Press, 2007). See also the aforementioned film 'Red Road', above n 50; Rosen, above n 50; and David Bond's account of 'Erasing David', above n 50.

[93] D Lyon, *The Electronic Eye: The Rise of Surveillance Society* (Minneapolis, University of Minnesota Press, 1994).
[94] Eg Cohen, above n 53; Hudson, above n 79; Davies, above n 74; Goetz, above n 38; P Stolle and R Hefendehl, 'Gefaehrliche Orte oder gefaehrliche Kameras? Die Videoueberwachung im oeffentlichen Raum' (2002) 34 *Kriminologisches Journal* 242; Buellesfeld, above n 36.

3
Crime Prevention's Possible Legitimising Role

HAVING SHOWN THAT public CCTV surveillance interferes with a person's entitlement to anonymity, this chapter will investigate whether and to what extent crime prevention can provide a countervailing justification for this intrusion.

Acknowledging that a more differentiated approach than Ronald Dworkin's 'Rights as Trumps' conception is required, I shall start by looking to existing models for resolving the conflict between privacy interests and crime prevention. Andrew von Hirsch has developed a model for limiting the reviewing of CCTV footage and certain particularly invasive practices, but he does not deal with live surveillance and recording. The European Court of Human Rights' treatment of conflicts under Article 8(2) of the European Convention on Human Rights (ECHR) provides useful ideas, but no readily usable mechanism or normative standards for judging whether crime prevention interests have sufficient priority to override anonymity concerns. I therefore develop my own conception and criteria for rating the competing interests, and undertake my own evaluation of circumstances in which public CCTV surveillance might be justifiable. My analysis is intended to look beyond positive law to put forward ethical reasoning for the allocation of weights to the competing interests.

The first step of my analysis will be to rate the importance of anonymity compared to other privacy interests. Using deontological and consequential arguments, my conclusion will be that anonymity in public may have a somewhat lower degree of priority than privacy interests in the home, but that it nevertheless has a significant degree of importance. This is not sufficiently reflected in the protection afforded to it today.

The next step is to assess the importance of public CCTV's crime prevention mission. My premise will be that CCTV is a measure undertaken in the general welfare interest of crime prevention, and I shall explain why it would be misconceived to view the State's law enforcement duties as 'rights' which potential victims hold against the State.

This will be followed by an examination of the objectives and the degree of priority of the crime prevention interests pursued by public CCTV. I shall explore whether there can be a reasonable cause and necessityfor proactive intrusion that unlike a search is not aimed at a concrete crime and a specific suspect but sets out to reduce risks of crime in general and affects people not suspected of any wrong-doing. This will include an analysis of the arguments often cited in support of public CCTV, such as lack of guardianship and fear of crime, a discussion of the state of of urgency and the reasons for suspicion usually stipulated for crime preventive intrusions, as well as an overview of the types and seriousness of the crimes targeted by public CCTV under the heading 'street crime'. My argument will be that the priority of CCTV's enforcement interests depends on the imminence and seriousness of the targeted crimes, and that an urgent need for CCTV has to be established on the basis of detailed empirical analysis of the importance of the crime threat in a particular location.

There will then follow an assessment of the merits of public CCTV as a crime prevention strategy. It is not only a question whether a measure might be categorically suitable: the effectiveness of the measure in achieving its purported end is an important factor. Surveillance via CCTV aims to enforce the criminal law by three different mechanisms: direct intervention, increase of the likelihood of punishment, and deterrence based on the certainty effect. I shall examine the prospects of success of each strategy in theory and also give an overview of the available empirical research into CCTV's effectiveness and comment on its findings. On closer examination, the contribution of CCTV to crime prevention turns out to be much less significant than it has been held out to be. Many uncertainties persist about CCTV's effectiveness, especially with regard to its capabilities as a deterrent.

The chapter concludes with a normative evaluation of when public CCTV surveillance may be justified and what limitations should be imposed. I shall argue in favour of parsimony and selectivity in the use of CCTV surveillance in public space, and make suggestions for restrictions in its *modus operandi*.

I. MODELS FOR RESOLVING CONFLICTS BETWEEN PRIVACY INTERESTS AND CRIME PREVENTION OBJECTIVES

A. Dworkin's 'rights as trumps' conception

Ronald Dworkin's 'Rights as Trumps' theory posits that individual rights ordinarily ought to prevail over general societal objectives, as a matter of principle.¹ Individual rights may be derogated from when they compete with more important rights of other individuals.² General welfare interests, however, says Dworkin, may override rights only when the costs to society of maintaining the particular right would be of such an extraordinary order of magnitude that an 'assault on rights' may be justified.³

This position is too absolute, in my view. As von Hirsch points out, the notion of rights 'trumping' societal objectives can be misleading, as it suggests an 'either–or' approach.⁴ A more differentiated approach is required, as the tension between rights and public interests can be complex, and the degree of priority depends on factual circumstances as well as normative considerations. Although all rights are important for a decent human existence, some are more vital than others. Equally, societal objectives have varying degrees of importance. There are also gradations in the severity of the interference with rights.

Nevertheless, Dworkin's conception of rights trumping general welfare interests remains valid in the sense that rights as entitlements of overriding importance for individuals should enjoy special status and protection, and that social purposes need to have significant weight to overcome the priority of rights.

B. von Hirsch's approach

Writing on CCTV surveillance, Andrew von Hirsch suggests that the model for searches of private premises may provide clues for formulating ethical criteria for weighing anonymity interests against crime-prevention concerns. The search model, he observes, suggests that the public interest in crime prevention can sometimes prevail over privacy interests, but that privacy emerges as a right that has an intermediate protective role, for it limits the manner in which criminal investigations are pursued, without necessarily ruling out such investigations entirely:

> Its 'trumping' effect is not so strong as the right against torture (which should bar torture-based investigations entirely) or the right of free speech (which should permit prosecution only when immediate and serious risk of harm is involved).').⁵

---

¹ R Dworkin, *Taking Rights Seriously* (Cambridge, Mass, Harvard University Press, 1977), ch 7.
² *Ibid* at 194.
³ *Ibid* at 200ff.
⁴ A von Hirsch, 'The Ethics of Public Television Surveillance' in A von Hirsch, D Garland and A Wakefield (eds), *Ethical and Social Perspectives on Situational Crime Prevention* (Oxford, Hart Publishing, 2000) 57 at 66ff.
⁵ *Ibid* at 68ff.

von Hirsch also stresses the particular importance of intimacy protection and calls for special safeguards against involuntary disclosure of this 'first circle' of privacy interests which concern highly sensitive matters.[6] He therefore advocates proscribing audio surveillance, which, by implication, he considers as violating intimacy, and limiting the use of zoom cameras which are capable of detailed physical scrutiny.

The search model also provides von Hirsch with criteria for establishing the weight of crime prevention objectives. The decisive stipulation, he points out, is the 'reasonable cause for suspicion' requirement.[7] For a search to be legitimate, it must concern a specific crime and target a particular individual who is reasonably suspected of being involved in it. While this principle is not directly applicable, because CCTV is not limited to particular targets, he argues that it nevertheless has broader relevance for the question of law enforcement priority, imposing somewhat analogous restrictions. He therefore suggests

> limiting the ambit of scrutiny of tapes to places and times where there already exists reason for suspecting that a crime may have been committed.[8]

von Hirsch points out that reasonable cause for suspicion is only one of several factors to be considered when assessing the weight of crime prevention objectives. The seriousness of the crimes to be prevented also plays a role. He suggests adopting a limitation in line with standard criminalisation doctrine: CCTV intelligence ought to be used only against conduct that involves substantial harm to others or certain forms of grave offence. It should not be employed to support exclusion strategies designed to keep out from public places persons who are deemed socially undesirable, or who are thought to represent risks of offending in future.[9]

---

[6] *Ibid* at 69.
[7] Whether reasonable grounds for suspicion exist depends on the circumstances. Although subjective factors in the decision-making process cannot be ruled out, there must be an objective reason upon which the suspicion is based. The US Supreme Court's definition of 'reasonable suspicion' as 'more than a hunch' (*Terry v Ohio*, 392 US 1(1968)), suggests a rather modest requirement of objective support. The English Court of Appeal held in *Samuels v Commissioner of the Police for the Metropolis* (1999, unreported, case no CCRTF 98/0410/2, CA) that whether a suspicion is reasonable 'has to be determined as an objective matter from the information available to the officer'. This should in theory also imply objective standards of judgement: reasonableness should be determined by the standards of a person of average intelligence, not by those of the policeman making the assessment. Probable cause for suspicion that a crime may be afoot appears to me to be the preferable test, because 'probable' is more indicative of an objective assessment than 'reasonable'. The PACE Code of Practice for the Exercise by Police Officers of Statutory Powers of Stop and Search provides guidance on what would or would not constitute an objective basis, stating that reasonable suspicion cannot be based on generalisations or stereotypical images of certain groups or categories, or a person's religion. There nevertheless remains scope for subjectivity in the way a person's behaviour is interpreted—see PACE 1984, Code A 2.3.
[8] von Hirsch, above n 4, at 70.
[9] *Ibid* at 73.

von Hirsch's third criterion in the weighting process is the degree of interference with privacy interests caused by the crime prevention measure. He suggests ruling out certain applications of CCTV, because they go too far in compromising anonymity. Public CCTV surveillance also should not be covert, he argues, because people are led to believe that they are free from surveillance when they are not and, taken unawares, cannot prepare for scrutiny and present themselves in a good light. Moreover, surreptitious surveillance exercises a chilling effect, for one can never be certain to be free from official scrutiny and might thus always feel under constraint when going about in public in connection with any dealings, not only with regard to committing crimes.[10] According to von Hirsch, CCTV footage should not be reviewed unless a crime has been reported, not only because there is then no priority for enforcement, but also because 'fishing expeditions' (browsing through tapes in the expectation of spotting someone committing a crime) have a broad undermining effect on anonymity. He advocates a bar on collateral, non law-enforcement uses of recorded tapes, and not just for the obvious reason that such uses are unrelated to crime prevention and therefore of lower priority. A bar is also warranted, von Hirsch points out, because by extending the permissible audience to persons other than law enforcement personnel, privacy interests are more seriously compromised. Larger numbers of people would view the filmed conduct, and the observed might have to respond to expectations of a much wider scope.[11]

The fourth criterion von Hirsch applies to the evaluation of public CCTV is the distribution of the benefits and burdens, referring to Duff and Marshall's idea that surveillance may become less problematic when the persons burdened by an intervention are also its beneficiaries.[12] The monitoring of locations such as cash-points would be justifiable, von Hirsch argues, as all four criteria are fulfilled:

a) higher law enforcement priority (because of a special risk of being robbed);
b) conduct that involves substantial harm (robbery)
c) interference limited to a circumscribed spot; and
d) a fair distribution of benefits and burdens, for the people burdened are also the beneficiaries, as surveillance reduces their risk of being robbed of the money they withdraw.

von Hirsch is concerned with the reviewing of recorded CCTV footage only, and does not discuss the justification of live surveillance and preventive recording of events. I have argued in the previous chapter that

---

[10] *Ibid* at 69.
[11] *Ibid* at 72.
[12] *Ibid* at 70ff.

these practices also interfere with anonymity. Whether crime prevention arguments have the weight to support these forms of intrusion therefore still needs to be examined.

C. The ECHR model for resolving questions of priority between privacy and public interests

The ECHR is designed to ensure protection of the fundamental rights and freedoms of individuals against State intrusion. Article 8(1) of the Convention enshrines the right to respect for private life, Article 8(2) specifies grounds on which public authorities may justify interference with that right in pursuance of public interests.[13] The ECHR is positive law, even if on the higher level of constitutional law. It is a statement of principles, but does not provide readily useable normative criteria to help with deciding questions of priority. Nevertheless, the judges of the European Court of Human Rights have developed normative arguments for delimiting the parameters of constitutional entitlements and the justification of State interference. It might therefore be instructive to look to the interpretation of Article 8(2) and the first decisions concerning CCTV surveillance handed down by the Strasburg Court for guidance on how to approach the question of priority between anonymity interests and crime prevention. What can we glean from the reasoning of the European Court of Human Rights that might provide a useful heuristic model for my analysis?

For the justification of an interference with the right to respect for private life, according to the Court's jurisprudence three tests have to be passed:

a) the 'rule of law' test, requiring that the interference must be grounded in some positive provision of the domestic law;
b) the 'purpose' test, verifying that an interference serves one of the objectives specified in Article 8(2), ie the prevention of disorder or crime, the protection of health or morals, or the protection of the rights and freedom of others; and
c) most importantly, the 'necessity' test, demanding that the interference must be shown to be 'necessary in a democratic society' in the interest of one of the designated legitimate purposes.

---

[13] Art 8 ECHR provides:
(1) Everyone has the right to respect for his private and family life, his home and his correspondence.
(2) There shall be no interference by a public authority with the exercise of this right except such as is in accordance with the law and is necessary in a democratic society in the interests of national security, public safety or the economic well-being of the country, for the prevention of disorder or crime, for the protection of health or morals, or for the protection of the rights and freedom of others.

The rule of law requirement (see a) above) stipulates that any conduct intruding upon a person's private life needs to be sanctioned by public law. Imposing a formal framework on the decision-making process is designed to protect against unpredictable and arbitrary behaviour by the authorities, and to ensure standards of drafting so that people are given reasonable guidance about the limitations of their entitlements. The rule of law is not only an important condition for the State's accountability, it also helps individuals to know what their liabilities are, allowing them to act accordingly. However, the concept of public law has been interpreted as also including administrative rules and judge-made law, thus giving more leeway to the judgement of the authorities. This has resulted in greater uncertainties about the scope of one's entitlements and liabilities under Article 8 ECHR with regard to CCTV surveillance too.

The purpose test (see b) above) refers to the list of legitimate objectives for public interest interference spelt out in Article 8(2) ECHR. It does not present a serious hurdle, for the wide range of the listed interests can be extended to cover most State interventions. For measures serving a listed and therefore prima facie legitimate purpose, such as the prevention of crime and disorder, the purpose test tends to be perfunctory.

For a normative approach, one has to look to the third test, questioning whether the interference is necessary in a democratic society in the interest of a legitimate purpose (see c) above). According to the Strasburg Court, two principles have to be satisfied:

a) Measures infringing the right to respect for private life must respond to a pressing social need for action; only then would community interests in law enforcement have the weight to compete with privacy rights.
b) The interference must be proportionate to the legitimate objective pursued with it, and not exact a higher price than is necessary and acceptable in a democratic society.[14]

Whether there is a pressing social need is first of all an empirical question. Nevertheless, this also involves normative judgements, especially regarding the required degree of urgency and the potential effectiveness of the measure. However, when public CCTV has been at issue, there was hardly any normative discussion. The Strasburg Court has treated public CCTV surveillance as a suitable intervention serving the justified purpose of crime prevention, and has categorically endorsed it as responding to a pressing need for action, without addressing the issue why such need exists. No analysis has been provided as to whether different standards of necessity might apply to pro-active measures of crime prevention aimed at crime

---

[14] D Feldman, *Civil Liberties and Human Rights in England and Wales* (Oxford, Oxford University Press, 2002) at 540.

risks in general than to reactive measures dealing with identified criminal acts. Moreover, no technical questions have been asked about the degree of CCTV's effectiveness for achieving its objectives, and whether there were less invasive means.

The principle of proportionality in the narrow normative sense is the most opaque criterion. Neumann's statement regarding penal proportionality is equally applicable to constitutional proportionality:

Proportionality is an equation with three unknowns. The question is how to define the undetermined weight of one interest—in our case anonymity—in relation to the undetermined weight of another interest—in our case crime prevention—according to undetermined standards (what *is* proportional?).[15]

The ECHR does not provide us with criteria for assessing the weight of a right. Andrew Ashworth suggests that the Convention has established a hierarchy of rights differentiated according to the permissibility of their derogation. The rights that can never be suspended for public interest reasons (the right to life, the right not to be tortured, or not to be punished for violation of retroactive prohibitions) are the highest ranking. The rights that may be interfered with only in the most pressing circumstances (the rights to a fair trial, to liberty and to security of the person) have second priority. The rights that can be suspended when necessary for national security or because they interfere with rights of others (the rights to respect for privacy, freedom of expression, assembly and religion) make up the third tier.[16]

While the level of ability to derogate from them may be an expression of the hierarchy of rights, and can serve as a guideline to their weight, this does not suggest any rationale for the hierarchy. The reasons for this still have to be identified, and the normative criteria distilled for what makes certain interests important, and why some are more so than others.

No indication is given about the ranking of the rights of the so-called third tier, nor of those falling within a particular group. Article 8(1) ECHR acknowledges everyone's rights to respect for his private and family life, his home and his correspondence, but Article 8(2) makes no distinction as to the level of derogation possible from each. We are thus left without guidance as to the assignment of weights to the different types of rights that are listed. The status of privacy-based claims that are not expressly mentioned, such as anonymity, is even more unclear. They tend to be viewed as lower-ranking merely because they do not form part of the

---

[15] U Neumann, 'Das Verhaeltnismaessigkeitsprinzip als strafbegrenzendes Prinzip' in A von Hirsch, K Seelmann and W Wohlers (eds), *Mediating Principles—Begrenzungsprinzipien bei der Strafbegruendung* (Baden Baden, Nomos, 2006) 129.

[16] AJ Ashworth, *Human Rights, Serious Crimes and Criminal Procedure* (London, Sweet & Maxwell, 2002) 75ff.

established catalogue. Questions persist about the scope of anonymity and to what extent it is covered by the Convention at all. While the Court has provided normative arguments as to why, even in a public context, there is a sphere which may fall within the scope of 'private life',[17] the Commission ruled that live CCTV surveillance in public space fell outside the scope of protection afforded by Article 8 and that there was no appearance of an interference with a person's private life, for all that can be observed is essentially public behaviour.[18]

Regarding the importance of crime prevention, the Court never questioned or attempted to evaluate the weight of the crime-prevention interests underlying public CCTV. Article 8(1) may guarantee minimum standards of respect for private life, but Article 8(2) has been interpreted in a way that leaves a substantial 'margin of appreciation' to the States to decide policy issues, and to interfere with private life for the sake of wide-ranging public interests. If the UK Government has taken the stance that pervasive public CCTV is necessary for public safety and crime prevention, the Court has not been set to challenge this policy.

The Court's norms of proportionality do not provide a readily useable mechanism for decisions, and no absolute standards for what would or would not be proportional. Neumann calls proportionality a 'soft' principle, because its application requires a multitude of judgements and valuations that are not determined by the principle itself.[19] For constitutional proportionality there is no mechanism equivalent to the ordinal and cardinal scaling of punishment which provides criteria for penal proportionality,[20] and the open-ended character of the term leaves much to interpretation.[21]

---

[17] *von Hannover v Germany* (2005) 49 EHRR 1, [2004] ECHR 294. The Court held that Princess Caroline of Monaco had a legitimate expectation of protection of and of respect for her private life even when appearing in public places.

[18] See *Pierre Herbecq and the Association Ligue des Droits de l'Homme v Belgium*, Cf.ECommHR, Apps Nos 32200/96 and 32201/96, (joined) Decisions and Reports, 1999, 92–98. The case is cited by de Hert and Gutwirth as an example of the difference between Art 8 *privacy* protection, which distinguishes between personal data that affect the private lives of individuals and personal data that do not, and *data protection*, where the only criterion is whether the data is personal data, ie data relating to an identifiable individual. See P de Hert and S Gutwirth, 'Privacy, data protection and law enforcement. Opacity of the individual and transparency of power' in E Claes, RA Duff and S Gutwirth (eds), *Privacy and the Criminal Law* (Antwerp, Intersentia, 2006) 61 at 75, fn 40.

[19] Neumann, above n 15, at 129.

[20] See A von Hirsch and AJ Ashworth, *Proportionate Sentencing—Exploring the Principles* (Oxford, Oxford University Press, 2005) 138.

[21] de Hert and Gutwirth argue that the central question to be considered under Art 8(2) should be the question of *reasonableness*. 'The determination of reasonableness should be pragmatic, contingent and subject to easy revision ... All infringements on the rights provided for by Article 8 by new modes of surveillance must be reasonable (rather than proportionate or necessary in a democratic society). Applying the reasonableness criterion avoids unworthy word games about the nature of privacy and privacy infringements': de Hert and Gutwirth,

Constitutional proportionality could be viewed primarily as a cost–benefit consideration, stipulating that the salutary effects of interferences must be worth the burdens: the greater the sacrifice for the right holder, the more important the public interest and the benefit of the measure must be to justify the interference.[22] This approach could become a cover for purely utilitarian reckonings in which the 'gain to the many outweighs the inconvenience for the few'.[23] There are, however, also deontological aspects to the requirement that there should be reasonable equality in the distribution of burdens and benefits of a measure, and that the sacrifices should be 'acceptable in a democratic society'. The Strasburg Court therefore rightly treats proportionality as a normative criterion; but which criteria should be used to determine proportionality and which sacrifices are 'acceptable in a democratic society' is not explained. The dynamics between burdens and benefits are often complex, and there is not always a direct comparative relation. The concept is also challenged when different interest groups are involved and benefits and burdens are distributed unevenly among them.

The seriousness of an intervention ought to be a crucial element in the evaluation, but in its dealing with CCTV surveillance, the Court has examined only one extreme aspect. In the *Peck* case, which affirmed that a person has certain expectations of privacy in public,[24] it confirmed that those could be violated by showing his recorded picture on television. No attempt has been made by the Court so far to analyse the intrusive effects

---

above n 18, at 80ff. I am not so certain that this is the solution. After all, there are no readily available standards of reasonableness; and before getting to the question of whether a measure is reasonable, one still has to address first whether it infringes the right to respect for private life and explain why.

[22] Penal and constitutional proportionality are different principles. Constitutional proportionality considers whether the intrusion is excessive in relation to the prospective social benefits. Penal proportionality is a retrospective and desert-orientated principle relating to the link between the gravity of the past crime and the degree of penal censure expressed through the severity of punishment (see von Hirsch and Ashworth, above n 20, ch 9). Nevertheless, there is some common ground. As von Hirsch and Ashworth state, it is not just a prudential principle, but an ethical principle too, that it is wrong to prevent crimes by inflicting incommensurate punishment Therefore, even if an increase of sanctions beyond the quantum that would be proportionate might help achieve prevention more efficiently, this step could not be justified (see *ibid* at 133ff). In this vein one might argue that constitutional proportionality acknowledges that it is wrong to promote a public interest (such as crime prevention) by inflicting deprivations on individual entitlements that are excessive compared to the importance of the particular public interest. Even if an incommensurate interference with privacy, for example, might help prevent crimes more effectively, this would not be a fair and morally defensible solution.

[23] Dworkin, above n 1, at 191.

[24] *Peck v UK,,* (2003) 36 EHRR 41. It cannot be excluded that the emotive circumstances of Peck (the broadcast showed the applicant attempting to commit suicide) played a part in this. It is interesting to imagine the outcome of the case if the plaintiff had been recorded simply walking down the street.

of live surveillance and recording—it rather seems implicitly to sanction it, provided the footage is not broadcast.[25]

As far as public CCTV is concerned, the Commission and the Court have in my opinion been unduly permissive of State intrusions.[26] Anonymity interests have been acknowledged only within a very narrow range and receive but half-hearted protection. The barriers against State interferences are too porous, and I question the unqualified presumption that public CCTV is invariably necessary and its benefits worth the burden.

Many aspects of the conflict of interests between anonymity and crime prevention as presented by public CCTV surveillance still need to be charted and criteria for the evaluation established. I shall undertake to define 'the three unknowns', namely to determine the weight of the competing interests—anonymity and crime prevention—and establish meaningful criteria for judging questions of priority. The concepts of reasonable suspicion, urgency and proportionality can provide guidelines for the direction of arguments and serve as restraining norms.

II. THE VALUE OF ANONYMITY

A. What constitutes the weight of a right?

Rights are granted in acknowledgement of individuals' normative entitlement to certain interests or resources that are important for the quality of a person's life and which should, therefore, be afforded special protection. Rights have a special status, and the presumption in favour of rights means that the selected individual interests should be given priority over community interests. Treating an interest as a 'right' serves to ensure the individual's entitlement to its enjoyment, even if depriving him of it could result in societal benefits. The degree of protection afforded to rights

---

[25] The Court's comment that the events 'far exceeded any exposure to a passer-by or to security observation and to a degree surpassing that which the applicant could possibly have foreseen when he walked in Brentwood on 20 August 1995' (*Peck v UK*, para 62) refers to the broadcasting of recorded CCTV footage on a national TV channel as part of a programme promoting the public surveillance initiative. This suggests the conclusion that recording and use for security purposes would not surpass the 'reasonable expectation of privacy'. It ties in with the decision in *von Hannover v Germany* (above n 17), where the issue at stake had also been the mass circulation of photos of Princess Caroline's private life, taken in public venues by gossip magazines.

[26] de Hert points out that the ECHR framework is clearer on 'harsh' measures (involving physical interference) but uncertain on 'soft' measures, eg electronic invasions. The anal inspection of a prisoner has been viewed as invasive, but de Hert questions whether the same decision would have been taken had a body scan been involved. See P de Hert, 'Balancing security and liberty within the European human rights framework. A critical reading of the court's case law in the light of surveillance and criminal law enforcement strategies after 9/11' (2005) 1(1) *Utrecht Law Review* 68 at 90.

against interferences to promote the *bonum commune* should depend on how important that interest is for individual well-being.

The weight of a right must thus be tested by reference to its contribution to a person's quality of life, taking into account the fundamental values the right protects, such as human dignity, physical integrity, autonomy and freedom of choice. The importance of a right can sometimes best be gauged by the effects on a person's life and his moral entitlements that occur when the protected interests are infringed: the severity of the potential consequences gives an indication of how vital it is for a person to be able to preclude such infringements. A person's life has several layers, comprising the personal sphere of the body, his emotions, relationships and material possessions, as well as his social environment and available collective goods. When a right is infringed, the effects might be felt on one, several or even all of these levels: the infringement could have a physical impact, an emotional or intellectual impact, an impact on his relationships, his style of life and his options in general. In the hierarchy of rights, those rights protecting those interests that are most indispensable for a decent human existence should enjoy the highest priority.[27]

B. Examples of highest-ranking rights

The right against torture is usually considered as an example of a right of the highest rank, which should always prevail over crime-prevention interests.[28] It is not difficult to see why. Torture has a devastating impact on a person's life, and is utterly dehumanising and degrading. It inflicts extreme physical pain, might even be fatal, and involves emotional and intellectual humiliation. People are reduced to terrified creatures, their mental resistance is broken, and they are made to betray their strongest beliefs and allegiances.[29] The experience has lasting effects: the pain, mutilation and humiliation inflicted weigh on the victims of torture long after the event, and often stay with them for the rest of their lives.[30]

---

[27] The levels of possible derogation may be an expression of the hierarchy of rights, as Ashworth observes (see above, n 16), but the severity of the potential consequences of infringement is a decisive factor in providing the rationale for the hierarchy.

[28] von Hirsch, above n 4, at 67ff.

[29] No amount of legal rhetoric and strained reasoning can hide the fact that the Bush administration's decision to authorise and practise torture and cruel, inhuman and degrading treatment of prisoners, and to defend it as a necessary adjustment required for the self-defence of the nation, was constitutionally and morally wrong.

[30] 'Whoever was tortured stays tortured', observed the Austrian writer Jean Amery, himself a victim of torture in a concentration camp. For an analysis of the effects of torture, see J Murphy, 'Cruel and Unusual Punishments' in J Murphy (ed), *Retribution, Justice, Therapy* (Dordrecht, D Riedel 1980) 225.

The right not to be physically injured is a vital interest in any event, for we are extremely vulnerable in matters concerning our body and health. Our immediate, elemental well-being, and ultimately the quality and length of our life, depend on it. This calls for the highest threshold against gross interferences by the State with a person's physical sphere.

Other vital rights concern the basic principles of criminal procedure. An unfair trial can lead to a wrongful conviction, and thereby trigger drastic undeserved consequences. A mischaracterisation of a person as blameworthy unjustly disqualifies him and has long-term effects on his social standing. He is stigmatised even if he has been given a non-custodial sentence and after he has served his time. If an unfair conviction leads to a prison sentence, the person loses his liberty and is subjected to very harsh treatment. He is deprived of the company of his family and friends, of his usual environment and occupation, and thrown together with people whom he may have reason to fear.

> The enormity of what happens to these individuals and their families is difficult to grasp ... The life courses of those involved are permanently changed. They suffer losses, of relationships, prospects, and years of their expected life history.[31]

C. The value of free speech

The right to free speech does not have quite the same priority as the foregoing highest-ranking rights, as it is not essential for basic subsistence and autonomy. However, the expression and development of ideas is fundamental for a human life, giving scope to the ability and desire of humans to use their intelligence and express individual thinking. A lack of freedom of information and exchange of ideas can stunt spiritual and intellectual growth, and barring a person from using his knowledge and faculties curtails his chances of fulfilling his potential. Dworkin emphasises this 'constitutive' justification of free speech, which, he argues, gives the individual an intrinsic moral entitlement based on the rationale of individual dignity and liberty.

Dworkin also identifies 'consequentialist' arguments, relating to the societal usefulness of free speech. The exchange of ideas and opinions and access to information can further knowledge and understanding. Citizens who know what is going on and are aware of alternatives are better equipped to participate in the political process. Being able to challenge

---

[31] A Grounds, 'Effects of Wrongful Convictions' in *Criminology in Cambridge, Newsletter of the Institute of Criminology*, November 2005, 3. Most of the 26 individuals Grounds assessed for his study suffered from severe and chronic psychological trauma.

those by whom they are ruled and making them answerable is a means of control and promotes integrity in government.[32]

Consequentialist arguments thus have a role to play in ascertaining the weight of a right. They add value to the right by providing yet more grounds—and grounds pertaining to the general welfare—for why it is important to protect certain individual entitlements.[33] In the case of political speech, instrumental reasons for protecting the right are particularly strong, since free speech and the associated freedom of information are a prerequisite for the integrity and responsiveness of the political process.[34]

The problem with an argument that relies too much on the societal benefits of a right is, however, that those benefits may be cancelled out by the burden the right imposes on the community, or by the societal benefits resulting from disregarding the right (which might be perceived as even greater than those gained by respecting it). Moreover, if the emphasis is on the gains to the many, the inconvenience for the individual is, as Dworkin observed, too easily outweighed. Rights may be 'valuable both as an end and as a means',[35] but in cases of tensions between individual interests and societal objectives, individual interests have a better chance of prevailing if their justification is not primarily based on instrumental considerations but first of all on the intrinsic value of the right for individual well-being. In the case of free speech, a constitutive reasoning also widens its scope, because it covers any type of expression or information. With an instrumental approach, the range of free speech could arguably be narrowed to expression and information that is of political significance, or which is perceived to have some value for society at large.[36] However, the fact that the expression is of little discernible social value would not necessarily diminish the importance it may have for the originator.

The high intrinsic value of free speech in our society is reflected in the rule to which most democratic States subscribe, namely that only when speech creates an immediate risk of serious harm is there deemed to be sufficient ground to justify interference. More compelling reasons are thus required, in line with the standards set by the US courts that free speech

---

[32] R Dworkin, *Freedom's Law* (Oxford, Oxford University Press, 1996) 200.

[33] Feinberg lists the degree to which an interest is reinforced by other interests, private and public, as one of three different respects (the other two being the vitality and the inherent moral quality of an interest),which add to the importance of a right. J Feinberg, *Harm to Others* (Oxford, Oxford University Press, 1984) 217.

[34] For a discussion of consequentialist and constitutive justification of free speech, see Dworkin, above n 32, at 200 ff.

[35] Justice Brandeis, concurring in *Whitney v California*, 274 US 357 (1927).

[36] See Dworkin's analysis of how the scope of protection is narrowed when free speech is based on an instrumental justification; Dworkin, above n 32, at 203ff.

should be curtailed only where there is 'clear and present danger' that the speech involves immediate risks of seriously harmful consequences.[37]

D. Placing privacy in the hierarchy of rights

In the past, the acceptance of privacy as an enforceable right, as opposed to treating privacy as something merely desirable, has been hampered by concerns about a serviceable definition and the apparent 'subjectivity' of the notion of what is private. Claims that privacy defies delimitation because it is ultimately a matter of taste, and thus not suited to be given normative force, have been shown to be unsustainable.[38] The 'neutral' concept of privacy, to which I subscribe, defines it in normative terms, as the claim of a person to control access to himself (see chapter one, section II.A.).

Privacy has often been characterised as a negative liberty, as 'the right to be left alone', which has been interpreted as placing no obligation on the State to create a legal framework for its protection and as entailing a lower status than was accorded to positive rights. I agree with Paul Roberts that the concept of 'being left alone' is anachronistic.[39] We live in an environment of continuous social interaction and mutual interdependence. Such closeness requires regulations and enforceable rules. If the claim to privacy is important for a decent human existence, the State has to assume an active role in creating conditions that provide people with a fair chance of its enjoyment. Moreover, to be protected from interference by the State is in fact one of the most important claims an individual can possibly have. The rise of privacy as a legal right in Western jurisdictions owes much to past experience of totalitarian regimes and the awareness that safeguards against State interference needed to be strengthened.[40] The UK is the exception in Western Europe, having no privacy law as such, although the right under Article 8 of the ECHR applies.

---

[37] F Schauer, *Free Speech: A Philosophical Enquiry* (Cambridge, Cambridge University Press, 1982) 141ff.

[38] For a discussion of those concerns, see A Rosenberg, 'Privacy as Matter of Taste and Right', in EF Paul, FD Miller Jr and J Paul (eds), *The Right to Privacy* (Cambridge, Press Syndicate of the University of Cambridge, 2000) 68.

[39] P Roberts, 'Privacy, Autonomy and Criminal Justice Rights' in P Alldridge and L Brants (eds), *Personal Autonomy, the Private Sphere and the Criminal Law: A Comparative Study* (Oxford, Hart Publishing 2001) at 67. Nevertheless, Roberts suggests earlier that to argue from an autonomy-based rationale is more powerful, since it confers to privacy the status of a positive right (*ibid* at 58).

[40] Privacy is acknowledged as a positive right in Art 17 of the International Covenant on Civil and Political Rights, in Art 8 of the ECHR, and by most European national constitutions and domestic laws.

Privacy has much in common with free speech. In both cases neither health nor physical integrity is directly at stake,[41] nor the freedom to move about and tend to most everyday matters of life. The setbacks a person suffers tend to be gradual and on the cognitive and emotional level, rather than immediate and physical.[42]

Like free speech, privacy has constitutive and instrumental qualities. For a constitutive justification I refer to my analysis in chapter one, where I have shown the centrality of privacy to the affirmation of the self, both in relation to the individual himself and in relation to others. Privacy shares with free speech the constitutive normative rationale of human dignity and autonomy. Both privacy and free speech interests are essential for the fulfilment of the individual as a self-respecting human being. Controlling access to oneself and having a say in who should participate in matters that are closely bound up with oneself and one's life is important for a person's thriving and self-realisation—not much less, I would argue, than the freedom to express himself.

Both rights have important societal functions supporting the moral claim. The communal benefits of privacy have much in common with the contributions to ideological openness and stimulation of the intellectual process attributed to free speech. Privacy plays an essential role in creating a liberal and pluralistic environment, by securing freedom against intrusive authority and social pressure. Personal space for unself-conscious expression promotes originality and diversity, and freedom from interference also reduces social friction and is thus conducive to peaceful coexistence in society.

However, in most Western democracies free speech enjoys a higher status and considerably better protection than privacy. von Hirsch makes reference to the search model as an indication of the inferior trumping effect of privacy compared to free speech. An interference with free speech is barred unless the speech involves *immediate* risk of *seriously* harmful consequences.[43] Such unequivocal language raises the threshold for infringement of free speech, securing protection at a high level. The barriers against interference with privacy are much more porous and the requirement of immediate urgency, deriving from the immanence of the threat and the seriousness of the threatened harm, is missing. An invasion into a person's home is usually permitted when there are probable grounds

---

[41] Although some would argue that an intrusion into a person's intimate sphere comes close to a physical violation, even if there is no bodily harm or even contact.

[42] Cases of interferences with personal choices are different, for here the setbacks can be immediate and physical. The same is true for certain infringements of free speech, such as the prohibition on teaching or generally exercising one's profession.

[43] von Hirsch, above n 4, at 68; Ashworth's earlier quoted hierarchy of human rights under the ECHR, based on the different threshold for an interference (above n 16) also confirms a higher ranking of free speech.

for suspicion that an arrestable offence has been committed.[44] The protection of anonymity tends to be weaker. In England especially, the few barriers against unwanted access when people are in a public space were further undermined under the Labour Government. Privacy and anonymity are essential conditions for individual well-being, and to ensure commensurate protection, strict conditions for justifying an infringement should be imposed. Modern technologies and their ease of intrusion are threatening to undermine the private sphere, and adequate conceptions for its defence need to be formulated urgently.

The degree of importance of privacy interests may vary, however. A right usually comprises a group of related interests, which are based on the same set of ethical grounds but have different functions and may have differing priority. Privacy interests range from the protection of a person's relations with his family, his domestic and intimate sphere, to the protection of anonymity in public. More highly-rated privacy interests tend to be those regarding the protection of intimacy and the home. I have argued earlier that the value of a right depends on the effect it has on a person's life and his moral entitlements when the protected interests are infringed. To place anonymity and privacy on the weight scale, I shall therefore first examine the impact of the violation of intimacy and of the privacy of the home, and then compare this to the effects of the infringement of anonymity interests.

1. The importance of the protection of intimacy

Controlling access to intimate matters is generally acknowledged to be of highest priority among the various privacy concerns. There are several reasons for this. To begin with, there is the strong shaming potential of unwanted intrusions into the intimate sphere. This applies to physical aspects as well as to emotional states. Controlling boundaries is most important when one may be unable to present a dignified spectacle. It is humiliating to have uninvited witnesses when one is literally or emotionally naked, without the trappings expected by society. This is the least opportune time for scrutiny. It diminishes the standing of the observed and gives the observer licence to feel superior. What adds weight to intimacy protection is that unwanted scrutiny of intimate aspects is often in contradiction to the expressed wishes of the person concerned. People usually signal unequivocally that intimate matters are not for general participation, by covering up, by seeking shelter for intimate business or by expressing through body language that outsiders are excluded. Acting

---

[44] In England and Wales it has to be an 'indictable offence', which has replaced 'serious arrestable offence', loosening the requirement from the *most* serious offences to a wider class of *more* serious offences (see PACE 1984, Pt II, s 8(1)(a), amended by the Serious Organised Crime and Police Act 2005).

contrary to such demarcation is blatantly ignoring the wishes of the person who has most to lose from disclosure, and is disrespectful for that reason as well as for the degrading effect of the unwanted scrutiny.

Intimacy protection is first and foremost dignity-based, but may sometimes also have a strong autonomy rationale. Intimacy violations can take the form of direct interferences with moral autonomy when an individual is prevented from making choices that pertain to intrinsically personal aspects of his existence. Penalising a person's sexual orientation or denying a pregnant woman the option of an abortion would be in that league. Moral autonomy is indirectly affected when one must fear being scrutinised while engaged in intensely personal forms of expression. Being watched by outsiders on those occasions is certainly embarrassing, but the thought of its happening is also inhibiting and may cause a person pre-emptively to forgo acting as he would have wished. Intimacy protection can become relevant in any circle of activity. Preventing intrusion into the personal preserve that is most closely bound up with the self—where exposure would therefore be most revealing—is always of great importance.

The taboo surrounding exposure of intimate matters also has an instrumental societal function: warranting a certain decorum and reticence, it has a civilising effect on manners and protects individuals not only from exposure, but also from being exposed to sights and activities that may be embarrassing, disagreeable or offensive to outsiders, who do not care to witness the intensely personal displays of others.[45]

2. *The value of privacy of the home*

The home is the 'backstage' area of people's lives where they do not 'present' themselves to outsiders and the proprieties are not always observed. It is also the forum where relationships are at their most intimate and intense, and defences are let down in the confidence of being among people one trusts. Intimacy protection is a salient point of the special status of domestic privacy. Close relationships and family life, which enjoy particular privacy privileges against interference from outsiders, in acknowledgement of the intimate bonds that link those within that circle, tend to be centred in and round the home. If one cannot count on privacy

---

[45] von Hirsch and Simister observe that obligations of mutual restraint concerning a person's intimate sphere (Nagel's conception of reticence) should include the entitlement to *exclude* others from one's intimate domain, as well as the entitlement not to be involuntarily *included* into the intimate domain of others, and to be spared intimate revelations; A von Hirsch and AP Simister, 'Penalising Offensive Behaviour: Constitutive and Mediating Principles' in A von Hirsch and AP Simister (eds), *Incivilities, Regulating Offensive Behaviour* (Oxford, Hart Publishing, 2006) 122.

in one's home, there is no refuge from the pressures to conform, and no safe haven where one need not hold back and need not worry about what others may think.

As with other forms of intimacy-based privacy, the explicit demarcation of the home as an exclusive space reinforces the value of domestic privacy and aggravates the affront of an intrusion. Significantly, under English law the intrusion into a person's home had been considered a wrong on its own terms, as an act of trespass, before an entitlement to respect for private life was acknowledged by the law, precisely for violating the explicit demarcation of the home as a space reserved for its owner.

The existing rules concerning intrusions for crime-preventive purposes into the domestic sphere take account of the special importance of controlling access to one's home. In most Western democracies, police power to enter a house or flat without the owner's consent is subject to special conditions and formal approval procedures. In England and Wales, entry is restricted to cases of arrest for an indictable offence and to the search for important evidence relating to such an offence, subject to reasonable grounds for suspicion that the suspected person or the evidence is in that dwelling.[46] Random checks and 'fishing expeditions' are not permitted.

3. Rating anonymity in public space

Anonymity is more difficult to place on the weight scale than the established types of privacy. Anonymity as a type of privacy in public has had only a short history, and systematic treatments of this subject are still scarce. One reason for the uncertainty about the value of anonymity is that it can seem somewhat remote from privacy's original meaning. As Schauer observes, there is a notion that when the scope of a right has been extended by stretching its meaning, the weight of the right diminishes.[47] Dworkin thus asserts that a claim may be weaker if the values protected by the original right are only marginally at stake under the new scenario, or where the burden imposed on society by extending the right is far beyond the social cost of the right in the narrow original sense.[48]

To acknowledge a right to privacy in the public domain admittedly extends the idea of privacy to an environment beyond its traditional range. Not surprisingly, it is far from universally accepted that privacy may be invoked at all in the absence of some kind of seclusion or separation from the general public. But I have shown that anonymity interests share the same rationale and values as other privacy interests:

---

[46] PACE 1984, s 17(1)(b) and s 8(1)(a)–(c); see also n44.
[47] Schauer, above n 37, at 134ff.
[48] Dworkin, above n 1 at 201.

Once one escapes from the idea that privacy is essentially rooted in a place or in a right to solitariness, the nature of the place and the proximity of other people in it should not absolutely determine the quality and extent of the rights which one can enjoy there.[49]

Moreover, I would dispute that by extending the concept of privacy to cover anonymity interests in public, society is burdened with costs far beyond those incurred by privacy rights in the original meaning. Respect for anonymity does not heighten the risk to the public domain in an excessive way. Rather, it represents what used to be the status quo: before CCTV, a person's accessibility in public was limited because he could rely on factual barriers and the prevailing social code of civil inattention. An imbalance has been created, not by the acknowledgement of an entitlement to anonymity, but by the advent of new surveillance methods and technologies, which jeopardise the anonymity which hitherto one could take for granted.[50]

What may happen, however, when a right is interpreted in a way to include types of interests previously not acknowledged, is that there is now a greater chance of conflict with other—communal and individual—interests. But this should not be taken as an indication of the inherent weakness of the entitlement itself. When asserting the right to anonymity against competing other interests, the weight of each claim has to be assessed in order to decide which interest deserves precedence.

The public domain demands a degree of social tolerance for intrusion, and the boundaries of the space one can claim for oneself are in flux. The argument that informal rules are a better, because more flexible way of regulating social interaction in public than formal rights, therefore has certain merits. The combination of conventions of discretion, boundary negotiations and situational barriers gives people a fair chance of factual enjoyment of anonymity. However, one cannot always count on informal enforcement. Help with the assertion of the anonymity claim is needed, for example, when someone blatantly and persistently breaches the code of

---

[49] D Feldman, 'Privacy-related Rights and their Social Value' in P Birks (ed), *Privacy and Loyalty* (Oxford, Clarendon Press, 1997) 39ff.

[50] Notwithstanding its lackadaisical attitude towards CCTV, the British public takes its right to remain anonymous very seriously, and the Labour Government's proposal to introduce mandatory ID cards provoked vociferous opposition. Perhaps the fact that there used to be no centralised databank linking a person's picture with personal information about him (even for driving licences, photos were introduced only in 2001) made surveillance more palatable, for people reckoned that this would provide a factual barrier against identification. Today a large variety of such databanks exists, and even if they are not centralised, the authorities can access them for data-matching purposes (see ch 2, section I.A.10.(v)). In most other European countries compulsory ID cards have existed and been accepted by the public for some time, but the laws of those countries tend to provide much stronger safeguards against interferences with anonymity.

civil inattention (stalking), or when someone overcomes the factual barriers by means that cannot be fought off—be it by acting surreptitiously or with the help of technology. A case for formal protection also arises in relation to the authorities who, unlike other individuals, have no mutual interest in observing anonymity conventions and have the power to resist informal attempts at their enforcement. Public CCTV threatens factual enjoyment of anonymity on all three counts: everyday anonymity conventions can be overridden because virtual intruders cannot be challenged; the technology can defeat factual barriers; and there is no equality of status or interests between the observer and the observed. Failing an enforceable claim, the authorities would have the power and the means to disregard anonymity entitlements.

People should have a fair chance to enjoy anonymity, for it is a condition for quality of life in the public domain. Therefore, formal protection needs to be provided against those who do not adhere to the informal rules and who can overcome the conditions necessary for its factual enjoyment. The entitlement to anonymity may have flexible boundaries, but this is no reason to deny it legal protection. Grey areas and boundary definition problems are a feature of privacy and other rights, due to the complexity of the issues they cover.

The entitlement to anonymity implies somewhat more modest demands than those connected with privacy of the home, as it does not assert the exclusion of others in absolute terms. Since a person has implicitly accepted a degree of exposure when he goes out into the public domain, his right to resist demands for disclosure has certain limitations of scope (see chapter one, section III.). He cannot stop co-present others from observing what meets their eye; he has to submit to their cursory checks for the absence of hostile intent; and there may be spatial restrictions on the territories of self. However, the value of being able to resist disclosure beyond those limits should not be assigned lesser importance on that account. When seclusion is not an option, protection against excessive scrutiny is of great significance for preserving dignity and autonomy. This applies most obviously to people living in institutions who are under constant supervision (prisons, psychiatric asylums, hospital wards), but also to everyone spending extended or repeated periods in the public arena, which is part of life today. Anonymity and intimacy interests are intertwined, for control over the presentation of self protects not only the façade, but also what is beneath the surface. If one could not rely on the distance and restraint warranted by anonymity, one's intimate sphere would also be in peril of being invaded. This danger is particularly acute when the observer is hidden and has the use of a powerful camera.

Seeing others in a state of exposure holds great fascination for some, and the social dictate of civil inattention acts as a restraint, to keep persons from forcing themselves on others in an attempt to get a closer view (curiosity tends to make people reckless, as one can witness at the site of an accident).

For each of the spheres in which privacy interests become important, it is possible to identify specific reasons for vulnerability, which highlight the value of access control.

The domestic sphere is where intimacy interests are most at stake. In our home we are most likely to be in a state of physical or emotional nakedness, for we trust that we are safe from scrutiny by uninvited witnesses. Intruders could gain insights into the most personal fabric of our lives that we may want to guard most closely.

In the professional sphere, special vulnerability results from the fact that the pressure to conform to someone else's expectations is greater in a relationship of dependence. It is risky to ignore the expectations of one's boss (even if they do not concern one's professional duties), and the approval of superiors and colleagues may be decisive for one's status in the workplace and the authority one can command. To contain that pressure, and to prevent discrimination, it is essential that a person can insist that those aspects of his life which are unrelated to his work and his professional performance are his own business and need not be disclosed to his employer.[51]

In public, one is vulnerable because one is exposed to a large, diverse, unknown and possibly hostile group of other persons. Having to engage with the others beyond the exchange of a superficial impression, and share with them more than a fleeting encounter, would be demanding and hazardous. The consequences of an infringement of anonymity can be extremely unpleasant: to be singled out, badgered or accosted by strangers and subjected to personal comments in front of others would not only be embarrassing and humiliating; being on the receiving end when others give vent to their animosities and negative feelings would be frightening. This is aggravated by the public character of confrontations, and the possible escalations which could readily happen under those conditions. Not to become fair game to others' curiosity and maintaining the territories of the self are essential conditions for remaining at ease when one is surrounded by people.

To appreciate anonymity, one needs only to imagine how stressful going out would become if civil inattention were no longer practised. Every

---

[51] A topical issue is the practice of 'maternal profiling'. It involves employers obtaining information on a woman's age, marital status and family commitments to determine whether to hire her, how much to pay her and how much responsibility to give her. There is evidence that such profiling goes on behind the scenes, even though in the UK, asking questions in a job interview about a woman's maternal status would leave an employer open to a sex discrimination case. See 'Mothers need not apply', *Guardian*, 22 February 2008.

venture outside would be like running the gauntlet, especially if one's appearance did not comply with the norm. We could no longer rely on the public space as a 'chill out' zone and refuge from intense encounters in the domestic sphere. The public domain can provide breathing space only if people are allowed to disappear into the crowd. In this sense the 'street' has today taken on an important liberalising function. Among anonymous strangers, non-conformity is tolerated. Being submerged in the crowd allows one to be relaxed about self-presentation. The general public one encounters in the streets have no expectations of a personal nature. One cannot count on the same level of indifference or tolerance from people one knows, especially those with whom one has a personal relationship. It is often to escape those pressures that we seek the anonymity of the public domain. The restriction of the audience to people who are co-present is essential for this purpose. If that factual limitation were to be overcome—as an extensive use of CCTV surveillance allows—we would lose an important aspect of control over the presentation of ourselves. The risks of being recognised and judged on personal merits and out of context would thus become incalculable.

Like all privacy interests, anonymity takes on a special significance in relation to the State. It acquires greater weight in that context, for scrutiny and judgement by those with official powers are more uncomfortable and create greater pressure to conform. In public, people are readily accessible. If the authorities did not have to respect anonymity, they could harass people at will, and it would be hard to develop a 'healthy civic self assurance'[52] even if privacy in the home was not at risk. One only has to see how submissive people have become in the face of increasingly invasive and often arbitrary airport security controls to get a notion of the intimidating effect a loss of protection of anonymity would have. This also highlights anonymity's instrumental value as an inalienable condition for a liberal democratic society that treats individuals not as objects to be supervised and threatened with sanctions to make them abide by the law, but as legal subjects, who are deemed capable of moral judgement and decent behaviour, and who are therefore worthy of respect. Moreover, anonymity also plays an important part in diffusing social friction in public space.

A number of factors do nonetheless speak for ranking the interest in anonymity in public somewhat below the interest in the privacy of the home. In public, only the 'surface' of a person is on display, and the public domain is not the forum where personal decisions of far-reaching consequence are at issue or where one expects to realise oneself in full. The

---

[52] R Gavison, 'Privacy and the limits of law' in FD Schoeman (ed), *Philosophical Dimensions of Privacy* (Cambridge, Cambridge University Press, 1984) 346 at 369.

function of anonymity is not usually the protection of the intimate sphere, although even in public we are sometimes engaged in intimate business, and it is then that we need the discretion of others most. It must not be forgotten that anonymity and intimacy interests are intertwined: control over the presentation of self protects not only the surface, but also what lies beneath. If one is not able to keep people at a distance, the intimate sphere that is not on display could be in peril of being invaded too. Any CCTV operator with a powerful zoom lens is capable of obtaining intimate insights. However, the public nature of the space as such has an inhibiting effect and limits behavioural choices: we do not usually 'let go' entirely, because others may watch, and unorthodox conduct provokes curiosity and unwelcome attention. (Those who display intimate aspects for everyone to see, or who perform intimate acts in full view have themselves to blame for their loss of privacy.) Self-restraint is also advisable due to the fact that, when going abroad in public, we cannot always rely on remaining wholly anonymous, as we might meet someone by whom we are known and be judged on a personal level. Importantly, people who venture outside have a chance to 'get their act together' before they face the world. This means that they are in a less vulnerable position when they encounter scrutiny and judgement than if they are scrutinised when they do not expect an audience at all, or scrutiny only by specific chosen individuals.

Also from a consequentialist standpoint, anonymity in public is somewhat less important than domestic privacy. Intrusions into a person's home—a place that is clearly set apart and marked out as the forum for personal and intimate activities—be it by the State or by other individuals, create greater upheaval and have more serious antagonistic effects on mutual relations than interferences in public, where a person is easily accessible and a degree of attention must be expected.

Domestic privacy now enjoys significantly better legal protection against interference than anonymity. In England and Wales, an entry to search has to relate to an indictable crime, and there are significant legal safeguards regarding entry and search of the home, whereas constraints on interference with anonymity are extremely lax. Stop and search powers give the police discretion to subject people in public to blatant invasions not just of anonymity, but also of the most intimate sphere,[53] and regulation of CCTV

---

[53] There has been a sharp rise in the use of stop and search as the police have been relying on s 44 of the Terrorism Act 2000, which frees them even from the requirement of reasonable suspicion. Thus, a policeman may stop and search a person if he considers it 'expedient for the prevention of terrorism'. The fact that in 2008/09 only 0.6% of s 44 stop-and-search actions resulted in an arrest is a clear indication that the police are using them much too liberally, without consideration of the serious intrusion these measures cause. See *Operation of police powers under the Terrorism Act 2000 and subsequent legislation: Arrest, outcomes and stops & searches, Great Britain 2008/09*, Home Office Statistical Bulletin, 26 November 2009 (18/09), 44.

surveillance leaves many grey areas. It is appropriate that the threshold for an intrusion in the home should be somewhat higher, as the violation of the domestic sphere is more traumatic, but the nuances in weight between privacy at home and anonymity in public are not as significant as the difference in legal protection implies. The permissive attitude towards intrusions on anonymity in the UK betrays a lack of understanding of what anonymity is about and why it is worth protecting. It means that anonymity interests are not given their proper weight and that the law enforcement grounds are not given sufficient scrutiny as to whether they justify interference. The value of anonymity warrants genuine constraints against intrusion. Law enforcement reasons may not have to be as urgent as in the case of domestic searches, but the bar ought to be raised substantially from what it is today, and interferences with anonymity interests by the authorities should be subject to considerably stricter conditions than have been imposed so far.

III. THE IMPORTANCE OF PUBLIC CCTV'S CRIME PREVENTION MISSION

A. Whose interests are served by public CCTV?

Public CCTV is sometimes claimed to be a measure used to safeguard the 'rights' of the potential victims of street crimes. That view asserts that the conflict brought on by public CCTV is not one between individual rights and public interests, but between rights of individuals—the right to anonymity in public space versus the right of potential victims not to be harmed. This argument is erroneous.

Victims have a right against the perpetrator not to be harmed. The perpetrator of the harmful act is the offender, not the State. Since the State is not directly responsible for the act of the offender, it can be held morally responsible only to the extent it has defaulted on a duty to prevent the offending. The State does have an obligation towards the community to create a law enforcement system which helps to promote citizens' safety from criminal harm. In fulfilment of this obligation, a variety of State measures and institutions have been put in place to address the crime problem. This includes the establishment of a code of criminal prohibitions against various kinds of harmful behaviour, and the creation of appropriate enforcement structures.

However, the community's claim to an effective crime prevention system does not make the State morally responsible for the perpetration or risk of perpetration of all crimes. This would not only be impossible to achieve, but conferring a claim to individuals against the State to be protected against crimes would also create contradictory and unmanageable demands that could never all be satisfied.[54] Surveillance by CCTV serves to illustrate the point: if individuals had a claim to be protected, would it mean that the State owed each citizen not only a public CCTV scheme, but also one offering the best protection, with live monitoring, recording and dispatch facilities? Where would that leave people in adjoining areas without CCTV, affected by the displacement of criminal activity from the locations under surveillance? They would also be owed protection against crime, and might have a claim to have the cameras next door dismantled if they could not have their own CCTV.

Apart from these instrumental limitations, more important constraints on the State's crime prevention duties derive from civil liberties. Individual liberties place special constraints on the way crime prevention is carried out; and when such measures infringe individual interests in anonymity, the State itself is the agent of a wrong against all those affected for which it bears direct responsibility. Andrew von Hirsch and Andrew Ashworth, in their critique of the Bottoms–Brownsword Model, alert us to the danger of viewing the State's law enforcement duties as 'rights' which potential victims hold against the State. Bottoms and Brownsword invoke the collision of individual rights as the reason for denying an exceptionally dangerous defendant a proportionate sentence. The prospective victim, they argue, has a competing 'right' not to be seriously injured, which can sometimes outweigh the entitlement to a proportionate sentence.[55] von Hirsch and Ashworth point out that giving victims a right against the State to be protected against criminal harm, which then may be balanced against the offender's moral entitlement not to be treated unfairly, would reduce 'the entire analysis (of rights) into a form of cost–benefit reckoning'. An offender's entitlement to fair treatment then could readily be 'trumped' by crime prevention concerns, because these now could be reclassified as purported 'rights' of potential victims.'[56] This danger applies not only to offenders' claim to fair treatment, but to all civil liberty claims against the general welfare. Passing the State's crime prevention measures off as measures taken in the interest of the potential victim undermines the special protection of rights, lending itself to the circumvention of the constraints they impose on State interferences.[57]

---

[54] Victims also generally have no claim against the State to have offenders prosecuted. With few exceptions, the victim has no right against the State to preferment of an indictment.

[55] AE Bottoms and R Brownsword, 'Dangerousness and Rights' in J Hinton (ed), *Dangerousness: Problems of Assessment and Prediction* (London, Allen & Unwin, 1983) 17ff.

[56] A von Hirsch and A Ashworth, *Proportionate Sentencing, Exploring the Principles* (Oxford, Oxford University Press, 2005) 52ff.

[57] Even though the Bottoms–Brownsword Model was only ever intended for use with a very limited scope—for offenders presenting a 'vivid danger' of inflicting serious harm—von

Not surprisingly, in the official advocacy for CCTV surveillance in the UK, the interests of potential victims take centre stage, and it is implied as a foregone conclusion that their claim not be harmed outweighs any claim to anonymity. Surveillance by CCTV, I submit, is undertaken in the communal interest of the prevention and detection of crime in public space. Individual anonymity interests place special constraints on the way crime prevention is carried out, and overriding them requires justification by substantiating an overriding public interest. The former Labour Government defended its surveillance policy with the expansive and categorical statement that

> there is a need to gather and access personal information to: support the delivery of personalised and better public services; fight crime and protect public security; reduce the burden on business and the citizen, and tackle social exclusion through early intervention.[58]

However, those arguments still have to be substantiated, and the State and the officials put in charge of public CCTV must show that the communal interests in crime prevention are of sufficient urgency and magnitude to override anonymity interests, and that interfering with important individual entitlements in this particular way would be justifiable.

B. What are the objectives of public CCTV and to what extent are they concerned with crime prevention?

The stated aims of public CCTV surveillance are complex and not just concerned with crime prevention. The statement of purpose of the Cambridge City Centre CCTV Scheme, a well-run operation that is sensitive to privacy issues, sets out the following key objectives:

— Protecting areas and premises used by the public
— Deterring and detecting crime
— Assisting in the identification of offenders leading to their arrest and successful prosecution
— Reducing antisocial behaviour and aggressive begging
— Reducing fear of crime
— Encouraging better use of city facilities and attractions
— Maintaining and enhancing the commercial viability of the city and encouraging continued investment.

Hirsch and Ashworth are concerned that it could open the door to invoking derogations more extensively, so that victims' rights could regularly be invoked to outweigh offenders' claims to fairness.

[58] See *Surveillance: Citizens and the State*, House of Lords, Session 2008–09, Constitution Committee, Second Report, ch 3, para 68.

Most public CCTV operations in the UK will use identical or similar wording to state their mission.[59]

Of the objectives listed under the Cambridge scheme, only three pertain directly to the enforcement of criminal laws (deterring and detecting crime; assisting in the identification of offenders leading to their arrest and successful prosecution; reduction of antisocial behaviour and aggressive begging). The connection between reducing fear of crime and law enforcement needs to be explored further. The other missions, such as maintaining commercial viability, the encouragement of investment and the revival of inner cities, refer to a wider social and economic agenda. However, CCTV stands in need of justification by virtue of its interference with anonymity, and general welfare aims do not suffice to warrant the intrusion.[60] The justification for the intrusion has to derive from crime prevention, and the overriding purpose therefore must be crime-preventive. The other objectives may be achieved as a result of CCTV's capabilities in enforcing the criminal law, but they have no role to play in legitimising the practice.

C. What is the persuasive force of the crime prevention arguments supporting public CCTV?

If enforcement becomes a sufficiently urgent priority, crime prevention can justify an interference with privacy rights. Searches of the home are subject to three conditions:

a) they have to concern a specific crime of some significance;
b) they must target those who are reasonably suspected of the crime or of harbouring significant evidence relating to it; and
c) there must be reasons to believe that the search will yield significant evidence.

The stop and search procedure is of little use as a normative model, since the judgement whether a search is justified is left to the discretion of the acting policeman.

Public CCTV surveillance is a more expansive and looser model of crime prevention than a search, for it is not undertaken in reaction to a specific criminal event but is a precautionary measure. As a form of pro-active policing, CCTV surveillance addresses general risks of crime and intrudes

---

[59] See Code of Practice for the Cambridge CCTV Scheme, Cambridge City Council (2006), section 1.1.
[60] The economic well-being of the country may be an acceptable reason for interference with the right to respect for private life under Art 8(2) ECHR, but not even the most partisan supporters of public CCTV have tried to make a case for it based on this purported justification.

on people's anonymity before any possible hostile intentions have manifested themselves. While people are observed in real time, perhaps also recorded, or just recorded (either of these acts affects their anonymity), crimes have not yet materialised and may never do so. People are subjected to intrusions on the chance that a crime may be committed, and in order to secure evidence for the investigation and prosecution of a crime in that event. Only when footage is reviewed after a crime has been reported does the intrusion respond to a specific investigative need.

Richard Jones remarks that the problem with pro-active policing is that the 'notion of risk is made autonomous from that of danger'.[61] Danger relates to a concrete event and implies that between the possibility of a crime being committed and its actual commission there is only a limited period within which one can prevent its occurrence. There is thus urgency for action. The same is true for enforcement measures, after a crime has been committed and the culprit has to be found and brought to justice. A risk lacks the connection with a present criminal event, evoking merely a certain degree of likelihood of such an event occurring. Risk is an imprecise notion, ranging from some chance of criminal activity to a high likelihood. As it refers to an event that may happen in the future, there is scope for speculation and subjective interpretation, giving the authorities much greater discretion to interfere than the 'actual danger' principle of search provisions. In Germany, CCTV is widely criticised for permitting intrusions without concrete danger and thus without there being urgency for action. The requirement of danger is seen as an important control mechanism for police powers—if freed from it, the police would enjoy a degree of discretion for action which would no longer ensure that due consideration is given to privacy and liberty entitlements.[62]

Andrew von Hirsch's analogy to the search model, ie limiting the ambit of scrutiny of tapes to places and times where there already exist reasons for suspecting that a crime may have been committed, works only for retroactive footage review, not for live surveillance and recording.

---

[61] RP Jones, *Modern Penality and Social Theory* (Cambridge, Institute of Criminology, 1997) 91.

[62] In Germany, concerns have been raised about the rule of law (*Rechtsstaatsprinzip*, Art 20, para III of the German Basic Law). Some argue that CCTV surveillance exceeds legitimate police powers, which are confined to protection against concrete dangers for public safety and order (*Gefahrenabwehr*), and to the interference with the rights of those making trouble (*Stoerer*). See eg M Dolderer, 'Verfassungsfragen der "Sicherheit durch Null-Toleranz"', *Neue Verwaltungszeitung* 2001, 130. For others, the police mandate to protect against danger comprises both prevention and pro-active precaution, and would thus also cover preparatory measures to that effect, such as the collection of information with a view to preventing possible dangers, which, they argue, is what CCTV is employed for. For an overview of the discussion about pro-active policing (*die Vorverlagerung polizeilichen Handelns*), see D Buellesfeld, *Polizeiliche Videoueberwachung oeffentlicher Strassen und Plaetze zur Kriminalitaetsvorsorge* (Stuttgart, Boorberg, 2002) 95ff.

To protect anonymity against unwarranted intrusions, it is imperative to assess the risks. The mere possibility of crime occurring cannot provide sufficient grounds for public CCTV, or there would hardly ever *not* be a reason to install it. However, the principles of probable grounds for suspicion, urgency, necessity, effectiveness, and reasonable relations between burdens and benefits are workable concepts. Thus, one might say that CCTV surveillance could be justifiable if there was probable cause for believing that crimes might occur in a public space, there was urgency for action, based on the imminence and the gravity of the criminal threat, and there were reasons to expect that this intervention would be effective. In the following sections I shall deal first with the question of urgency and then discuss CCTV's potential for success in reducing crime in public space.

1. Does public CCTV respond to an urgent need for enforcement?

(i) Lack of guardianship in public space

A recurring argument in support of public CCTV asserts that there is urgency for enforcement in public space, because a lack of guardianship creates opportunities to commit crimes without being detected, thereby motivating people to offend. This type of reasoning refers back to Marcus Felson's 'Routine Activity Theory', which links the frequency of offending to the frequency of people encountering attractive targets in the structure of everyday life.[63] According to that theory, there are three elements necessary for creating a criminogenic situation: vulnerable victim, motivated offender and the absence of a capable guardian. Rather than treating each element as a separate condition that needs to be proved, the advocates of CCTV adopt a more simplistic approach, treating the first two elements as implicit consequences of the third: the lack of guardianship motivates offenders to commit crimes and makes people vulnerable victims. The lack of guardianship is attributed to the disappearance of jobs with guardian functions, such as caretakers and porters, but also to the loss of the mechanisms of community control of mutual checking and sharing of the responsibility for public safety, said no longer to operate in the anonymous environments of our streets.[64] Surveillance via CCTV is promoted as a new form of guardianship to replace the old but now inadequate forms of social controls, and to create conditions that are less conducive to offending.

---

[63] M Felson, *Crime and Everyday Life. Insight and Implications for Society* (Thousand Oaks, CA, Pine Forest Press, 1994).
[64] About the loss of social control, see AE Bottoms and P Wiles, 'Understanding Crime Prevention in Late Modern Society' in T Bennett (ed), *Preventing Crime and Disorder* (Cambridge, Institute of Criminology, 1996) 1 at 29.

While on one hand people are increasingly expected to take on personal responsibility for avoiding and managing crime risks, and to invest in private protection schemes for their property,[65] the pro-active and pervasive CCTV policy pursued by the Labour Government signalled that in the public arena the State would take over. Where people were once considered by and large to be capable of looking after themselves during their stay in public space, they are now treated as vulnerable victims and a 'targeted population at risk',[66] who need to look to the State to manage the risks on their behalf. People are encouraged to place their trust in a 'disembedded' expert system,[67] instead of relying on their own monitoring and social control skills, which, it is claimed, are insufficient. Not just the prevention of crime, but identifying individuals posing higher risks too are said primarily to be the responsibility of the State—implying that people are no longer capable of discerning for themselves the signals of harmful intentions, nor of doing much to protect themselves. Trust, not only in the other users of public space, but also in civilian ability to recognise and deal with potential harmful intentions, is, however, one of the very foundations on which the practice of anonymity rests.[68]

Whether this account is correct is hard to tell. Community mechanisms for preventing crimes may be most effective if they are based on pre-existing social networks, and such connections are increasingly absent in cities and larger towns. The willingness to act as guardian and take a protective stance if another person is threatened is likely to diminish in relation to strangers. Standing up to someone who shows hostile intent is risky, and in the absence of a personal connection with the person under attack, people tend to be less motivated to endanger themselves. There is no vetting or selection process for the public space. The exposure to all sorts of people whose motives and intentions may be difficult to discern makes one vulnerable, especially as the anonymity of the place and the audience might lower inhibitions and lead some individuals to commit harmful acts which they would not perform within their own sphere and on people they know. However, general observations and theories about social trends are no substitute for factual substantiation. An empirical verification that there is a loss of social control mechanisms would be very difficult.

---

[65] For an analysis of the changes in attitude, see P O'Malley, 'Risk and Responsibility' in A Barry, T Osborne and N Rose (eds), *Foucault and Political Reason: Liberalism, Neo-Liberalism and Rationalities of Government* (London, University College of London Press, 1996).
[66] M Dean, 'Risk, calculable and incalculable' in D Lupton (ed), *Risk and Sociocultural Theory; New Directions and Perspectives* (Cambridge, Cambridge University Press, 1999) 147.
[67] See ch 2, section II.B.5(ii).
[68] See ch 1, section III.B.2.

(ii) Fear of crime

A driving motive behind the proliferation of public CCTV in Britain has been the Labour Government's desire to enhance perceptions of safety in public places. A subjective feeling of security is one conception of public protection, and creating such feelings among the members of the public is a legitimate objective for public policy. However, assuaging fears of crime is no licence for interfering with anonymity. Fear of crime is often baseless. Crime rate statistics suggest that crime in most categories has been falling since the mid-1990s. In many people's perception, however, the risk of crime continues to increase. Minor disturbances are often viewed as being indicative of major threats. A Surrey University Research Program found that 'youths hanging around' were perceived as one of the three principal threats to neighbourhood safety.[69] Several authors have explored and analysed the complex dynamics underlying the changes in perceptions of crime.[70] Giddens attributes the increased consciousness of risk to the seemingly menacing character of contemporary living.[71] Empirical studies confirm that in assessing risks, we systematically commit misjudgements, and that it is not the most frequent and serious occurrences that we fear most. Our intuition is not based on calculation of actual risks. We fear the things we can easily imagine more than those we cannot, irrespective of their relative probabilities.[72] We worry most about the more unlikely but

---

[69] AE Bottoms, 'Incivilities, Offence and Social Order in Residential Communities' in von Hirsch and Simister (eds), above n 45, at 258.

[70] See eg Bottoms and Wiles, above n 64; A Giddens, *The Consequences of Modernity* (Cambridge, Polity Press, 1990); B Hudson, *Justice in the Risk Society* (London, Sage, 2003) 43ff.

[71] Giddens, above n 70, names several reasons for the menacing character of contemporary living: the globalisation of risks; the risks stemming from the created environment; the development of institutionalised risk environments affecting millions, such as investment markets; and the well-distributed awareness of risk and of the limitations of expertise. One could add to this list the unpredictable hazards created by the interferences with the environment and the groundbreaking technological and scientific developments.

[72] Eg, people fear the (lower) risk of crime more than the (much higher) risk of a traffic accident, spectacular rare risks (being attacked by a gunman running amok) more than unspectacular frequent risks (food poisoning). Neuroscientists and psychologists have an explanation for this phenomenon, ie human brains have not yet caught up with the conditions of the modern world. The intuitive fear which ensured man's survival as a species, telling us to keep away from dangerous animals, for example, takes place in the brainstem region. It is very fast and subconscious, telling the heart to pump adrenalin around the body and triggering flight-or-fight reflexes. The risks of the modern world are too complex to be gauged by these primordial instincts. However, the more nuanced but slower instrument we have for dealing with this, namely the rational analytical weighing system, is located in a much younger region of the brain, the neo cortex. This region, according to the psychologist Daniel Gilbert, is still in a 'beta-test phase' and is regularly overruled by the older, instinctive reaction. For this reason we have problems with the rational judgement of danger and measuring the likelihood of the occurrence and extent of harm. See D Gardner, *Risk—the Science and Politics of Fear* (London, Virgin Books, 2008), chs 2 and 3. See also 'Instinktiv falsch', *Neue Zuercher Zeitung*, Folio 09/2007.

more dramatic eventualities, not least because those tend to dominate the news and get extensive media coverage. Characteristic for today's risk perceptions is high potential harm but low probability, as captured by Susan Sonntag: 'a permanent modern scenario: apocalypse looms—and it doesn't occur. And still it looms ...'[73]

Public policy using people's fears to justify invasive measures should always raise our suspicions. In his book *Risk—the Science and Politics of Fear*, Dan Gardner shows how the image of crime created by the media, and exploited by some politicians, misrepresents the reality.[74]

Generating fear of supposedly dangerous events and people is in the interests of those who promise risk management, because it confirms and expands their mandate; or in Stephen Crook's words, 'regimes of risk management "produce" risks in order to tame them'.[75] Raising fears and promising security have proved an effective tactic for justifying ever-more invasive measures and for securing ever-bigger budgets for spending on 'homeland' security and police equipment. The promise of public safety creates political capital,[76] and the British Labour Government's wish to engender confidence in the electorate that it had crime risks under control was doubtless a strong motive for its push for public CCTV.

However, in terms of perception of safety, it is not CCTV but increased foot patrols that produce the most positive results.[77] Only a few people have said that they would frequent an area they used to avoid more often after the introduction of a CCTV scheme.[78] Visibility and accessibility of the police have always been key factors in reassuring citizens. The reduction of local police presence has meant that this form of reassurance is no longer readily available. Impersonal technological systems like CCTV do not inspire the same degree of trust as a policeman on the beat, for good reasons—they are less capable guardians, as I shall show in section IV B 1 below.

It is one of the 'six paradoxes of security', pointed out by Lucia Zedner, that the anticipatory prevention strategies bent on eliminating risks promise reassurance but in fact increase anxiety:

---

[73] S Sonntag *Aids and its Metaphors*, (Harmondsworth, Penguin, 1989).
[74] Gardener, above n 72, ch 9.
[75] S Crook, 'Ordering Risks' in Lupton (ed), above n 66, 182.
[76] By adopting a tough crime policy and putting the protection of potential victims above concerns for rights, the Labour Government trusted to be on politically and tactically advantageous grounds, boasting that the public was much more tolerant of the curbs on civil liberties in return for the promise of greater safety than liberal opinion would like us to believe.
[77] See *Reassuring the Public: a Review of International Policing Intervention*, Home Office Findings, November 2004, 241.
[78] M Gill and A Spriggs, *Assessing the Impact of CCTV*, London, Home Office Research Study No 292, 2005, 5.

Alerting citizens to risks and scattering the world with visible reminders (CCTV cameras) of the threat of crimes nourish the concern about crime.[79]

People see themselves as potential victims and require ever more reassurance. When policy makers develop prevention strategies in direct response to public demand, they may be asked to provide for unrealistic levels of safety.[80] And they may respond to the 'irrational notion of the feeling of security with phantom measures of risk containment'.[81] Surveillance via CCTV has aspects of such 'ritualistic risk management'[82]: it is supposed to reassure but, as we shall see in section IV. below, its contribution to personal safety is much less significant than it is held out to be.

Increasing the feeling of security is also an important aspect of CCTV's commercial strategy. The way the Cambridge statement of mission (see section III.B. above) builds up is telling: 'Reducing the fear of crime' (the reason why people avoid downtown areas), followed by 'encouraging better use of city facilities and attractions', followed by 'maintaining and enhancing the commercial viability of the city and encouraging continued investment'. Reassuring consumers to get them back into shops and restaurants might be a salient motive, especially for CCTV schemes run in partnership with local commerce, but supporting local commerce is an ulterior aim, and it is a truism, as von Hirsch states, that

> if the purported justification for a potential intrusion into privacy is crime prevention, then the use at issue should be crime preventive and not one serving ulterior aims.[83]

Crime prevention relates to the interest in security, not to the interest in feeling secure. Measures of crime prevention should be based on a rational understanding of risk, not on subjective anxieties. 'Risk rationality' means that risk should be a category of our understanding, not intuition or sensibility. If there are objective and well-founded reasons to be anxious because there is high risk of crime in a particular location, reducing those specific risks becomes a more urgent public concern that may possibly override anonymity interests.

---

[79] L Zedner, 'Too much Security' (2003) 31 *International Journal of the Sociology of Law* 163ff.
[80] D Garland, 'The culture of high-crime societies: some preconditions of recent "law and order" policies' (2000) 40(3) *British Journal of Criminology* 350.
[81] Buellesfeld, above n 62, at 73.
[82] Crook, above n 75, at 172.
[83] von Hirsch, above n 4, at 72.

(iii) Probable cause for suspicion that crimes will occur

Crime risks have to be assessed based on comprehensive local data and local knowledge about past criminal occurrences: their frequency, the types of crime and the specific circumstances that might have helped their commission. It is not possible to do this on a large geographical scale, for every location presents a different scenario that has to be analysed and understood.[84] The methodologies developed under the 'problem-orientated policing' approach, for the analysis and rating of crime concentration, with a view to allocating scarce police resources to the areas where they are most needed, can also be used to define target areas for CCTV surveillance.[85] They include 'crime-mapping' methods and geographic profiling, using computer models to assign probability values to particular geographic areas,[86] which can serve forecasting as well as investigative purposes.[87] Detailed spatial analysis can reveal the clustering of particular offences in particular locations, the relationship between offences and infrastructure (vandalism and deprived housing estates) and between different types of offences (eg drug sales and mugging). Analyses of the temporal trends in criminal activity in an area are also important tools for understanding local crime patterns, and in combination with crime maps, assist with the identification of hotspots. There are also methods and techniques for establishing comparative degrees of risks, to help select the areas where crime risks are highest.[88]

The level of urgency of a crime-preventive intervention is determined by two factors: the degree of likelihood of a crime occurring, and the seriousness of the criminal harm involved. The more serious the potential harm, the higher the priority given to preventing it. For serious crimes a lower degree of likelihood may therefore justify pro-active interference,

---

[84] The shift of emphasis of crime statistics from the national to the local level, with local data to serve as operational tools to understand and respond better to local crime, was one of the fundamental changes recommended by an independent review carried out for the Home Office. See 'Crime Statistics: An independent review', carried out for the Secretary of State for the Home Department, November 2006.

[85] For an account of the development and the implications of 'problem-orientated policing', see H Goldstein, *Problem-Oriented Policing* (New York, McGraw Hill, 1990).

[86] Such as 'Crime-Stat', a spatial statistics program for the analysis of crime incident locations. See 'Predicting a Criminal's Journey to Crime', *National Institute of Justice Journal*, No 253, January 2006, 253.

[87] JE Eck et al, *Mapping crime: understanding hotspots*, Report for The US National Institute of Justice (NNCJ 2093993, August 2005), is a useful guide to determining and dealing with hotspots. 'Place' theories explain why certain crimes occur repeatedly at specific locations; 'street' theories deal with crimes in a somewhat larger context; 'neighbourhood' theories cover extensive areas; and 'repeat victimisation' theories explore the patterns of vulnerability to crime among groups and individuals.

[88] *Ibid* at 36ff.

because fewer chances should be taken. However, there has to be reasonable probability that serious crimes may occur. Footage obtained from CCTV may be helpful in clearing up some serious crimes, but enforcement priority is not determined *post facto* but at the time when the cameras are installed. The question to ask is how likely it is that serious crimes might happen in the area placed under surveillance. Most of the time, the statistical risks of seriously harmful crimes tend to be low.

2. *How serious are the crimes targeted by CCTV?*

Priority for enforcement is not determined by the imminence of crimes alone; the seriousness of those crimes also needs to be taken into account. A lower level of probability may warrant preventive measures if the expected crimes are likely to create significant harm. The use of CCTV is advocated as a protection against 'street crime'. The term 'street crime' is not clearly defined, but it may be interpreted as denoting crimes that typically threaten people and property in public space, making that public space more hazardous. The following crimes fit the description:

a) Property crimes, including snatch thefts, pick-pocketing, thefts of and from vehicles. These may be 'crimes of temptation', with offenders responding to 'the presence of attractive, poorly protected objects'.[89] Some of those crimes involve violence (muggings and robberies). Shoplifting does not really qualify as street crime, but shoplifters on the run are frequent targets of camera operators.

b) Crimes involving violence that are unrelated to thefts. They are mostly 'crimes of friction' (acts of violence caused by friction that tends to develop 'when large numbers of strangers congregate in places of public entertainment, often under the influence of alcohol, meeting in a limited geographical area'[90]), but could also include rape and other forms of assault.

c) Vandalism (criminal damage) of public installations and publicly accessible private property.

d) Anti-social behaviour, involving aggressive, threatening and offensive behaviour towards others.

e) Drug dealing and drug use in public venues.

f) Acts of terrorism: although not of the ordinary street-crime variety, these crimes typically target the public space. Terrorists chose public

---

[89] PO Wikstrom, 'Causes of Crime and Crime Prevention' in Bennet (ed), above n 64, 123.
[90] *Ibid.*

locations to get attention for their cause and to destabilise governments of which they disapprove by spreading fear among the population and showing the impotence of the regime.

g) Traffic offences: CCTV is increasingly used to monitor motorists. Speed cameras no longer measure only the velocity of vehicles and scan licence plates; they also take photographs of the inside of the cars to verify whether seat belts have been fastened, or whether drivers are indulging in 'distracting activities'.[91] A recent priority has been the policing of drivers using hand-held phones, and the enforcement of the fixed penalty for this newly-created offence.[92]

Street crimes thus encompass a broad spectrum of offences, from the very serious (acts of assault) to minor (petty property crimes, obnoxious behaviour). The pattern emerging in Britain, however, shows the main focus of public CCTV operations to be low-level crime, public order offences and incivilities. Cohen's scathing comment, that 'surveillance is turned against "stupid" crimes and those who commit them', may be an exaggeration, but it is not unfounded.[93] There is a strong emphasis on brawls in front of pubs, anti-social behaviour issues, thefts from car parks and tracking shoplifters.[94] Operators look out for fly-tippers and billposters, alert councils if rubbish bags are not being collected, and monitor drunks. 'Talking' cameras are specifically employed to tell people to pick up their litter (see chapter two, section I.A.6.).

To defend this policy, the supporters of CCTV like to refer to the 'broken windows' theory, which postulates

> a basic causal sequence of community decline, whereby untreated disorder in an area eventually leads to more serious crimes being committed in the area concerned.[95]

Another argument for enforcement against minor crimes is that most criminals who later become chronic offenders (the small group of criminals

---

[91] Rule 126 of the UK Highway Code states that: 'Safe driving needs concentration. Avoid distractions when driving such as loud music, trying to read maps, inserting a cassette or CD or tuning a radio, arguing with your passenger or other road users, eating and drinking'. A decision to add smoking to r 126 is now under consideration. It was reported that a woman was fined because she was filmed applying make up, another for eating an apple. See T Dowling, *Guardian*, 10 March 2006.

[92] As for speeding offences, substantial income is expected from the penalties.

[93] S Cohen, *Visions of Social Control: Crime, Punishment and Classification* (Cambridge, Polity Press, 1985) 142.

[94] According to Cambridge's CCTV System Annual Report 2005, the pursuit of shoplifters accounted for nearly one-quarter of the crimes dealt with by CCTV operators. Shoplifting tops the list of arrests made, amounting to a running total of 931 over seven years, followed by fighting/assault, which led to 853 arrests for the same period. The numbers of arrests for other offences are much lower, 'drunkenness' (with 333 arrests) being the next in line.

[95] M Innes, 'Signal Crimes and Signal Disorders: Notes on Deviance' (2004) 55(3) *British Journal of Sociology* 335.

who commit a large percentage of crimes) start with petty crimes, and if those remained unchecked or without consequences, this would be likely to encourage them to commit more serious offences.[96] The perception of under-enforcement with regard to minor offending is also seen as the reason why people feel exposed and fearful of crime in public space.[97] By adopting a policy of 'zero tolerance', cracking down on minor offending and disorderly behaviour in public space, the UK Government intended to reassure the public, establish safety in the streets, reclaim neighbourhoods and stop the decline into more serious offending. Surveillance via CCTV not only helped with this enforcement initiative (CCTV operators have been asked to report youngsters drinking in the streets[98]), it also served as a 'control signal' by which the authorities communicated that disorderly and deviant behaviour will not be tolerated and that perpetrators will be pursued.[99]

IV. HOW EFFECTIVE IS PUBLIC CCTV SURVEILLANCE FOR COMBATING STREET CRIME?

A. Findings of empirical studies

To date, surveillance by public CCTV has been a rather loosely-conceived activity. Its implementation and expansion have been pursued without the support of empirical research evaluations, relying largely on untested assumptions and wishful thinking. Its effect on crime has not yet been thoroughly analysed. Partisan quarters have tended to exaggerate the achievements of public CCTV surveillance as a crime-prevention strategy. The British Journal of Criminology described the statistics of the Strathclyde Police force claiming a 75 per cent drop in crime following the installation of a CCTV system in Airdrie as 'post hoc shoestring efforts by the untrained and self interested practitioner'.[100] There have been a number of individual evaluations of local schemes, with varying results,[101]

---

[96] See DP Farrington, 'Human Development and Criminal Careers' in M Maguire, R Morgan and R Reiner (eds), *The Oxford Handbook of Criminology* (Oxford, Oxford University Press, 1994) 237.
[97] Garland, above n 80, at 360.
[98] See *Downing Street Daily Newsletter*, 17 November 2004.
[99] For an analysis of the various types and significance of 'control signals', see AE Bottoms, 'Incivilities, Offence and Social Order in Residential Communities' in von Hirsch and Simister (eds), above n 45, 269.
[100] E Short and J Ditton, 'Seen and now Heard; Talking to the Targets of Open Street CCTV' (1998) 38(3) *The British Journal of Criminology* 404.
[101] Eg J Ditton and E Short, 'Yes it Works, No it Doesn't: Comparing the Effects of Open-Street CCTV in Two Adjacent Scottish Town Centres' in K Painter and N Tilley (eds),

but systematic studies of the impact of CCTV on crime, using proper methodology and a reasonable sample size, are still scarce.
The few such analyses undertaken so far have concluded that CCTV had a noticeable lowering effect on vehicle thefts in car parks, but that there was no significant reduction of street crimes in general.[102] Surveillance by CCTV had some impact on property crimes and little or no impact on crimes involving violence.[103] The studies examined the change in crime figures before and after the introduction of CCTV, but not to what extent the use of CCTV might have contributed to the conviction of offenders. The studies mostly used active monitoring schemes; the effects of recording-only operations have not yet been analysed in any depth.

The disappointing results of these studies are not necessarily proof that CCTV does not work. A number of factors affected the performance of the schemes:

a) *Inadequate camera coverage of the area.* In Gill and Spriggs's 2005 study, the percentage of the area covered by CCTV cameras varied from 9 per cent to 95–100 per cent. Car park schemes, which achieved the best results, had the highest density of cameras.[104]

b) *Ineffective dispatch facilities.* Some operations had no link to the police and camera operators had to dial 999; operations run by the private sector had greater difficulties with obtaining police cooperation.

Surveillance, Lighting, CCTV and Crime Prevention (Monsey, NY, Criminal Justice Press, 1999); N Tilley, 'Evaluating the effectiveness of CCTV schemes' in C Norris, J Moran and G Armstrong (eds), *Surveillance, Closed Circuit Television and Social Control* (Aldershot, Ashgate Publishing, 1998).

[102] See, BC Welsh and DP Farrington, *Crime Prevention Effects of Closed Circuit Television: A Systematic Review*, Home Office Research Study 525 (2002). The study was funded by the Home Office and contains 24 evaluations of CCTV operations in three different settings (city centre/public housing; public transport; car parks). See also BC Welsh and DP Farrington, 'Surveillance for Crime Prevention in Public Space: Results and Policy Choices in Britain and America' (2004) 3 *Criminology and Public Policy* 497. See also BC Welsh and DP Farrington, 'Public Area CCTV and Crime Prevention: An Updated Systematic Review and Meta-Analysis' (2009) 26(4) *Justice Quarterly* 716. This review included 44 evaluations of operations in the UK, the US and Sweden; see also BC Welsh and DP Farrington, *Effects of Closed Circuit Television Surveillance on Crime*, Campbell Systematic Reviews 2008: 17, and DP Farrington, TH Bennet and BC Welsh, 'The Cambridge Evaluation of the Effects of CCTV on Crime' in G Farrell (ed), *Imagination: Essays in Honour of Ken Pease* (Monsey, NY, Criminal Justice Press, 2007). Gill and Spriggs evaluated 14 CCTV projects in a range of contexts, including town and city centres, car parks and residential areas; see M Gill and A Spriggs, *Assessing the Impact of CCTV*, Home Office Research Study 292 (2005).

[103] A study published by the Australian Institute of Criminology came to the same conclusion. CCTV had no effect on violent crime, but showed better results in preventing property crime, particularly vehicle crime. See *Closed circuit television (CCTV) as a crime prevention measure*, AI Crime Reduction Matters No 18 (Canberra, Australian Institute of Criminology, 2004).

[104] Gill and Spriggs, above n 102, at 26.

c) *Wrong choice of location.* Control over entry and exit routes was important for the success of a scheme, and a reason why car parks had the best results.
d) *Wrong type of targeted crime.* On some type of crimes CCTV seems to have little impact (see the discussion below).

One consistent finding of the various evaluations was that if public CCTV is to have an effect, it must be carefully planned and integrated with other crime-prevention measures.

The best results were achieved when CCTV was accompanied by a package of other measures (special police patrols, improved street lighting) as part of a multi-agency response, tailored to a specific type of crime in a particular environment. To what extent a reduction in crime was attributable to CCTV or the other parallel interventions was not examined in the particular evaluations. However, a separate study, comparing the effectiveness of CCTV and improved street lighting, concluded that improved lighting was more effective in reducing crimes in city centres and residential areas.[105]

Many aspects of the impact of public CCTV on street crime, and the optimal conditions for its effectiveness, remain unclear. If CCTV is to become part of an effective crime-prevention strategy, the practice has to be supported by proper analysis and empirical research. The ratios between the costs and the effects of public CCTV have never been examined, in spite of the fact that three-quarters of the Home Office's crime-prevention budget was spent on CCTV during the 1990s, and a further £500 million were invested in the decade up to 2006.[106]

In the absence of conclusive data, I shall examine if CCTV surveillance can in theory be an effective crime-prevention strategy.

B. What are the mechanisms by which CCTV sets out to combat crime and are they likely to work?

Public CCTV surveillance seeks to utilise three different mechanisms for combating street crime:

a) the active prevention of crimes thanks to early detection by camera operators and operator-initiated police intervention;
b) an increase in the likelihood of apprehension and conviction of offenders;

---

[105] Welsh and Farrington, 'Surveillance for Crime Prevention in Public Space: Results and Policy Choices in Britain and America', above n 102.
[106] See *Surveillance: Citizens and the State,* House of Lords Constitution Committee—Second Report, Session 2008–09, ch 3, para 70.

c) general deterrence as a result of the improved likelihood of apprehension and punishment.

Surveillance by CCTV thus attacks crime on two different levels: the proximal situational level, by changing factual circumstances so that they are less conducive to crime; and the future offender level, by setting out to influence the reasoning process of potential offenders, dissuading them from offending.[107]

The situational part of the strategy is to reduce the opportunities for street crimes. An opportunity for crime occurs when there is the right conjunction of causes: a ready offender, a vulnerable and attractive or provocative target, a favourable environment and the absence of willing modulators.[108] The role of CCTV is to provide willing and able modulators who can step in when criminogenic situations occur, and whose capabilities and powers to take action give them credibility in the eyes of potential offenders. Professional surveillance personnel, with their superior facilities of detection and links to the police, are to play the role of 'interveners' and 'reactors', who can summon help and instigate legal action against offenders based on recorded evidence. This is expected to create conditions that are less favourable to crime: the presence of modulators and reactors should make it more difficult to prepare for street crimes without being spotted, to commit them without being stopped, and to escape without being punished.

Increasing the likelihood of apprehension and conviction of offenders is not crime prevention in the strict sense, for crimes have already been committed. However, bringing about the punishment of those who have breached the criminal prohibitions enforces the criminal law and its normative message. The punishment of offenders emphasises the wrongfulness of their actions.

The third mechanism—deterrence of potential offenders—aims at preventing future harm. The higher likelihood of apprehension and punishment as a result of CCTV is expected to act as an inhibiting stimulus on potential offenders, and deter them from the commission of street crimes.[109]

---

[107] Because of CCTV's dual aspect of situational and offender orientation, it does not fit within Brantingham and Faust's classification of prevention measures into primary prevention (targeting causes linked to situational circumstances), secondary prevention (targeting people at high risk of engaging in criminal activities to stop them from offending) and tertiary prevention (dealing with treatment of known offenders). See RJ Brantingham and F Faust, 'A Conceptual Model of Crime Prevention' (1976) 22(3) *Crime and Delinquency* 284.

[108] P Eckblom, 'Towards a Discipline of Crime Prevention: a systematic approach to its nature, range and concepts' in T Bennett (ed), *Preventing Crime and Disorder* (Cambridge, Institute of Criminology, 1996) 43 at 54.

[109] CCTV is a type of offender-orientated measure different from the two examples mentioned by Eckblom, for its intended mechanism of deterrence is not 'criminality

What are the chances that these strategies work? I shall examine how each of the three desired mechanisms for preventing crime is supposed to function, which conditions are logically necessary to make this happen, and whether it is reasonable to assume that a noticeable impact on crime in public space can thus be achieved. As different patterns of criminality may not respond alike to an intervention, a distinction has to be made with regard to the various kinds of street crimes and offender types.

1. Active interventions in crimes in progress

Early detection of criminal attempts and their foiling by the initiation of police interventions is the most direct form of crime prevention CCTV sets out to achieve. It is only feasible if real-time monitoring is provided. Passive monitoring schemes are of no avail, for when footage is eventually reviewed (if it is reviewed at all), events have taken their course.

However, even with active monitoring the foiling of crimes may be hard to achieve. Unlike many other measures of situational crime protection, CCTV does not impose physical obstacles to ensure the better protection of potential targets of crime. It sends a warning message, signalling instrumental inducements for abstaining from crime, but if an offender is not swayed by these inducements, he is free to act. Surveillance by CCTV provides only virtual, not hands-on, guardianship. Operators are in fact managers rather than guardians. They cannot step in, defuse friction, talk to, reason with, threaten or overpower perpetrators, and they need the cooperation of another agency to stop offenders, which creates delays when time could be of the essence. Most of the typical street crimes are of an instantaneous nature: it takes just seconds to assault someone, to destroy something, to snatch a handbag, break into a car or throw a bomb. Even the most effective dispatch system cannot overcome the 'distanciation'[110] between CCTV operators and the action in the street. Remote-controlled interventions can only lag behind. The police might be able to pursue an offender and prevent him from committing more crimes, but the chances that the police will arrive in time to foil a crime in progress are quite limited.

2. Increasing the risks of detection and punishment for offenders

An increase in the risk of detection and punishment of crimes could be achieved by passive as well as active monitoring. However, more crimes are

---

prevention that tries to change potential criminals by tackling their inclination at the roots', neither does it remedy the 'current life circumstances of individuals by removing influences that might motivate them to offend': *ibid* at 56.

[110] See ch 2, section II.B.2.(i).

likely to be discovered if operators observe events in real time. Under unmanned CCTV schemes many crimes might slip thorough the net, for a significant number of crimes are never reported and much of the recorded footage may never be reviewed. It is probably fair to assume that this is the case with most of the CCTV footage in the UK—not out of respect for anonymity, but due to limited processing capacity and because 'fishing expeditions' are time-consuming.

Even if crimes are discovered, this is by no means a guarantee that culprits will be brought to justice. Recording of evidence is only one step in the complex undertaking of identifying perpetrators that depends on a variety of other factors and conditions. While recordings can provide valuable clues for the prosecution, they do not reveal the offender's actual identity and where to find him. Discovering an offender's identity may be difficult and resource-intensive, especially if he has no criminal record, or if he has covered or disguised himself.[111]

Aside from a handful of spectacular cases, there is no proof that CCTV surveillance has contributed significantly to the rates of clearance and conviction of offenders. Those who have practical experience with CCTV evidence in court, or who have carried out empirical research on the subject, tend not to rate the forensic value of CCTV highly.[112] The head of New Scotland Yard's Visual Images Identifications and Detections Office estimated that only 3 per cent of London's street robberies have been solved using CCTV images.[113] The quality of images recorded on video-tapes is often insufficient, and even if digital recordings are of superior standard, the cameras may have happened to be in the wrong location, or their view obstructed or impaired. The evidential value of recordings may also be flawed by gaps in the sequence of picture frames, or because of doubtful date- and time-keeping. Digital technology has created problems of its own, namely with regard to proving the authenticity of a digital recording. Manipulating a digital image is easy, and while changes might be detectable in the original image, once it is copied, there will be no evidence that tampering has taken place. As there is no difference in quality

---

[111] Clive Norris relates that it took some 4,000 man-hours of video analysis to produce an image of sufficient quality of the London 'nail bomber' in 1999 to enable identification. The identification itself took a team of 50 detectives over 10 days, and the offender was tracked down only after detonating two more bombs and thanks to a trail he left at the last site. C Norris, 'From Personal to Digital. CCTV, the Panoptikon and the Technological Mediation of Suspicion and Social Control' in D Lyon (ed), *From Surveillance as Social Sorting. Privacy, Risk and Digital Discrimination* (London, Rutledge, 2003) 259ff.

[112] See M McCahill and C Norris, 'Literature Review' in *On the Threshold to Urban Panoptikon? Analysing the Employment of CCTV in European Cities and Assessing its Social and Political Impacts*, urbaneye Working Paper No 3, University of Hull, 2003.

[113] Quoted by R Cowan, 'Fiasco and function blurs CCTV's image', *Security Insider* (Australian Security Association, June/July 2008) 23.

between the original and the copy of a digital image, failing a reliable audit trail, it may prove impossible to determine whether an image is the original or not.[114]

In spite of the problems of identification and evidential accuracy, public CCTV nevertheless has the potential to make a significant contribution to increasing the risk of detection and punishment. Imperative are quality recordings and enough cameras to cover a high percentage of the targeted area. To ensure systematic and focused monitoring, the number of cameras per operator has to be limited. Electronic data matching and recognition technologies may facilitate identification in the future.

3. Deterrence by making detection and conviction more likely

The promise of a greater likelihood of detection and punishment through use of CCTV does not only have the purpose of ensuring retribution for past crimes. It may also enhance future-orientated crime prevention through deterrence—a strategy of seeking to induce compliance by making the potential offender wish to avoid the penalty. The deterrence of potential offenders would be an impressive achievement by CCTV, as there would be less criminal harm. The question is, how realistic is it to expect that extensive use of public CCTV will induce potential offenders to abstain?

The deterrence strategy of CCTV surveillance falls into the category of marginal general deterrence: general, because it sets out to discourage potential offenders at large from offending, not already-identified offenders from re-offending (which is the remit of special deterrence); marginal, because it relies on a change in enforcement policy to reduce crime, ie inducing greater compliance by increasing the likelihood of an offender's being apprehended and punished ('the certainty effect'). The 1999 survey by von Hirsch, Bottoms, Burney and Wikstroem of recent research on deterrence examines the mechanism and conditions that are logically necessary for achieving deterrence through an increased certainty effect.[115] I shall base the examination of the claim that CCTV can be an effective disincentive on their findings, on Doob and Webster's 2003 study of deterrence,[116] and on

---

[114] Evidence of Liberty and the University of Northumbria at Newcastle, House of Lords Select Committee on Science and Technology: Sub-Committee II—Digital Images as Evidence (1997).

[115] A von Hirsch, AE Bottoms, E Burney and PO Wikstroem (eds), *Criminal Deterrence and Sentence Severity* (Oxford, Hart Publishing,1999).

[116] A Doob and C Webster, 'Sentence Severity and Crime: Accepting the Null Hypothesis' in M Tonry (ed), *Crime and Justice: A Review of Research* (Chicago, Ill, University of Chicago Press, 2003).

Anthony Bottoms and Andrew von Hirsch's recent (2010) analysis of the crime-preventive impact of penal sanctions.[117]

We do not know how much CCTV *actually* increases the likelihood of being caught and convicted for crimes committed in the street. As noted earlier, a variety of factors and intervening contingencies must converge to achieve this, such as the type of surveillance regime, the quality and integrity of the recorded footage, and the identification of the offender. However, not only the objective increase in the likelihood of punishment, but also the subjective risk perception of people who are likely to commit street crimes is decisive in this respect. Deterrence is the result of the thought process of a potential offender, who considers the costs and benefits of committing a crime and decides against it because he judges that the costs would outweigh the benefits. The perception, attitude, beliefs and preferences of potential offenders are therefore decisive factors in the working of deterrence. It is not necessary that all potential offenders are responsive to deterrence. Deterrence aims at an aggregate crime-preventive effect, which would be achievable if only a proportion of the group of people who are likely to commit street crimes abstains through fear of the consequences, provided this proportion suffices in number to reduce the offence rate.[118]

There is no hard evidence that public CCTV really has an impact on the decision-making processes of those who might commit street crimes. Recent deterrence studies have confirmed statistically significant negative correlations between the likelihood of punishment and crime rates,[119] and association studies comparing crime rates following changes in law-enforcement levels may provide reasonably sound inferences of deterrent effect. A number of before-and-after studies have followed up the effects of the introduction of CCTV on crime rates in a particular area, but the studies by no means always showed a negative correlation between the establishment of CCTV and crime rates.[120] Even a negative correlation suggests only that a certainty effect might be operating, but is not in itself proof that deterrence is at work, and more evidence would be necessary to show that the certainty effect is functioning on the subjective level. Also, other variables that may have affected crime rates, such as changes in age

---

[117] A Bottoms and A von Hirsch, 'Deterrence', *Oxford Handbook of Empirical Studies* (Oxford, Oxford University Press, 2010).
[118] *Ibid.*
[119] See DP Farrington, PA Langan and PO Wikstroem, 'Changes in Crime and Punishment in America, England and Sweden between the 1980 and the 1990s' (1994) 3 *Studies in Crime and Crime Prevention* 104; PA Langan and DP Farrington, *Crime and Justice in the United States and in England and Wales 1981–96* (Washington, DC, Bureau of Justice, 1999) and TC Pratt, FT Cullen, KR Blevins, LE Daigle and TD Madensen, 'The Empirical Status of Deterrence Theory: a Meta-Analysis' in F Cullen, SP Wright and KR Blevins (eds), *Taking Stock—The Status of Criminological Theory* (New Brunswick, NJ, Transaction Publishers, 2006).
[120] See nn101–103.

composition or unemployment, have to be taken into account.[121] One of Nagin's 'four major impediments' to drawing confident policy inferences from the deterrence literature is that too little is known about the links between changes in actual sanction policies and potential offenders' perception of the risks of being punished.[122]

Andrew von Hirsch et al have identified four preconditions, regarding the state of mind of a potential offender, that are stipulative and must all be satisfied for a successful achievement of deterrence through an increase in the likelihood of punishment:

a) a potential offender must realise that the probability of apprehension has increased;
b) a potential offender must take these altered risks into account when deciding whether to offend;
c) a potential offender must believe that there is a non-negligible likelihood of being identified and apprehended;
d) a potential offender must be willing to alter his choices regarding offending in the light of the perceived change in certainty of punishment.[123]

To verify the 'policy to perception' and the 'perception to action' link,[124] namely whether public CCTV is perceived as increasing the risk of apprehension and punishment, and whether this induces people to abstain from crime, further research is needed. It might take the form of questionnaires and interviews, measuring perceptions of changed likelihood of apprehension after the introduction of CCTV, and inquiring how people knew of these changes and how they perceived these might have affected their behaviour. However, the perception of persons who would never consider committing street crimes is irrelevant for the functioning of deterrence. Of interest is whether potential offenders would abstain. Perceptual research therefore ought to focus on persons who (eg because of their life-style or criminal history) are likely to offend, or examine why those who committed crimes in areas under CCTV surveillance and were caught had not been influenced by the presence of CCTV.

As there have been few attempts to examine offenders' perceptions of CCTV,[125] I can only surmise how likely it is that CCTV surveillance might

---

[121] von Hirsch et al, above n 115, at 18.
[122] DS Nagin, 'Criminal Deterrence Research at the Outset of the Twenty-first Century' in 'A Review of Research' (1998) 23 Crime and Justice 55.
[123] von Hirsch et al, above n 115, at 7.
[124] Bottoms and von Hirsch, above n 117.
[125] See M Gill and K Loveday, ' What Do offenders think about CCTV?' in M Gill (ed), The Handbook of Security (London, Palgrave Macmillan 2006); and M Gill, A Spriggs, R Little and K Collins, 'What Do Murderers Think About the Effectiveness of CCTV?' (2006) 2(1) Journal of Security Education. 11

induce potential offenders to think along the lines of the four preconditions listed above. I shall take clues from the findings of the existing perceptual deterrence studies and contextual research into offender decision-making, and the association studies conducted into CCTV operations so far.

For this exercise it is essential to distinguish between different types of street crimes and offender personalities, for they follow their own logic, and offenders' mindsets, priorities and motives vary.

(i) Do potential offenders realise that the probability of apprehension has changed?

This question concerns the most basic precondition for deterrence: potential offenders' knowledge that a change in enforcement has occurred. As a rule there should be signs that CCTV is operating in a given area.[126] Apart from helping to avoid people being watched without their knowledge, this should also serve as a warning to potential offenders that the risks of apprehension and conviction have increased. The signs tend to be quite discreet, however, and are easily overlooked, but given the pervasiveness of CCTV in Britain, it may safely be assumed that in city centres, business districts, around important public buildings, in railway and subway stations and car parks, some form of CCTV will be operating. However, offenders may not be so perceptive, and many people seem to be unaware of the presence of cameras.

The expansion of CCTV surveillance schemes in the UK has been widely publicised, which might serve to raise public awareness. The local media usually report when CCTV is first installed in a community or an existing service is expanded, and information about an operation's range and activities should be available to the public. However, not everybody, especially those new to the area, would have knowledge of that.

(ii) Would the potential offender take the altered risks of punishment into account when deciding to offend?

Deterrence strategies envisage a type of offender who balances the pros and cons before choosing to break the law. He would not necessarily have to be a fully rational offender, who calculates consciously what he stands to gain or lose, but merely one who possesses 'bounded rationality', meaning that he can consider benefits and costs to some degree, and be influenced by this consideration.[127]

---

[126] In the UK the Information Commissioner's Guidelines for CCTV Surveillance stipulate that the public have to be alerted to the presence of cameras.
[127] von Hirsch *et al*, above n 115, at 6.

In the absence of individual information, certain conclusions about the likely state of rationality of street-crime offenders may nevertheless be drawn from the nature of the offences and the typical profiles of those who commit them. Surveillance by CCTV is used primarily against the following crimes: lesser property crimes (such as snatch-thefts and pickpocketing), muggings, thefts of and from vehicles, violence resulting from social friction, vandalism and offensive public behaviour, drug-related crimes and terrorist attacks.

The weighing up of the costs and benefits before committing a crime may be most characteristic of property crime offenders, as one can assume that these utilise a certain calculating, means-to-an-end-rationality. Moreover, such property crimes are often premeditated, which requires a degree of planning capability. This also applies to property crimes where the offender uses violence as an instrument to serve his economic self-interest.

Other street crimes involving violence, however, may often be committed on impulse. Statistical deterrence studies have shown that CCTV has no significant effect on violent crime.[128] An offender acting impulsively tends to have little regard for legal consequences when he chooses to offend, and would therefore not be susceptible to deterrence.[129] High-rate offenders, in particular, often suffer from compulsive/impulsive disorders, preventing them from considering the long-term consequences of their actions. Social friction crimes tend to be committed under the influence of alcohol or other substances. Prudent deliberation might be also impaired by the phenomenon of arousal experienced when committing crimes in groups, which could be the case for members of street gangs. Individuals acting without the support of a group may be more capable and inclined to take the threat of CCTV into account.[130]

In the case of drug-related crimes, one has to distinguish between dealers and users. The first may be more risk sensitive, for the crime is also a business, and for the crime to pay, the cost of it must not exceed the benefits. This may make this group more inclined to take the increased threat of CCTV into account. Drug users are less likely to respond in this way, for they may often be dependent and act with diminished, perhaps not even 'bounded', rationality when in need of a 'fix'. The distinction is not always so clear, however, for quite often people are both users and dealers, and act with varying degrees of rationality.

---

[128] Farrington *et al*, above n 119, at 23; Welsh and Farrington, 'Public Area CCTV', above n 102, at 34.
[129] von Hirsch *et al*, above n 115, at 22.
[130] A study of vandalism on buses showed that potential offenders were responsive to an increased threat of detection, for better supervision on the lower deck did lead to a lower incidence of damage than on the upper deck where supervision was lax; see RV Clarke and P Mayhew, *Designing out Crime* (London, HMSO, 1980) 38.

Terrorists occupy a separate category of those who commit crimes in public, but while religious and political fanaticism distorts values and priorities, this does not mean that terrorists act irrationally. Even a suicide bomber who is oblivious to the risk of punishment is conscious of the risk of failure and may weigh the opportunities for the best chance of accomplishing his mission. One can assume that CCTV cameras are seen as posing an increased risk, and would be taken into account in the preparations. Acts of terror are usually carefully planned, and participants have sought to counteract the risk of detection by surveillance personnel by trying to appear inconspicuous and to blend in with the crowd, thereby deflecting CCTV operators' interest and suspicions.

(iii) Does the potential offender believe that there is a non-negligible likelihood of being caught as a result of CCTV?

Most ordinary people seem to believe that CCTV considerably increases the likelihood of offenders being caught.[131] Government and police officials regularly extol the merits (real and speculative) of CCTV in bringing criminals to justice. The media have largely been supportive of CCTV and have written extensively about the pivotal role CCTV footage has played in the investigation of a number of high-profile, serious crimes. Although the number of critical voices has increased lately, they are countered by at times quite sensationalist reports about ever-improving technologies and methods for identification. The fact that these developments may still be a long way off becoming operative tends not to get mentioned.

According to Martin Gill, who is one of the few criminologists to have researched offenders' attitudes towards CCTV, most of them do not consider it a real threat. It is not difficult to understand why. Surveillance by CCTV, with its virtual modulators and remote-controlled interventions, may not be viewed as posing serious risks, as apprehension and punishment are contingent on numerous intervening conditions. There are several ways of avoiding getting caught by CCTV. Offenders can take precautions and cover up, or they can avoid looking at the cameras. If they are familiar with the area or have made it their business to check out criminal opportunities, they will know about the density and siting of cameras, and can choose angles that are not covered. They can find out if and during which hours there is live monitoring, and obtain information about the weaknesses of a given scheme and exploit them. Prudent offenders—the

---

[131] The author is always surprised by the unquestioning faith in the crime-preventive capabilities of public CCTV expressed by even otherwise sceptical people, but it has to be said that those are all law-abiding citizens, unlikely ever to commit street crimes themselves.

main target for deterrence—may therefore view CCTV as a certain challenge but not fear it enough to think it would prevent them from getting away unpunished.

Moreover, perceptual research studies have shown that offenders have a tendency to treat punishment as a contingent future cost, and there is evidence that persistent offenders are more inclined than others to discount punishment as an unlikely future event.[132] A significant percentage of street crime is committed by persistent or impulsive offenders. Surveillance by CCTV might be too abstract and remote to convey a convincing threat of impending punishment.

Offenders who have been convicted on the basis of CCTV evidence are likely to believe that it represents an increased risk, but we do not know about the frequency of such cases and whether they would be known to others than those offenders themselves and their immediate circle. Some operations publish information about how often CCTV footage has served as evidence in court proceedings in their annual report (this is the case in Cambridge), but those reports may be studied by only a small minority of educated and engaged citizens.

Potential offenders, who might at first have taken CCTV seriously, may do so less once it transpires that it performs less efficiently than expected. If an enforcement measure is not as effective as it was held out to be, or enforcement levels have dropped, 'self-interested rational actors may notice this and cease to believe that they will be caught and processed'.[133] 'Deterrence decay' is a recurring phenomenon in studies of the deterrence effect, indicating that whilst it is true that what matters for deterrence is not the actual but the perceived increase of likelihood of apprehension and punishment, without a noticeable actual increase a deterrence effect may not be sustainable. It would be a subject for longer-term association studies to examine if there was a tendency for crime figures to rise again to pre-CCTV levels, after an initial decrease following the introduction of a CCTV scheme.

(iv) Would the potential offenders who commit crimes in public be willing to alter their choices in the light of perceived changes in the likelihood of being caught as a result of CCTV?

General deterrence works only if the altered risk of detection crosses the 'threshold' where it will make a difference to the potential offender's choice. As Bottoms and von Hirsch point out, thresholds are very difficult to measure, and different groups of people may have different thresholds.[134]

---

[132] See Bottoms and von Hirsch, above n 117.
[133] Ibid.
[134] Ibid.

The tolerance of risks varies, and the willingness to alter choices also depends on how important crime is in the life of an offender, and on the degree of disutility a punishment would represent for him. This depends on the type of crime and offender. The 'professionals' among those who commit street crimes, for whom the proceeds from their crimes—be it drug dealing or property crimes—are an important source of revenue, have strong interests at stake which might keep them from desisting. Instead of altering their choice of committing crimes, which tends to be bound up with their social environment and the way they conduct their lives, they are more likely to alter their choice of location and move to one where the risks are lower.

Addicted drug users are also not likely to stop buying and using drugs because of CCTV. They might at most be deterred from going about it blatantly in locations known to be under surveillance, unless their need to obtain drugs overrides all prudent risk considerations. The same could also be true for compulsive shoplifters. Success in the surveyed area might therefore conceal the deflection of crime to areas that are not under surveillance.

The disutility of punishment depends in part on the social consequences that punishment might have for a potential offender. For persons with conventional social bonds and lives, not only are sanctions unpleasant and inconvenient, but exposure and punishment entail a significant loss of status, and may put valuable relationships, jobs and material security at risk. Deterrence research has consistently found that 'individuals who report higher stakes in conventionality are more deterred by perceived risk of exposure for law-breaking'.[135] However, this section of the population is the least likely to engage in street crimes, and if a conformist individual gets caught up in a fight or commits an act of vandalism, it is usually because he is in a state of reduced rationality and thus less able to act prudently.

Street crimes are not 'white-collar' crimes. The typical perpetrators tend to belong to social groups with lower stakes in conventionality. Research has shown that this makes individuals more indifferent to the threat of punishment. For some, a criminal record and even imprisonment may be part of life and not carry much stigma as regards alienating them from their group or causing a loss of employment. Moreover, a significant number of offences committed on the street incur no more than a warning or a relatively modest fine, which the police might not be able to collect because of the offender's lack of funds. Offenders are not particularly inconvenienced by sanctions of that type and may, therefore, not fear them enough to change their behaviour.[136]

---

[135] Nagin, above n 122, at 70; see also Bottoms and von Hirsch, above n 117, at 11.
[136] This is not meant to be an argument in favour of more severe sanctions for low-level crime. As von Hirsch *et al* have shown, the evidence concerning the effects of severity

Of the 'committed' offenders, terrorists might be most resistant to deterrence, because of their particular determination and notion of utility. Suicide missions have their own strategic logic—the objective is to complete the mission, and to perish in the attempt. Fear of punishment is thus only a slight disincentive. Suicide bombers take care to avoid discovery by CCTV operators during their preparations and, if thwarted by unexpected tight security at their primary objectives, have been known to find another target where the chances of successful completion of an attack are more promising.[137] Others may not be ready to die, but many are still be prepared to take high risks for their cause. Within their own group, the moral disapproval of and stigma imposed by a society whose destruction they seek would not count against them; on the contrary, it would elevate their status and perhaps ensure rewards for their families.

C. General conclusions about the potential effectiveness of public CCTV for combating crime

Martin Gill and Angela Spriggs have summed up five requirements that are essential to a public CCTV scheme's ability to have any significant effect on crime:

a) the technical quality of the equipment;
b) the density of distribution of cameras;
c) camera coverage and positioning;
d) management and operation of the control room; and
e) clear objectives and suitable targets.[138]

Provided these technological and operational conditions are fulfilled, an increase in the detection and punishment of crimes may be achievable. This should be helped in the future by increasingly sophisticated data-processing and face-recognition facilities. Reducing the chances of those guilty of wrongful conduct escaping the penalties for their behaviour is in itself a desirable achievement and can be a legitimate purpose for crime preventive intrusions Searches of the home are also primarily geared towards detection and punishment of already committed offences, not the prevention of future crimes.

There is more doubt, however, about CCTV's other purported crime-prevention mechanisms—direct intervention in crimes in progress and deterrence. Passive monitoring schemes negate the chance of pro-active

---

generally does not indicate substantial negative correlations between sentence levels and crime rates. See von Hirsch *et al*, above n 115, 47ff; also Bottoms and von Hirsch, above n 117.

[137] For a comprehensive analysis of the *modus operandi* of terrorists, see D Gambetta (ed), *Making Sense of Suicide Missions* (Oxford, Oxford University Press, 2005).
[138] Gill and Spriggs, above n 102.

prevention altogether. Even with real-time monitoring, CCTV surveillance is not particularly well suited to the thwarting of crimes in progress. The guardianship it provides is substantially impaired by the remoteness in time and space of the guardians and their inability to intervene swiftly. Operators may be able to dispatch police forces to the scene of a crime, but the police are frequently likely to arrive too late to prevent harm. Nevertheless, provided the demand for police support is not out of proportion to the available man-power on the ground, active monitoring CCTV schemes may contribute to some degree to the pro-active prevention of street crime.

A sustainable deterrent effect could be CCTV's most valuable achievement, for the general interest is served best if potential offenders can be induced to refrain from violating others' rights. However, deterrence is a complicated subjective mechanism. The 'soft' evidence we have indicates that public CCTV may have a limited deterrent effect, but there are several reasons for caution about its impact. I tend to agree with Cohen,[139] who suggests that surveillance as a deterrent might work better with 'amenables'—people who have strong social bonds to conventional society and who do not really view crime as a viable option—than with 'non-amenables' or those who have a stronger criminal propensity, namely

> people with a low level of self control and weak social bonds to conventional society, who feel less threatened by sanctions and often engage in criminal activity.[140]

The character and the circumstances of street crimes suggest a preponderance of offender types who have a stronger criminal propensity than average. Such persons appear to be more willing to take risks. Whether a significant enough proportion of that group is deterred by public CCTV to bring about a noticeable long-term decrease in street crime, or whether it merely displaces crime and committed offenders seek criminal opportunities elsewhere, remains to be seen. It might be yet another paradox of CCTV that it works as a deterrent for conformists who do not really need surveillance, since to them the existing signals of general deterrence (laws, police, courts, penalties) are sufficient disincentives, but not for its real targets—the people who commit most street crimes. Invisible and remote managers behind cameras may not represent an immediate enough threat to impress committed or impulsive offenders. A dramatic increase in the likelihood of apprehension and punishment could in all probability induce even chronic and professional criminals to abstain. Even if punishment entails no stigma for the penalised, it remains a tiresome and unpleasant

---

[139] Cohen, above n 93, at 150.
[140] Wikstrom, above n 89, 136f f.

experience that most people would rather avoid. However, CCTV has to date fallen short of achieving such results.

Although many questions pertain to the scope of the deterrent effect, it must not be discounted as a potential benefit of CCTV, with certain important provisos:

a) First, a CCTV operation should have suitable targets, which implies that public CCTV should be used in particular against the types of crimes that are committed by offenders who are likely to act with bounded rationality and to be susceptible to a prudent appeal.
b) Secondly, the operation has to be set up properly and run effectively. An actual increase in the likelihood of being caught may be the best way to influence offenders' perception of the higher risks they are taking.

4

Policy Principles and the Regulation of Public CCTV Surveillance

PUBLIC CCTV SURVEILLANCE is a model of crime prevention different from a search, with its own dynamics between means and ends. A search is focused on a particular crime that has already happened or is about to happen; CCTV is a measure of pro-active precaution. A search is a physical interference; the intrusion by CCTV is primarily virtual. Closed circuit television is a regular feature that may stretch over long periods of a person's sojourn in public; a search is a relatively rare and one-off occurrence. A search affects only those people who are suspected of close connection with a crime; CCTV affects everybody. A search may violate the most highly-ranking privacy interests—the privacy of the home and the intimate circle; public CCTV interferes with anonymity and potentially also intimacy interests. There are many variables with regard to the burdens and benefits of CCTV, depending on situational and operational constellations.

The search model can serve as a point of reference, but public CCTV has to be judged on its own account. There are several reasons for adopting a restrictive policy with regard to CCTV surveillance in public space.

I. POLICY CONSIDERATIONS FOR PUBLIC CCTV SURVEILLANCE

A. Interference with people who are not suspected of wrong-doing

Surveillance via CCTV interferes with the entitlements to anonymity of people who are not suspected of wrong-doing. Those who do not violate the criminal law (or where there are no reasons to suspect them of doing so) should have a rightful expectation of enjoying their liberties without interference by the authorities. Certain concessions regarding his anonymity may be expected from a person if there are grounds to assume a close connection—a 'special link'—with a crime under investigation, even though he is not a suspect. A bystander's observations may be instrumental in bringing the culprit to justice; it is therefore not unreasonable to ask a witness to contribute to the investigation, even at some expense to his own anonymity through having to disclose his name and address and give evidence. However, a witness's connection with a crime would not permit a search of his home, which as a more invasive measure is justifiable only as regards suspects: because suspects are linked to the crime by their potential responsibility for it, it is fair to burden them more heavily with its investigation. A victim certainly has a special connection with the crime, being the one who feels its impact most closely, and therefore he has a particular interest in seeing this transgression punished; but he is also connected because his testimony is essential for establishing who should be charged and for what. It is therefore justifiable that the victim should have to accept intensive questioning and perhaps intimate examination to establish the degree of the harm inflicted on him, so that the right person can be charged, and charged correctly.

Surveillance via CCTV does not operate conditionally to any such special link. The scrutiny is exploratory, with a view to finding out if there might be grounds for suspicion against some members of the public being surveyed and recorded.

I concur with Duff and Marshall's observation that a preventive interference might be morally more acceptable if everyone was burdened equitably,[1] for there is then no discriminatory edge to the intrusion and no specific personal blame associated with it. In the case of airport security checks, for example, everyone is burdened equitably and everyone is treated equally as potential offenders. All subjects are also potential victims, and as everyone is benefiting from the rigorous vetting (with the exception of the potential saboteur, but his is not a legitimate interest), one can assume they consider it a price worth paying. A similar situation occurs when CCTV is used to monitor cash points. Everyone approaching the cash point is recorded as a potential offender, but also as a potential victim, for people withdrawing cash are attractive targets and at particular risk of being robbed. They are therefore also likely to value the protection CCTV affords over and above privacy in this specific location.[2]

In public space in general, the benefits and burdens of CCTV surveillance are not so evenly distributed, however. Those perceived as the more likely offenders will be scrutinised to protect the more likely victims. Type-casting is built into a system of risk monitoring, where the observers have to take cues from appearances, and judgement will inevitably be

---

[1] A Duff and SE Marshall, 'Benefits, Burdens and Responsibilities: Some Ethical Dimensions of Situational Crime Prevention' in A von Hirsch, D Garland and A Wakefield, *Ethical and Social Perspectives on Situational Crime Prevention* (Oxford, Hart Publishing, 2000) 27.
[2] A von Hirsch, 'The Ethics of Public Television Surveillance' in von Hirsch *et al*, above n 1, 57 at 71.

influenced by statistical risk factors. Individuals who stick out, or who belong to ethnic or other groups that are more often associated with crime (which might only be due to their skin colour), will be monitored more intensely than those who blend in and whose looks do not trigger mistrust.[3] This means that some people may pay a much higher price than others for the benefit of better crime protection. Not only do they bear the brunt of the virtual intrusion, but as a result they may also be subjected to more frequent interference by police forces on the ground.

The argument that CCTV is acceptable because it is less invasive than a search is a non sequitur, for it implies that the people subjected to CCTV would be candidates for a search. This is not the case, for public CCTV surveillance burdens people who are not suspected of having done anything wrong, not even of being connected with a criminal event in a particular way. This calls for particular, urgent reasons to justify the measure and restraint in its use. The principle of parsimony, which should guide any interference with valuable entitlements, is even more appropriate when the interference concerns people going about their lawful business. On the other hand, submitting people to closer scrutiny might be defensible in locations where the chances are high that there are potential offenders among the observed. In those circumstances, people would also be more willing to pay the price of loss of anonymity, especially if the impact is mitigated by the limited scale of the operation.

B. Preserving anonymity in public space

Public CCTV should be reserved for so-called 'hotspots of crime', which connotes areas that have a considerably higher-than-average incidence of criminal events and where there is a considerable risk of victimisation.[4]

---

[3] CCTV operators are unlikely to be less prone to racial discrimination than police forces on the ground. A report for the Equality and Human Rights Commission has found that police forces have used the stop-and-search powers under s 60 of the Criminal Justice and Public Order Act 1994 and s 44 of the Terrorism Act 2000 excessively against people from ethnic minorities. The report concludes that 'the evidence points to racial discrimination being a significant reason why black and Asian people are more likely to be searched than white people'. Black people are at least 6 times (in some Counties up to 10 times) as likely to be stopped by police as white people, Asians twice as often. See Equality and Human Rights Commission, *Stop and think: A critical review of the use of stop and search powers in England and Wales* (http://www.equalityhumanrights.com, 2010).

[4] In Germany, hotspots (*Kriminalitaetsschwerpunkte*) are sometimes defined as 'dangerous places' (in Bavaria this refers to areas of 'criminal milieu and prostitution'), also as 'public places where crimes are committed more often' or as 'places, where the committing of crimes has to be particularly expected, because of specific local conditions'. See V Goetz, 'Oeffentliche Videoueberwachung im Kontext der praeventiven Polizeiarbeit' in J-M Jehle and M Gras (eds), *Oeffentliche Videoueberwachung im Europaeischen Vergleich (Little Brothers are Watching You—A European Comparison)* (Goettingen, Universitaet Goettingen, 2003)

Reserving CCTV for circumscribed locations with high crime rates helps to ensure that there is priority of enforcement and limits the ambit of surveillance.

Surveillance via CCTV intrudes on people before an actual crime has happened. Taking into account that anonymity interests rank somewhat lower than rights to privacy at home, and that CCTV surveillance is not as disagreeable as a search and conveys no blame, it may be defensible to subject people in public space to this type of preventive measure at an earlier stage of a criminal threat, when there is a risk of crime but not yet an actual criminal act. However, it is indefensible to interfere with anonymity without there being a significant risk of crime and to impose CCTV if enforcement grounds are of low priority. Moreover, the consequence of this approach could be surveillance on a large scale—a situation we already have in England—and the more widespread the network of public CCTV, the more anonymity is put in jeopardy. Anonymity interests are interests in opacity: to preserve a personal sphere in public and feel confident about one's liberties, one needs to be able to rely on substantial periods free from close scrutiny by the authorities. Frequent and prolonged supervision and recording in public space threatens the very essence of anonymity, and is most conducive to achieving the chilling 'Big Brother' effect.

Crime prevention benefits do not increase coextensively with wider coverage but become more difficult to achieve, because large surveillance networks tend to overtax resources. Councils often do not have the necessary funds or expertise to set up and run a CCTV scheme professionally to exacting standards, which is one of the reasons for the poor performance of many schemes. Moreover, enforcement agencies have limited manpower at their disposal: too many demands for police interventions create dispatch bottlenecks, hampering speedy interventions. Indiscriminate recorded intelligence exceeds the capacity of a strained criminal justice system to follow up leads and bring cases to trial. If there is no noticeable increase in the likelihood of punishment, the certainty effect, if any, is bound to diminish in the long run.

There are important arguments against employing CCTV for policing minor offending (the UK Labour Government's 'zero tolerance' strategy[5]). First, a likely consequence of this policy would be a proliferation of surveillance, which, for reasons just explained, would be undesirable.

---

106. For a discussion of the implications of the differences in definition, see R Hefendehl, 'Observationen im Spannungsfeld von Praevention und Repression. Oder was von CCTV und laengerfristigen Observationen zu halten ist' (2000) 5 *Der Strafverteidiger* 270.

[5] See above ch 3, section III.C.2.

Secondly, the (increasingly contested[6]) 'broken windows' approach threatens to erode 'the distinction between illegal and unpleasant behaviour, crime and nuisance, delinquency and disorderliness'.[7] The concept of anti-social behaviour is in the same vein, and has been justly criticised for its expandability and scope for subjective judgement.[8] Operators' might raise the alarm unnecessarily, and their reactions become difficult to predict, creating insecurities for the observed about what is expected from them. I am not arguing that petty crime should remain unchecked or without consequences, and do not deny that there are good reasons for going after the perpetrators. Sweeping pro-active policing of people who are not suspected of wrong-doing is another matter, however. What should be questioned before proliferating cameras in public space is whether enforcement against minor offences and breaches of public decorum is of such priority that it is necessary to interfere with citizens' entitlement to anonymity.

A certain degree of tolerance should be granted as regards minor incivilities.[9] However, repeated exposure to cumulative offensive behaviour can be extremely unpleasant, exceeding what people may be expected to accept in a public environment. In locations where this occurs, there could arguably be an urgent need for enforcement measures, even though the level of seriousness of the individual offence is low. Whether CCTV surveillance is the best option for tackling those problems is yet another question, though. Special 'neighbourhood task teams'[10] and initiatives encouraging and involving the community, and promoting better mutual understanding, have so far shown more promising results than CCTV surveillance.[11] In places of public entertainment where 'crimes of friction' occur,[12] action programs, as drawn up by Wikstroem, including problem-orientated policing of particular public premises and locations, and targeted policing of specific groups of people known as 'trouble-makers', are

---

[6] There seems to be little evidence that a lack of enforcement against minor crimes may lead to more serious offending. See RJ Sampson and SW Raudenbush, *Disorder in Urban Neighbourhoods: Does it Lead to Crime?* (Washington, DC, National Institute of Justice, 2001).

[7] B Hudson, *Justice in the Risk Society* (London, Sage, 2003) 69.

[8] For a summary of the objections to ASBOs, see AJ Ashworth, 'Social Control and "Anti-Social" Behaviour: The Subversion of Human Rights?' (2004) 120 *Law Quarterly Review* 163.

[9] See S Mendus (ed), *Justifying Toleration: Conceptual and Historical Perspectives* (Cambridge, Cambridge University Press, 1988).

[10] See 'Made in NY, perfected in Kent—broken windows tactic tames streets of Dover', *Guardian*, 22 September 2009.

[11] See S Mackenzie, J Bannister, J Flint, S Parr, A Mille and J Fleetwood, *The Drivers of Perception of Anti-Social Behaviour*, Home Office Research Report 34 (2010) 12.

[12] See ch 3, section III.C.2.

more likely to have an impact than CCTV.[13] Surveillance by CCTV might be used to support such action programs, perhaps only for limited periods, but whether it would add significant benefits has to be assessed carefully. When dealing with offender types who act impulsively or irrationally, the deterrence argument does not carry much weight. Surveillance by CCTV might increase the likelihood of apprehension and punishment, but low-level offences are often not brought to trial, and recording is of little use if the crimes are not significant enough to merit the costs and time required for exploiting the evidence and tracing offenders.

Increasing public confidence and creating subjective feelings of security among the public as a rationale for pervasive CCTV coverage is no justification for infringing anonymity, when this is actually unlikely to improve protection or reduce crime in a significant way. To quote Andrew Ashworth:

> ... is it justifiable to pursue policies aimed at fostering such feelings or aimed at increasing 'public confidence' (a nebulous notion at best), when it is known that such policies are unlikely to have a significant effect on objective risk or protection?[14]

A selective and strategic public CCTV policy might be more likely to achieve a favourable balance between benefits and burdens, for while intrusions are fewer and of shorter duration, the prospects of positive results are higher. When intrusions do occur, they would yield only limited information about individuals. People would retain scope for moving outside supervised areas and be able to spend most of the time in public free from official gaze and judgement.

C. Preventive evidence collection

The recording of events for evidence collection may cause less interference with anonymity, but, as noted in chapter two, passive monitoring is not innocuous. The potential for intrusions on anonymity is actually greater than when people are monitored live without being recorded. People who have been recorded have no control over the use and distribution of their images, and safe storage systems and access restrictions can never quite

---

[13] Police action is to be supported by measures specifically designed to reduce the availability and the carrying of weapons, and by measures designed to reduce the sale and consumption of alcohol and drugs. See PO Wikstroem, 'Causes of Crime and Crime Prevention' in T Bennett (ed), *Preventing Crime and Disorder: Targeting Strategies and Responsibilities* (Cambridge, Institute of Criminology, 1996) 115 at 151.

[14] A Ashworth, *Sentencing and Criminal Justice*, 4th edn (Cambridge, Cambridge University Press, 2005) 531. Andrew Ashworth's critique concerned the indeterminate sentencing provisions in the Criminal Justice Act 2003 on the grounds of fostering subjective feelings of security.

overcome the risks of exposure and unwanted audiences which recordings create. Recording, no less than active monitoring, therefore requires justification, and should be based on urgent and specific reasons for crime-preventive interventions in the location in question.

Referring to Duff and Marshall's 'third kind of normative perspective',[15] I would argue that random pervasive recording in public for preventive evidence collection is an 'intrinsically inappropriate measure'. According to Duff and Marshall, certain means can be intrinsically inappropriate to the proper end of crime prevention, and to achieve crime prevention by those means is not a proper end. The demand that people have to be treated as responsible moral agents not only sets constraints on the means, but also helps to determine the ends. What matters is not just that people do not commit crimes, but also how and why they have come not to commit them. For example, it is intrinsically inappropriate to the proper end of crime prevention, according to Duff and Marshall, to achieve it by excluding certain people from shopping malls, because this denies some people a central aspect of fellow citizenship, ie access to the benefits of a place dedicated to the public.[16]

Pervasive recording entails no exclusion—crime prevention would be achieved by increasing the certainty of detection and punishment. How could this be intrinsically inappropriate, one might ask, since the threat of detection and punishment are built into our criminal justice system? My argument is that there is a qualitative difference between occasional controls and pervasive evidence collection, and that the prevention of street crime by means of systemic dismantling of anonymity, not just affecting the chances of committing a crime unpunished, but also threatening human dignity and liberty, is not a proper end.

Another reason speaks against pervasive recording in public space as a strategy for crime prevention. Increasing the threat of punishment does not deprive punishment of its moral message, and highlighting the detection risk of offending does not have to dilute the deontological condemnation expressed in punishment.[17] Nevertheless, one should not rule out the possibility that an over-reliance on CCTV, with its emphasis on the instrumental appeal to desist from crime in order to avoid paying the cost,

---

[15] Duff and Marshall, above n 1, at 20.
[16] *Ibid* at 21.
[17] von Hirsch and Ashworth reject a narrow conception of moral agency, according to which the introduction of any prudent considerations would divest the appeal to the actor of its essential moral character: A von Hirsch and A Ashworth, *Proportionate Sentencing— Exploring the Principles* (Oxford, Oxford University Press, 2005) 25. However, speaking about sanction severity, von Hirsch expressed concern that if penalty levels rose so high that minimal prudence would virtually command compliance, the normative reasons for desistence supplied by penal censure could become largely immaterial: A von Hirsch, *Censure and Sanctions* (Oxford, Clarendon Press, 1993)13.

might entail a dilution of the moral reasons for desistence. This could become a problem, for it is not possible to record and monitor people all the time. It is important that policy makers realise that CCTV can only ever be a small part of the solution for enforcing the criminal law, and that instrumental obedience is no substitute for moral endorsement of criminal prohibitions. Strengthening, communicating and convincing people of the normative reasons for desistence should always remain a priority.

D. Covert CCTV surveillance

The main argument one might make in defence of covert observation is that offenders might be caught more easily if they did not know that cameras were operating and hence took fewer precautions to avoid detection. There is also a notion that, by keeping CCTV covert, a more pervasive deterrent effect might be achieved, because the threat of detection would then not be limited to a circumscribed area. The two strategies supposedly would complement each other: the unpredictability of covert CCTV would keep some potential offenders 'on their toes' and deliver others into the arms of the law, achieving optimal results for crime prevention.

However efficient covert observation might be from a consequentialist point of view (there are many question marks regarding the deterrence claim, for unknown threats have no deterrent effect[18]), the pursuit of the reduction of crime has to be consistent with the values of our society. Secret surveillance goes against the grain of human dignity and denies people what should be a 'central aspect of citizenship', namely the right to know when the State interferes with their entitlements. People are taken unawares and cannot prepare for scrutiny, and once the practice becomes known, they must fear being spied on every time they go out. A measure as invasive and troublesome as secret surveillance should not be used against unsuspected individuals. It has no role to play in monitoring the general public for unspecified risks of street crime. It should be reserved for targeting specific individuals who are suspected of serious wrong-doing. This also applies to directed surveillance.[19] As it became known that directed surveillance has been ordered for minor matters, such as enforcing smoking bans and spying on council employees, it may have dawned on many how easily the line is crossed from guardianship to intrusive snooping, and that having done little or nothing wrong does not mean that one need not fear CCTV.[20] There is a need for safeguards and clear

---

[18] See ch 3, section IV.B.3.(i).
[19] See ch 2, section I.C.3 and n34.
[20] See 'Thousands spied on by councils but few prosecuted', *Guardian*, 24 May 2010.

limitations of the powers to order directed surveillance, targeting particular individuals.[21] Like other forms of covert surveillance, directed surveillance should be reserved for the investigation of criminal offences which would attract a customary sentence of a minimum of two years.[22] To prevent interested parties also being responsible for taking the decision whether direct surveillance is justifiable, external (as opposed to internal) authorisation should be required. It should be in the form of a search warrant, signed by a magistrate.

E. Placebo surveillance

The term 'placebo' may be applied to all forms of pretended surveillance. Placebo cameras in the literal technical sense may not be employed very often, but there is doubtless a great number of CCTV cameras that are not monitored (or monitored only irregularly) and do not record (or with substandard quality), and are, therefore, of no direct use for the detection, thwarting or prosecution of crimes. Placebo cameras allegedly have a deterrent effect, though, in spite of the fact that there is no genuine increase in the likelihood of apprehension. Why should there be a need to justify them at all, one might ask, if they do no harm but help with the task?

Pretended surveillance is not in fact harmless. When people believe that they are watched, they feel and act as if they were under observation—only this makes the claim of deterrence at all plausible. However, whatever deterrent merit they might have (it may not last long), the use of placebo cameras is morally problematic. Placebo cameras not only mislead potential offenders (about the increased risk of detection), but also let down the public, who are led to believe that they are being protected when they are not. Intentional deceit of citizens cannot be an ethical means for law enforcement. It violates the principles of veracity and trustworthiness which should form part of the moral code of the criminal justice system and its governance.

F. CCTV's role in the fight against terrorism

National security has been invoked to sanction inroads into civil liberties because the benefits to our safety allegedly outweigh the cost to personal liberty. Dan Gardner describes how politicians and government agencies

---

[21] See ch 2, section I.C.3 and n34.
[22] See *Surveillance: Citizens and the State,* House of Lords Constitution Committee—Second Report, Session 2008–09, ch 3, para 177.

have systematically inflated the terrorist threat.[23] Declaring people's fundamental civil liberty to be that they are kept safe from terrorism and serious crime, the previous UK Labour Government substantially increased the powers of the State to interfere with privacy and liberty rights, so that people might be monitored and policed more liberally.[24] The powers provided by the terrorism laws have been used much more extensively than originally intended, and are more often used for local government and crowd control than for national security.[25] The fight against terrorism must not be treated as an unrestricted licence to use CCTV in public space. The prevention of acts of terrorism is doubtless of high priority, but upholding our values and freedoms is essential to a democratic society. Moreover, so far the contributions of CCTV surveillance to our security from terror attacks have not been impressive. London boasts the most complete public CCTV network of any city in the world, but in July 2005 bomb attacks were carried out in several locations right under the eyes of the operators. The recorded footage was useful for reconstructing events after the attacks, and contributed evidence for the investigation, but punishing perpetrators becomes less important when those committing or initiating the crimes often cannot be called to account because they have died in the course of the deed, or have escaped abroad and are beyond reach. The primary objective in the fight against terrorism must be to thwart terrorist attempts. To forestall attacks, pre-emptive and tactical intelligence needs to be generated about the organisations involved and their members, which is more likely to be achieved by targeted surveillance and cooperation with security services on an international level, than by general public CCTV schemes.[26]

---

[23] D Gardener, *Risk—the Science and Politics of Fear* (London, Virgin Books, 2008) ch 11.

[24] In the US, counter-terrorist measures sanctioned in defence of national security have included torture (renamed 'coercive interrogation'), incommunicando detention, warrantless wiretapping, ethnic profiling, subjecting everybody's phone calls and e-mails to computer screening for suspicious words, and permitting intelligence agents to follow up on all such communication. Richard Posner has proposed a reinterpretation of the US Constitution which would make all these measures permissible. See R Posner, *Not a Suicide Pact: The Constitution in a Time of National Emergency* (Oxford, Oxford University Press, 2007).

[25] Section 44 of the Terrorism Act 2000, allowing the police in a designated area to search anyone without suspicion that an offence has occurred, for a period of one month, has been used extensively, often in connection with demonstrations. The designated area comprised all of Greater London, and the maximum duration of one month had already been extended to six months by renewing the authorisation each time it expired. This practice would have continued, had it not been uncovered by human rights groups. See House of Lords Constitution Committee, *Surveillance: Citizens and the State* (Second Report, Session 2008–09).

[26] Exploring the motivations of suicide bombers, Caryl argues convincingly that to be successful in the fight against terrorism, the authorities need to rethink their approach. He suggests a differentiated range of long- and short-term measures that might be suited to

G. CCTV for monitoring people inside their cars?

The points for debate here are not those speed controls involving just the scanning of licence plates; at issue is the scrutiny of people inside their cars to check whether they are using handheld phones or engaging in other distracting activities.

Surveillance via CCTV might be effective for targeting those offences: drivers can be caught unawares, and the cameras provide recorded evidence.[27] The likelihood of punishment is significantly increased, for automatic number plate recognition (ANPR) software enables the authorities to trace the addresses of the cars' owners (who are held prima facie responsible) and to serve penalty notices. In the case of traffic offences, a higher likelihood of punishment might be an effective deterrent. As more drivers would receive penalty notices, they would realise that risks have increased, and many of them might thereby be induced to be more law-abiding, for even if they were able to afford the fines, they also risk points on their driving licences, and few drivers are immune against the disutility of the possible loss of their permit.[28]

However, scrutinising people inside their cars is not the same as surveillance of people walking about. The space inside a car is not a public domain; it is in fact more akin to a person's home, with similar significance for privacy and intimacy. People consider their cars to be secure and personal spaces in which they do not have to keep up appearances. The intrusion is aggravated by the fact that via the licence plates, people may be identified and readily accessed by the authorities. Given that driving is a potentially dangerous activity, it is fair that motorists should have to put up with closer scrutiny, but is it really appropriate to employ a seriously intrusive measure for enforcing fines for the use of mobile phones? Punishment levels indicate that drink-driving is rated as far more dangerous and therefore as a more serious offence. Enforcement is thus of greater priority. Yet alcohol controls are used only selectively, around events or locations where alcohol consumption is high, or where there are reasons to believe that drivers might be over the limit. Breath and blood tests are more intrusive than CCTV, but considering the danger a drunk driver represents, the burden is not out of proportion. In comparison, submitting people to frequent and random violations of the intensely private space

---

dealing with the problem, including targeted surveillance for individual suspects, but does not attribute much value to public CCTV. See C Caryl, 'Why they do it?', *New York Review of Books*, 22 September 2005, 28ff.

[27] Camera-detection devices that send out a signal when the car approaches a speed camera do not work with regular CCTV cameras.

[28] As of February 2007, s 26 of the Road Safety Act 2006 was amended, not only increasing the penalty for using a hand-held phone while driving to £60, but also introducing the imposition of a three-point driving licence endorsement.

inside their cars in a campaign against the use of mobile phones—an offence entailing a relatively low fine and whose importance is still subject to debate—seems somewhat excessive. There is talk of high risks of collision when driving while holding a phone, but not much empirical evidence about the safety risks involved. If it exists, it has not been made available to the public at large.[29] Many drivers may therefore not be convinced of the conduct's hazards and the legitimacy of this new prohibition, viewing it as a pretext for collecting money from fines. When drink-driving became punishable, it was at first difficult to get people to comply with the new law, because driving under the influence of alcohol had not been punishable before (unless it involved other motoring offences) and people did not understand its risks. Compliance with drink-driving laws may first have occurred chiefly for reasons of prudence, but the change of moral attitudes about drink-driving was greatly helped by intense publicity concerning the heavy toll it is taking on the roads and the realisation of how much it endangers lives.[30]

Without persuasive data about the hazards of using hand-held mobile phones, it will be hard to convince people of the moral wrong of their actions. Closed circuit television cameras alone will not achieve the desirable interaction between a prudent and a normative mechanism of compliance, best for bringing about sustained changes.[31]

H. CCTV for catching shoplifters?

Providing assistance with the apprehension of shoplifters is often a focus for CCTV schemes set up as private/public partnerships for monitoring

---

[29] The Department of Transport's claims that speed cameras contribute significantly to road safety are also neither proven nor undisputed. The RAC and other motoring groups have questioned the value of speed cameras after police figures published by the Department of Transport revealed that only one in 20 collisions last year was caused by a driver breaking the speed limit. These figures contradict claims by speed camera supporters that speed is a factor in one-third of collisions. The biggest breakthrough in road safety occurred long before speed cameras were introduced (between 1984 and 1994), and was largely due to better safety standards in car manufacturing.

[30] A von Hirsch, AE Bottoms, E Burney and PO Wikstroem (eds), *Criminal Deterrence and Sentence Severity* (Oxford, Hart Publishing, 1999) 3. They also report about a study of a two-week police 'blitz' on worn tyres on automobiles in a Dutch town, which came to similar conclusions. Extensive media coverage explaining the dangers of driving with worn tyres ensured that people understood the need for the initiative, which succeeded in reducing the use of worn tyres (*ibid* at 22).

[31] Some of the arguments against using cameras for traffic offences are similar to those levelled against public CCTV in general, namely that they merely displace, but do not solve, the problems (drivers slow down/put the phone down as they approach the cameras, but speed up/take up the phone again as soon as they are past), and that they relieve motorists of the responsibility of managing the risks of driving themselves.

central business areas.[32] Shoplifting is not a street crime, as it represents no threat to people's safety. Its frequency reflects the retailing strategy of shop owners, who, to stimulate consumption, offer their goods in a way that allows people to help themselves. The focus for combating this offence should therefore be inside the shops, and the pursuit of shoplifters does not warrant setting up a public CCTV scheme. However, store detectives may by rights ask CCTV operators for assistance with keeping track of shoplifters on the run.[33] Once an offence has been committed, enforcement becomes a priority. If demands for assistance are a frequent occurrence, it is only fair that as the beneficiaries, retailers should contribute to the cost of the CCTV scheme.

II. THE REGULATION OF PUBLIC CCTV SURVEILLANCE

Three fundamental premises should provide the conceptual framework for the regulation of CCTV surveillance in public space:

a) Anonymity in public, as an aspect of privacy, protects individuals' dignity and autonomy, and should not be interfered with lightly. Anonymity in public space must remain the rule, not become the exception.
b) Public CCTV surveillance, in the form of active as well as passive monitoring, interferes with anonymity interests.
c) Crime prevention and the supposed preventive ability of CCTV for law enforcement should not be treated as granting an unqualified licence for such surveillance. Governments committed to the values of human dignity and autonomy should consider the introduction of public CCTV surveillance only if there is an urgent need for enforcement and there are good prospects that CCTV can make a significant contribution. The scant concern for anonymity interests, and the overstated claims of crime-preventive effectiveness that have been characteristic of the English CCTV policy, must be reversed.

A framework of rules and regulations has to ensure that the protection of anonymity against unwarranted intrusions is observed at all levels of operation. The protection of anonymity has to begin by restricting the proliferation of public CCTV. The implementation of public CCTV schemes should be guided by a selective approach, focusing on the extent and seriousness of the crime threat, and on the types of the crimes and potential offenders to be targeted. Ensuring transparency of purpose and fair practice in the execution of CCTV is an important but secondary

---

[32] See ch 3 III C 2.
[33] See ch 3 III C 2 n94.

concern, and there have to be systems of checks and balances. Surveillance by CCTV is carried out away from public view, by or under the aegis of the authorities and their representatives, who are at the same time the principal users of the intelligence it yields.

I shall propose principles and limitations for the implementation and execution of public CCTV, and make suggestions how to promote transparency and accountability. The quality and structure of a regulatory framework dealing with CCTV will also be discussed. This chapter will conclude with an overview of the existing regulation of public CCTV surveillance in the UK and a brief critique of its merits and shortcomings.

A. The implementation of public CCTV schemes

1. Selection of locations

The implementation of public CCTV schemes should be conditional upon a comprehensively documented and significant criminal threat. The initiating agency should be under an obligation to undertake a risk assessment and site analysis for the locations to be put under surveillance. This should include not only identification of the targeted crimes and local crime data documenting the frequency of criminal occurrences over a given period, but also a survey of environmental, social and demographic factors, and how they may relate to the crime problem. Crime-mapping techniques should be used to establish spatial and temporal patterns, and an attempt should be made to assess long-term crime trends in the area. Moreover, a critical analysis should be provided as to why public CCTV may be expected to have a significant effect on crime in the particular context. There should be evidence that multi-agency cooperation has been organised and that surveillance is underpinned by a package of other crime-reduction measures, as these are essential conditions for a successful strategy.

If there are several high-crime locations in the vicinity of each other, CCTV ought to be reserved for the ones with the highest enforcement priority. Adjoining CCTV schemes may have a 'pointilistic' effect, resulting in the coverage of an extensive area even though the reach of each individual scheme is restricted. To allow for breathing space, surveillance-free zones should be interspersed, and less intrusive measures of enforcement employed for the locations with lower risk levels.

2. Proper budgeting and funding

To have any impact on street crime, a public CCTV operation has to be set up and run in a professional manner. The implementation of CCTV schemes should therefore be conditional upon submission of a detailed budget and secured funding for adequate technical equipment, appropriate premises and running costs. Budgets should be based on costs over a period of several years, and specify the following key cost components: preparatory work, equipment, installation, control room set-up, data storage, monitoring staff costs, maintenance, repair, system upgrades, governance, insurance and legal fees. In order to safeguard anonymity, the premises of the operation have to fulfil certain standard requirements, such as a self-contained control room, separate reviewing area with lockable partitions and secure storage facilities. Provisions have to be made for a sufficient number of cameras to ensure coverage of the targeted location.[34]

3. Periodic operational review

Any public CCTV scheme should from time to time be reassessed and evaluated, to establish to what extent there continues to be a crime problem in the area and what effect CCTV surveillance may have had on it. The basis for the evaluation has to be the statistics on the incidence of crime, as in the initial risk assessment and any subsequent reviews, compared to the status at the time of the review. Whether CCTV has worked as a strategy to reduce crime is a more complex issue. A statistical increase in crime does not necessarily prove that the operation has failed, but could merely reflect higher detection rates. A decrease in crime might be attributable not just to CCTV but to other circumstantial factors, and whether such factors could exist would have to be investigated. Valuable clues about the performance of a scheme can be found in the operation's records, if activities have been properly documented.

Cambridge has developed a model for creating a readily available set of records to evaluate the need and demand for a scheme, the quality of its service, its achievements and its operational shortcomings. The Cambridge City Council CCTV System Annual Report includes the following tables:

a) the numbers of arrests involving CCTV (with a breakdown by type of crime and location);
b) the numbers of incidents observed (both crime and non-crime);
c) the number of events referred to the police, and the number of alarms and calls from the police asking for assistance responded to; and
d) the number of failures to establish contact with the police.

An incident log is kept for each camera. If the number of incidents recorded over a certain period falls below the average, this is taken as an

---

[34] For a detailed budget checklist, see G Clancey, *Considerations for establishing a public space CCTV network*, Australian Institute of Criminology, Resource Manual No 08 (2009)18.

indication that there is no need for a camera in that particular zone and the camera is removed or placed elsewhere.

A 'CCTV Effectiveness' table rates the quality of evidence, and lists the number of tapes viewed by the police, the number of still photos and copies of tapes produced, and the number of tapes sealed as evidence.

All tables include a year-by-year comparison.[35]

B. The execution of surveillance

1. *Informing the public*

Planning permission procedures could provide the model for the form and scope of advance communication of public CCTV projects. A good way of securing openness and transparency would be the adoption of mandatory 'privacy impact statements', already common practice in Canada and supported by the UK Information Commissioner.[36] According to this model, the agency proposing to implement a surveillance scheme has to disclose the intended *modus operandi* and provide an assessment of its likely impact on privacy. This would prevent uncertainties, such as those surrounding the Central London Congestion Charge for instance, where the authorities have to date avoided spelling out what types of data are generated by the cameras, how the data are processed and who has access to them.

Operators of CCTV schemes should be under an obligation to make available more comprehensive information about the scheme at the town hall and on-line, and provide a contact for dealing with enquiries and complaints regarding the scheme. People have a legitimate interest in knowing when their anonymity is being invaded and should be given enough information to judge whether the grounds for doing it are reasonable, even if the decision to install a public CCTV scheme is ultimately not justiciable. The purpose of the operation ought to be specified, not just in formulaic terms, but by indicating the particular types of crime that are targeted. Knowing an operator's brief makes it more predictable what might attract his attention and thus is reassuring for the person in the street. A precise mission statement also provides a better lever for a claim under the Data Protection Act 1998 for use of CCTV intelligence for other than the documented purposes for which it was obtained.

---

[35] Cambridge is in the lead group of the Public CCTV Managers Association's initiative to design and establish a national set of performance indicators, which is to include a yet more comprehensive list.

[36] See *Privacy Impact Assessment Handbook and Surveillance Society Conference*, Information Commissioner's Office, 7 December 2007.

That people should be alerted that CCTV is operating in a given location is elementary. The State owes individuals who are not suspected of wrong-doing, information about intrusions on their anonymity. The signs should be easy to see and read, and the agency responsible for overseeing the operation should be identified and a contact number provided. Contrary to current practice, the signs ought to indicate whether cameras are equipped with special capabilities, such as night vision or wave radar, for these technologies allow for unexpected degrees of intrusion, and people should be warned if they have to reckon with unusual forms of scrutiny. Providing this information can only enhance the deterrent message, whereas disclosing if and during which periods cameras are not manned would be counterproductive.

2. Audio surveillance

Audio surveillance goes beyond the normal intrusions one has to expect in the public domain. A person ordinarily has substantial control over his 'conversational preserve' and greater factual power to control who should hear what he says than who can see him. Expectations of privacy regarding one's conversation are less affected by going abroad than expectations of being spared visual scrutiny. People often use the public space for discussing intimate matters, for its anonymity may afford more privacy than the home or the workplace. Although not everything people say to each other is charged with intimate meaning, audio surveillance is a form of infringement of intimacy, for eavesdropping on what people say reveals more about what they think and feel than their image alone. It is a way of getting into their minds and into that first circle of privacy that relates to the matters that are closest to a person and which are guarded most closely.[37] It is not only the potentially intimate subject matter, but also the fact that audio surveillance obtains access to a person's way of thinking that qualifies it as a violation of intimacy. Because of the particular intrusive potential of audio surveillance (in particular when combined with visual surveillance), it should be ruled out as a general feature of public CCTV.

3. Night vision cameras

Night vision cameras make it possible to conduct surveillance after dark, diminishing the criminal opportunities resulting from the darkness and the quiet of late hours. They can aid with detection and secure evidence in cases where bystanders could not see enough to act as witnesses, or where there were no bystanders because of the late hour.

---

[37] See ch 3, section II.D.1.

However, the use of night vision cameras could easily result in a violation of intimacy interests. People might think they are under the cover of darkness when they are not. Cameras with night vision capabilities are still the exception, and if they are so equipped, people ought to be made aware of it, perhaps by the use of illuminated signs. If the crime pattern indicated that criminal activity was taking place primarily during the day, there might be no justification for using the more intrusive night vision technology after dark. Also, improved street lighting might often solve the problem; or when used in tandem with night vision cameras (in spite of improved street lighting, it may require night vision cameras to produce distinctive enough pictures after dark), people would at least know that they can be seen, and not get a false idea about being invisible to scrutiny.

4. *Passive versus active monitoring schemes*

Passive monitoring schemes (unmanned cameras recording events for possible later review) are appealing because their operating costs are significantly lower. Time-delayed monitoring also represents a less acute interference with anonymity than real- time monitoring, due to the greater distance—temporal and spatial—between the observers and observed, and if combined with a restrictive reviewing policy, fewer people would be subjected to scrutiny. There are, however, significant drawbacks. Recording people's images opens up greater possibilities for intrusions on anonymity.[38] Unmanned schemes provide no 'modulators' who could dispatch the police to thwart or pursue offenders. These regimes might even give offenders a better chance to commit harmful acts unchallenged. Unaware that the operating cameras are not manned (as this is not disclosed by the signs), potential victims might rely on the experts behind the camera to watch out for persons with hostile intent, instead of being alert themselves. Also, when a crime occurs, fewer people might be prepared to take the initiative to help others and risk their own safety, believing that the police would soon be on their way to take matters in hand. Moreover, much of the recorded footage is never watched, and there is a greater chance that crimes and offenders slip through the net than when operators monitor events in real time.[39]

If there is a pressing need for enforcement, because of the imminence, gravity or frequency of criminal threat—which should be the reason for installing CCTV in the first place—settling for a delayed review of recorded footage instead of active monitoring seems contradictory. I would

---

[38] See ch 2, section II.B.5.(i).
[39] See ch 3, section IV.B.2.

generally argue in favour of active monitoring, for it is an important factor in achieving optimal results, having three salient advantages over passive monitoring:

a) there is a chance of foiling crimes in progress;
b) prospects for detecting crimes and apprehending offenders are better; and
c) operator-led interventions on the ground contribute to the 'visibility' of a CCTV operation and may make potential offenders more aware of the increased threat of detection.

Moreover, although today most active monitoring schemes also have recording facilities, recording could be reduced by on-demand recording mechanisms, to be activated by operators only if they have reason to believe that a crime may be about to happen. There may be situations when ongoing recording might be advisable, eg when the targeted criminal activity is not easy to detect. However, when using more invasive practices, it should always be a consideration whether the gravity of the targeted crimes is significant enough to warrant stepping up the intrusion.

5. The reviewing of recordings

The reviewing of recorded footage takes the interference with anonymity a significant step further. Where recording created the risk of intrusion, reviewing turns the risk into reality. It involves more intense scrutiny, usually by an audience that has not been co-present. 'Fishing expeditions' effectively treat people who are not suspected of crimes as potential suspects, with an implicit risk that the presumption of innocence might be replaced by a 'confirmation bias'.

The reviewing of CCTV footage, therefore, ought to be subject to stricter conditions than real-time monitoring and recording, and enforcement reasons should have progressively more weight. However, some schemes have very loose regulations regarding footage review. Recordings may be reviewed in their entirety, and there need not be a particular reason for it. A more restrictive approach, also advocated by von Hirsch,[40] would be to permit a review of recordings only when a crime has been reported, to give access only to enforcement personnel dealing with the case, and to limit the footage review to the location and time of the crime specified in the report. All other recordings would be destroyed unseen after a specific period of time. Adopting these constraints would achieve four important objectives:

---

[40] von Hirsch, above n 2, at 70.

a) Instead of uncertain speculations about the possibility of criminal activity, there would be compelling enforcement grounds and a specific public interest in scrutinising the recordings.
b) People without a special apparent link to crimes are spared; only individuals who have a prima facie closer connection with the crime (be it as potential offender or witness), and therefore a lower entitlement to anonymity,[41] would be subjected to closer scrutiny.
c) The intrusion would be limited to material which can reasonably be expected to reveal relevant information.
d) The audience, although extended, would consist only of people charged with the investigation and prosecution of the particular crime, not other agencies or law enforcement personnel who have no direct business with the case in question.

I suggest adding a further proviso, namely that the investigation must concern crimes committed at the location where the recording was made, not crimes committed elsewhere. The purpose of public CCTV is to ensure the protection of a particular place from crimes. Crimes committed in other places are outside that remit. If the 'purpose specification' principle (stipulating that data may not be used other than for the one particular permissible purpose that has been expressly specified[42]) of the Data Protection Act 1998 is to have any meaning, the grounds for review have to pertain to a designated local scope, not to law enforcement in general. To widen it would give the State much greater licence to exploit recorded intelligence and permit the circulation of recorded footage among a staggering number of State agencies claiming to be in one way or another connected with the investigation of crimes.[43] People would thus be unable to determine the extent to which data about them are being used and by whom—two mandatory conditions for informational self-determination—preventing them from becoming data objects.

6. *Identification of recorded individuals*

Identification amounts to removing the ultimate shield of anonymity: once the person is identified, he can be pursued by the authorities and subjected to targeted, inconvenient and potentially punitive interventions. Considering the onerousness of such intrusion, the benefits to be derived from this step should have considerable weight. It should depend upon the gravity of the crime to be investigated as well as the value of the contribution to the

---

[41] See ch 1, section III.B.3.
[42] Data Protection Act 1998, s 4 and sch 1, Pt I.
[43] See ch 2, section I.A.10.

investigation that can be expected from the person in question. Establishing the identity of individuals who are captured on CCTV ought to be reserved for cases that involve a more serious offence and have as an objective the acquisition of demonstrably important evidence. These conditions appropriately mirror those for an entry search, for by the time the investigation takes place, the person is no longer apprehended in a public location.

Pursuing someone who is wanted as a witness and who has a purely coincidental connection with the crime should require weightier grounds for law enforcement than establishing the identity of a suspect, which burdens only the person who might be responsible for the crime, or the victim who has a personal interest in the case. A particularly high threshold should be imposed for the identification of participants in a demonstration.

There are several ways of going about the identification of a person captured on CCTV, and it is imperative not to expose the person more extensively than absolutely necessary in the process. Circulation of pictures via the mass media, with an appeal to the public at large to help with identification, should be a last resort because it entails the most extreme invasion of anonymity and privacy: putting the press and the public onto someone can make that person's life miserable, and his reputation may never recover from the exposure. This route should therefore be chosen only when a person is accused of an exceptionally serious crime and when there is already other strong incriminating evidence against him. Utmost circumspection has to be applied to prevent exposing victims, innocent bystanders and residential premises in the process.

Computerised face recognition seems at first glance the most promising method of identification. It dispenses with human scrutiny and does not have to involve people outside the immediate investigating team. However, when people's images are treated as machine-readable data, concerns relating to the interests of the featured individual, to his dignity and to the effect the use of his image might have on his life tend to be forgotten. Face-matching may have tangible and unpleasant consequences for the person whose picture is used. There is a considerable risk of erroneous matching, but presumptions based on computer analysis are hard to refute.[44] Although the burden of proof is not reversed, it could be an arduous struggle to establish that one has been misidentified.[45] Screening a

---

[44] All face-recognition systems currently in use have produced many more errors ('false positives') than positive identifications or arrests. A trial at Palm Beach Airport caused 1,081 false alarms in four weeks. See D Kopel and M Krause, 'Face the Facts—Facial Recognition Technology's Troubled Past—and Troubling Future', Reason Magazine 2002, www.reason.com/archives/2002/10/01/face-the-facts.

[45] For a general discussion of the subject, see P Brey, 'Ethical Aspects of Facial Recognition Systems in Public Places' (2004) 2(2) *Journal of Information, Communications and Ethics in*

person's image against a 'wanted' list is by implication to treat him as a suspect, and there should be compelling reasons for believing that he might be one of the wanted individuals. Without prior evidence of wrong-doing, subjecting people to an electronic criminal identification program is no more justifiable than 'forcing unsuspected citizens to participate in a police line-up'.[46]

No clear standards have yet been developed to define and limit the conditions under which law enforcement agencies may acquire, access and use biometric data files holding digitised photographs, such as ID card files and driving licences, for the identification of individuals.[47] Paul de Hert makes a pertinent distinction between identification technologies relying on administrative identity (electronic signatures, fingerprints), which are less intrusive and might therefore be accessed more liberally, and those using the psychosocial identity captured in a person's physical features and facial expression, which law enforcement agencies should be prohibited from accessing or using.[48]

Using general ID databases for matching CCTV footage is really a case of 'function creep', a term referring to the use of data technology introduced for one purpose for other purposes that were not previously disclosed or discussed.[49] The intrinsic and only officially acknowledged function of these data banks is to enable the verification of a person's identity claim, presenting an identification document to show that he is that person. The identification of a person walking about in public is not covered by that brief. That person makes no claims regarding his identity—that his identity is of no relevance is precisely what anonymity is

---

Society 97; and P de Hert, *Biometrics: Legal Issues and Implications*, Background Paper for the Institute of Prospective Technological Studies, DG JRC (Sevilla, European Commission, 2005).

[46] A Alterman, 'A Piece of Yourself: Ethical Issues in Biometric Identification' (2003) 5 *Ethics and Information Technology* 142.

[47] The Law Enforcement Alliance of America (LEAA) has pointed out that while the International Biometric Industry Association (IBIA), the body representing manufacturers of facial recognition systems ('Smart CCTV'), had urged that clear legal standards should be developed, no such standards were as yet in place. The LEAA considered that the fact that smart CCTV schemes were implemented was nevertheless in contravention of IBIA's own policy. See Brey, above n 45, at 102.

[48] de Hert, above n 45, at 24.

[49] Brey has identified three types of function creep: a) widening of the data base; b) purpose widening; and c) user shifts. Type a) occurs when the database for matching CCTV recordings is expanded to include not only wanted criminals, but also other existing data bases holding digitised photographs, such as those for ID card files and driving licences; b) implies using smart CCTV not only for identifying suspected individuals, but also for the purpose of analysing the ethnic composition of crowds; c) refers to access to the systems by new types of users, such as the FBI, the media or commercial organisations carrying out demographic research. See Brey, above n 45, at 104ff.

about.[50] Moreover, if in the course of an investigation CCTV images of the suspect are matched against a general database (rather than a file of wanted suspects), the people whose data are used are treated as if they might be suspects even though there are no reasons to connect them to the crime. This should be allowed only in exceptional cases, and only for the investigation of the most serious offences.

7. Safeguarding the evidential value of recordings

A primary function of CCTV recordings is to provide forensic evidence. To warrant the intrusion inherent in the recording, the evidence has to be viable and its integrity preserved. If the footage is visually substandard or if it is of doubtful authenticity, it is of no use in court. Time and date measurement must be accurate. As a matter of good practice, the equipment has to be monitored and maintained to high standards. A service routine should be established and a maintenance log kept. Should the reliability of the equipment be challenged in legal proceedings, the maintenance logbook can prove that the equipment has been serviced regularly and kept in good working order.

Recordings can be secured against unauthorised access and manipulation by a combination of physical, electronic and managerial measures. Digital schemes require particularly strict safeguards because digital images can easily be tampered with, and manipulations are well nigh impossible to detect. The biggest problem is to ensure that a digital recording that is presented as an original is in fact the original and not a copy that has been tampered with. It is therefore important to identify the original master clearly and to keep this marked 'original' in safe storage, to be presented in court if necessary. Digitally-recorded footage should be automatically encoded so that it can be reviewed only with the help of secret de-blocking codes. Only designated senior officials should be in possession of a personal de-blocking code, so that when recordings have been accessed it is possible to identify whose code has been used.

It would indicate serious operational shortcomings if the quality or the integrity of the recordings of a scheme were regularly to be impugned. The creation of a proper audit trail is a valuable precaution, in case the probity of the recorded evidence were to be challenged. Any form of access, use and processing of recordings should be registered, including the time, place and purpose of it, the number of copies made and the names of the

---

[50] The assertion that by applying for a passport people have consented to the use of their biometrics for any identification purposes is as disingenuous as the argument that people have consented to the intrusion by CCTV surveillance when they knowingly use locations where cameras operate. In both cases people are not really given a choice: if they need to use that particular space, they have to put up with the cameras, just as they have no option but to surrender their biometric data if they need a passport or visa.

individuals present. The 'four eyes' principle should be adopted as a safeguard, requiring at least two people always to be present when footage is accessed.

8. Limited storage period for recordings

Recordings should be kept for a limited time only. Notwithstanding safe storage systems, a risk of unauthorised access remains, and the more data that are accumulated and the longer they are held, the more difficult it is to monitor their use. The authorities themselves may have an agenda for accessing the information, and claim legitimate reasons to tap into that source of knowledge. If cameras are unmanned, it may take longer for crimes come to light, especially if recordings are reviewed only when a crime is reported. Some victims or witnesses may need time before they decide to come forward. However, if there is live monitoring, one should assume that crimes would be detected immediately. The relevant sections of the recordings could thus be preserved for investigative purposes, while the unclaimed footage should be deleted unseen without much delay. Unless there are special circumstances, the 30-day storage period recommended in the English Data Protection Commissioner's Code of Practice for the Use of CCTV seems unnecessarily protracted.

As a collector and holder of potentially important evidence, the CCTV authority has a role to play in ensuring a fair trial. A fair trial requires that the defendant is not deprived of evidential material that might help him prove his innocence. Not only the police, but also the CCTV authority should therefore bear responsibility for ensuring that the defendant's legal representatives are given a fair chance to examine topical footage.[51] A recording might help to prove a defendant's innocence as well as his guilt. This can become an issue where the police have used a recording in the investigation of a crime, but have returned it and authorised its deletion because for them it had no evidential value. For the defendant, this fact may yield such important evidence, however, that he has an interest in preserving and seeing the tape. If someone has been charged, it should therefore become an express obligation that, before destroying the tape, the surveillance agency ascertains that the defence has been informed and

---

[51] The police have an obligation to disclose to the defendant any 'unused material', ie evidence in their possession that they will not be using at trial, which might be relevant to the defendant's case (see Disclosure of Unused Material, Code of Practice issued under s 23 Criminal Procedure and Investigations Act 1996 (as amended in 2003). Under PACE 1984, operators are merely obliged to share all relevant information for a criminal procedure in their possession with the police, and it is the police's responsibility to disclose evidence.

given access to the tape. One might even argue that such an obligation can be read into Article 6 ECHR as being essential to the right to a fair trial.

9. Safeguards for ensuring fair practice

The problem of the 'unobservable observer' can never be resolved entirely.[52] Not only might publicly identifying camera operators involve a risk for their safety; knowing the names of those in charge of the operations would also tell us little about their attitudes or qualifications. An independent, publicly accountable 'watchdog' agency with a remit to conduct random inspections of CCTV control rooms and surveillance practices, and to publish reports about the state of affairs, as suggested by Goold,[53] would be one way of making CCTV operations more accountable, but such a body may never be created. In England, councils employ 'Comprehensive Performance Assessment' (CPA) CCTV Inspection Teams, but external inspections are reactive and intermittent. The observance of fair practice is largely left to the discretion of surveillance personnel and those who supervise them. To ensure fair practice in the day-to-day execution of surveillance, a range of managerial mechanisms should be adopted.

(i) Record keeping

The creation of an audit trail of surveillance activities is essential for the transparency of CCTV surveillance. Record keeping is not only useful for monitoring whether an operation is run effectively (see section II.A.3. above), it also serves to establish accountability. Individual log books listing an operator's observations, actions and explanations for actions, provide a basis for judging operators' competence and reasoning, although one must bear in mind that the facts may not always be recorded objectively and that the reasons for picking out people for special attention might be misrepresented or interpreted with hindsight.[54] It should therefore be permissible for management to review footage from time to time to check out an operator's style of surveillance and to verify the accuracy of his entries.

---

[52] Installing video cameras in the control room for the surveillance of operators, as practised by some operations, is no solution, creating its own massive privacy problems, especially considering that operators are often on a 12-hour shift.

[53] B Goold, 'Privacy Rights and Public Spaces: CCTV and the Problem of the "Unobservable Observer"', *Criminal Justice Ethics*, Winter/Spring 2002, 21.

[54] This is a known problem in police reports regarding stops and searches. Feldman points out that as the explanations for stops and searches have to be presented in terms of the reasonableness of officers' suspicion at the time, the reasons recorded in the report will tend to be *ex post facto* rationalisations rather than real reasons, and the need for them will not

Cambridge has developed a model for monitoring surveillance activities that is integrated into the day-to-day routine and should become standard practice. Operators keep an 'occurrence log', where anything noteworthy is registered, including communications with police forces on the ground, dispatch requests and the speed of police response. and the outcome of their intervention. Each time a zoom is activated this is noted in the 'zoom log', together with the time, duration and reasons for using the zoom, as well as the operator's conclusions. 'Recording logs' adhere to the same pattern. The 'reviewing log' names the official requesting and inspecting the footage, and registers each copy or still drawn from the footage, as well as the identities of those to whom they were distributed. Operators are also obliged to maintain a personal 'incidence log', which is a useful precaution for supporting their testimony in court, in case they are asked to appear as witnesses. A record is kept of the number of complaints received and the number of complaints upheld, including the reasons for the complaints and why those rejected were not upheld. This record is published in the Annual Report.

(ii) Layering controls for discretion

While too burdensome for routine surveillance practices, there should be a formal procedure for reviewing and processing recordings. Requests should be subject to approval by senior management. This would back up surveillance personnel who, because of their lower status, often find it difficult to resist the pressure of the police and higher-ranking officials.[55] For the sake of confidentiality, reviewing should have to take place in a secluded area that is separate from the control room.

(iii) Supervision and training

All agencies entrusted with public CCTV surveillance have to ensure the supervision of surveillance personnel and conduct regular assessment of operators' performance. Particular attention should be given to preventing

---

unduly inhibit searches. See D Feldman, *Civil Liberties and Human Rights in England and Wales* (Oxford, Oxford University Press, 2002) 317.

[55] This is even more important when dealing with requests for directed and intrusive surveillance (Regulation of Investigatory Powers Act (RIPA) 2000, s 26(2) and (9)). If the measures have been authorised in line with RIPA 2000, s 28(1)–(3) (directed surveillance) and s 32(1)–(6) (intrusive surveillance), CCTV operators are obliged to comply with such requests. However, there may be attempts by the police or other organisations to disregard the formalities, or to ask for more intrusive techniques than those permitted under the Act. To put a stop to such requests, prior presentation of the written authorisation to the operation's manager should be a prerequisite for participation in direct or intrusive surveillance. See also ch 2, section I.C.3, and n34.

use of CCTV facilities for ulterior, non crime-preventive purposes. Disciplinary and complaints procedures need to be established for breaches of fair practice. Anyone working with public CCTV should be obliged to sign a confidentiality agreement, barring them from divulging information received while executing their professional duties.

The training of surveillance staff ought to be standardised and based on a common CCTV manual and training programme.[56] Clear ethical and legal guidelines are important, helping those in charge of surveillance to understand the value of anonymity and to realise the invasive potential of CCTV surveillance in public. Uncertainty about the meaning of privacy in public prevails. The notion that CCTV is harmless as long as it is not aimed at private homes is widespread, and it is perpetuated even in official documents.[57] There should be a clear commitment to anonymity, and the entitlements related to it should be explained. The message has to be unambiguous and consistent, including an unequivocal prohibition of uses for purposes other than crime prevention. The understanding should be that the more intrusive surveillance practices become, the greater the urgency and the more significant the benefits of the intrusion need to be. An adequate minimum training period should be imposed for operators, with the same standards applying to whatever body is charged with surveillance, be it the council, the police or a private surveillance company.

C. The structure of the regulatory framework dealing with public CCTV surveillance

Substantive principles regarding the protection of anonymity have to be supported by a regulatory structure that ensures the implementation of the rules in practice, in establishing the system as well as at the operational level. The norms regulating public CCTV should provide specific parameters for the exercise of powers. They have to be drafted with precision and clarity, so that people are able to understand what their rights and liabilities are with respect to public CCTV surveillance. For the organisations mandated with the implementation of public CCTV, crime prevention should not just be a readily available formula. The agency exercising the mandate should have to substantiate why there is an urgent need for a

---

[56] Cambridge has established core courses for all staff and a Training Programme Block Syllabus for operators. Its CCTV operation manager is involved with working groups of both the regional 'Public CCTV Managers' Association' and the national 'CCTV User Group' set up with a view to establishing nationally recognised training and qualifications for all CCTV staff.
[57] In its 'Model Code of Practice for CCTV' the British Security Industry Association (representing private security companies) refers only to privacy, and this in vague terms, declaring that CCTV should not cause 'undue intervention in the general right to privacy of the members of the public'.

CCTV scheme in the area in question. The operating agency must be obligated to ensure that CCTV is executed with proper regard for anonymity, and that the physical, technical and managerial safeguards necessary to reduce its invasive potential are provided.[58]

Judicial controls should be available to help prevent authorities from operating outside their mandate. Individuals who have been the target of unjustified intrusions must have means of redress.[59] For the affected parties, having to rely for sanctions exclusively on internal disciplinary procedures, to be undertaken by the operating agency itself, is not a sufficient guarantee that those responsible for the breach will be held accountable properly. The culprit might be someone high in the organisation, or the organisation may have 'closed its eyes' to the abuse. In any event, the trustworthiness of the regime has suffered as a result of the failure of its internal controls. People therefore ought to have recourse to an external grievance mechanism to ensure that infringements of anonymity and non crime-preventive uses are fully investigated and adequately penalised.

The nature of the regulations matters, for whether they are statutory law or administrative guidelines has an impact on their status, enforceability and the remedies available. Statutes are binding on everyone, covering all CCTV operations, including those run by private enterprises. Statutes also have symbolic power: the fact that the Government has undertaken the complex legislative process to set rules highlights the importance of the values they enshrine. It confirms the State's commitment to the specified entitlements, for legislation cannot be changed easily and when bound by statutory law, the administration can be subjected to external judicial control to determine whether it has adhered to the State's promise.

Regulation by administrative guidelines has advantages and disadvantages compared to regulation by statute. Guidelines can be more pragmatic and flexible, but the reverse may be that since they are a form of self-regulation, the administration may shy away from imposing definite limitations on its own powers. Guidelines lack the democratic legitimacy of

---

[58] German law distinguishes between the law assigning the mandate (*Aufgabenzuweisungsnorm*) and the law determining the powers of the executing agency (*Befugnisnorm*). For interferences with constitutional rights, both have to be statutory laws, for only those are considered to have the necessary quality to ensure certainty, clarity and prospectivity. The prevailing opinion is that the norms mandating and determining the powers of the police do not cover public CCTV as, unlike the police, CCTV is not concerned with protection from danger but with the management of risks. As an interference with constitutional rights to privacy, it would require a specific statutory mandate for the implementation and a statute for regulating its execution. See D Buellesfeld, *Polizeiliche Videoueberwachung oeffentlicher Strassen und Plaetze zur Kriminalitaetsvorsorge* (Stuttgart, Boorberg, 2002) 149ff.

[59] This becomes an issue only at the operational stage. The implementation of unwarranted CCTV schemes burdens the public in general but does not have this personal connotation.

legislation. They do not have to go through the rigours of the legislative process, which guarantee a fuller representation of all interests affected—individual and collective—and are, therefore, more likely to be one-sided, favouring public order interests over individual interests. Guidelines are often internal documents and therefore not generally known to the public. Certain types of administrative codes of practice may be changed unilaterally and informally by ministerial demand, and thus provide no certainty of the protection they afford.

However, statutory regulations depend on operational integration to achieve their goal. Through guidelines one can influence the way surveillance schemes are run and organised, and ensure that the legal principles are fully implemented. A combination of statutes setting the broader principles for CCTV surveillance and the protection of anonymity, and administrative codes imposing concrete physical and managerial measures and rules of fair practice may be the best way to create a properly limited public CCTV regime. Guidelines should be published and readily available so that citizens can assess what the legal mandate implies and which intrusions they have to permit. Private companies engaged to run public CCTV operations must be bound contractually and legally to abide by the terms of the guidelines.

Codes of professional ethics have to be backed up by managerial and judicial controls as well as legal sanctions. There have to be structures of oversight and control of compliance, and effective means of holding the acting agency accountable. Accountability is a keystone for the implementation of policy principles. Relying on self-monitoring does not guarantee compliance, and those who are responsible for a CCTV operation should not be the sole judges of whether their own system adequately safeguards anonymity. Different levels of control, both internal and external to the agency, are called for. The exercise of the mandate should be subject to review, and there must be a mechanism for external inspection and performance assessment to which public CCTV operations should be obliged to submit without exception.

D. The regulation of public CCTV surveillance in England and Wales

It is not my intention to undertake an in-depth analysis of the existing regulations for CCTV, but only to provide an overview of the most relevant laws and provisions, and a summary critique of their merits and shortcomings. What is the existing regulatory framework for public CCTV, and does it guarantee that proper regard is given to anonymity interests in the implementation and execution of public CCTV surveillance?

1. Relevant regulations

In 1994, local communities were given the statutory mandate to establish CCTV schemes in public spaces to prevent crime and disorder; the authority was later extended to allow for Crime and Disorder Reduction Partnership schemes, run with cooperation between local authorities, police and private individuals.[60] For the first few years, CCTV surveillance in England was characterised by the near total absence of regulation. Even minimal bureaucratic requirements, such as planning permission, had been eliminated to speed up the implementation of CCTV.[61] In more recent years, however, a number of laws with direct relevance to public CCTV have been enacted:

— The Data Protection Act 1998, in force since March 2000, covers all CCTV installations for monitoring the public, including private schemes in shops and other locations accessible to the public at large. The definition of 'processing' in section 1 of the Act is extremely wide and covers all sorts of recording and holding of images, even if just for a limited period of time, such as real-time transmission, when images are shown on a monitor. This brings CCTV regimes that employ live monitoring, but do not record footage for storage, under the aegis of the statute. The fact that an individual cannot be identified by his recorded image alone does not prevent CCTV recordings from qualifying as 'personal data' as long as they represent images of the features of a distinguishable individual and identification is possible by processing the image (for example by data matching).[62]

— The Human Rights Act 1998 imposes a legal duty on public authorities to act in a manner compatible with the rights under the ECHR,

---

[60] Criminal Justice and Public Order Act 1994, s 163; Crime and Disorder Act 1998.

[61] Birmingham City Council had refused planning permission to a public CCTV scheme, out of concerns for the privacy-infringing potential of CCTV recordings. The Town and Country Planning (General Permitted Development) Order 1995 /(No.418), abolishing the need for planning permission for public CCTV installations, is said to have been passed to forestall local government objection against the Home Office's CCTV expansion programme. See SG Davies, *Big Brother: Britain's Web of Surveillance and the New Technological Order* (London, Pan Books, 1996) 187, fn 33.

[62] A revision of the Data Protection Act 1984, which covered only written information, was necessary after the European Data Protection Directive extended coverage to CCTV images, in spite of Britain's persistent adverse lobbying. Under the 1998 Act, the term 'data' has been expanded to cover 'information which is being processed by equipment operating automatically in response to instructions; or is recorded with the intention that it should be processed'. The European Directive 95/46/EC on the Protection of Individuals with Regard to the Processing of Personal Data defines personal data as follows: '"Personal data" shall mean any information relating to an identified or identifiable natural person; an identifiable person is one who can be identified, directly or indirectly, in particular by reference to an identification number or to one or more factors specific to his physical, physiological, mental, economic, cultural or societal identity.'

and entitles the victim of any violation of such rights to seek redress. By institutionalising the protection from unwanted intrusion into private life, Article 8 ECHR supports the argument that CCTV must not be allowed to grow unimpeded. Even though anonymity is not covered expressly, and its implications remain uncertain, case law of the European Court of Human Rights has confirmed that rights to respect for private life may exist outside the enclosures of the home.[63] Apart from Article 8, other rights are granted by the ECHR which may be relevant for public CCTV surveillance, such as Article 6 (right to a fair trial), Article 10 (freedom of expression), Article 11 (freedom of assembly) and Article 14 (prohibition of discrimination).

— The Regulation of Investigatory Powers Act 2000 was enacted to ensure that organisations exercising investigatory powers, such as the police, the intelligence services, the tax authorities and others, use those powers in accordance with the Human Rights Act 1998. Section 26 of the 2000 Act applies only to covert surveillance, including directed surveillance undertaken for a specific investigative operation (s 26(2)). Local authorities were originally given powers to order directed surveillance for tackling terrorism and organised crime, but have liberally used those powers and employed public CCTV for tracking individuals to investigate trivial matters[64] The new British Government has promised to end this practice, by introducing stricter regulations in 'The Freedom (Great Repeal) Bill' announced in the Queen's Speech on 25 May 2010.

— The Freedom of Information Act 2000. Local authorities became subject to this law on 28 February 2003.[65] The Act provides a general right of access to all recorded information held by public authorities, without significant formality or inquiry into the motives of the applicant and at subsidised cost. It makes it a criminal offence to alter, deface, erase, destroy or conceal any record held by the local authority, with the intention of preventing the disclosure of all, or part, of the information to which the applicant would have been entitled. This also applies to recorded CCTV footage. An applicant has to specify the particular place and time frame in which he believes himself to have been recorded, but the right extends only to the footage relating to the applicant's own image, not that of other bystanders.

---

[63] See ch 2 C and nn 17 and 24d.
[64] See ch 2, section I.C.3. and n34.
[65] The Act was fully implemented in January 2005, and most public bodies are now covered by it.

— The Information Commissioner's CCTV Code of Practice (revised edition 2008).[66] This Code, which is based on s 51(3)(b) of the Data Protection Act 1998, governs any CCTV system monitoring members of the public, ie not only public CCTV schemes, but also private schemes operating in shops and other mass private spaces (facilities owned by private organisations, but generally available for public use). The purpose of the Code is to clarify to the 'data controllers' (ie the people or agency who determine the purposes for which, and the manner in which, CCTV data are to be processed) their legal obligations under the Data Protection Act 1998. It also sets out guidelines for good practice, and is intended to reassure the public that the necessary safeguards against privacy violations are in place.

2. The achievements of the existing regulation

The Data Protection Act 1998 has, for the first time in the legal history of the UK, established enforceable standards concerning the collection and processing of images relating to individuals. Today, practically all public CCTV operations record images 'with the intention that they should be processed', and are thus subject to the Act's rules. Closed circuit television schemes must be registered; notification of a scheme and its purpose has to be lodged with the Office of the Information Commissioner.[67] This should bring into existence a central public record of CCTV operations in public space, making it possible to assess the scale of the coverage.

The 1998 Act proclaims eight data protection principles, stipulating that data must be:

a) fairly and lawfully processed;
b) processed for limited purposes and not in any manner incompatible with those purposes;
c) adequate, relevant and not excessive;
d) accurate;
e) not kept for longer than necessary;
f) processed in accordance with individuals' rights under the Act;
g) secure;

---

[66] The 2008 edn replaced the Code of Practice first issued in 2000, which had superseded the more general 'Watching Brief —a Model Code of Practice for CCTV', issued by the Local Government Information Unit in 1986. The latter made only very cursory reference to privacy issues— the main concern was to blank out views of private premises within the radius of CCTV cameras.

[67] It was assumed that in the early days of the DPA 1998, only 10% of all CCTV schemes had been registered. This was partly due to 'grandfather' provisions in the Act, which exempted older regimes from registration.

h) not transferred to other countries without adequate protection.[68]

The Data Protection Act 1998 also provides that data subjects should have certain rights against the agencies obtaining the data:

a) Section 7 of the Act stipulates the right of access by data subjects to their recorded images.
b) Section 10 provides that an individual is entitled to serve notice on a data controller, requiring the data controller not to begin, or to cease, processing personal data relating to that individual. Such a notice, to have effect, must establish that the processing in question is likely to cause substantial, unwarranted damage or distress to that individual.[69]
c) Section 13 gives the individual the right to go to court to seek compensation if he has suffered unwarranted damage or distress as a result of any contravention of the requirements of the Act.

A violation of the provisions of the Act is a criminal offence that can entail fines of up to £5,000. However, the practicalities of enforcement of the 1998 Act are quite problematic. The conditions attached to a claim for infringement of the Act under section 13 are stringent, and the prospects for success difficult to predict, because there are many loopholes in the requirements of the statute.

The Code of Practice complements the Act, providing guidance to those involved with the operation of CCTV schemes on how to organise and execute surveillance to ensure that data are processed fairly and lawfully under the Act:

a) There has to be a record of the persons or organisations responsible for ensuring the day-to-day compliance with the requirements of the Code, as well as of those who are in charge of security and disclosure policies.[70]
b) Surveillance by CCTV has to be overt. Clearly visible and legible signs must alert the public to the presence of cameras, and identify those responsible for their operation. Audio surveillance is allowed only in special circumstances and in a very restrictive way, and if it is used, the public have to be notified. Other special capabilities of the cameras (eg night vision) need not be announced.
c) There are clear instructions on how to ascertain adequate quality and

---

[68] Data Protection Act 1998, s 4 and sch 1, pt I. The principles are to be interpreted in accordance with pt II of sch 1.
[69] The *Peck* case (see ch 3 I C, nn 24 and 25) might provide an example. Had Mr Peck realised that he had been filmed while he attempted to commit suicide, he would have had grounds to serve a notice to stop the authorities from distributing the footage to third parties and from processing it any further than necessary to establish that no crime had occurred.
[70] Code of Practice, Standards Nos 3, 5, 7 and 8.

orderly handling of the recordings. It is recommended that a maintenance log be kept, documenting that the equipment is being kept in good working order and that the procedure prescribed for ensuring the accuracy of the camera location and the date and time references has been followed. If an operator is asked to verify an electronic face match, there has to be a record of his findings, for those data protection principles require that the match established by an automatic facial recognition system is also verified by a human operator. (A person can serve notice if the warrant issued for his arrest is based solely on the results of automated facial recognition and data matching systems.)

d) No particular storage period is prescribed. For CCTV schemes monitoring town centre crime-prevention schemes a 30-day storage period is mentioned, but the exact period should be the shortest possible, based on the operator's own experience.

The Code also sets out standards for handling access requests by individuals whose image has been recorded.

3. *The shortcomings of current regulation*

The Data Protection Act 1998 has unquestionable value as a statute setting broader principles for the use of data, but, having a wide range of applications and its concern being transparency of data handling and data integrity, it is at the same time both too general and too specific to serve as a policy blueprint for public CCTV. The wording is often ambiguous, and whether a contravention has occurred is a question of judgement. Many exemptions from important data protection principles—such as the protection of sensitive data and even overt surveillance—are sanctioned in the name of crime prevention. A data controller has far-reaching discretion to interpret a situation. Although his actions are subject to judicial review,[71] the fairness requirements of the data protection principles leave even more leeway for subjective judgement than the 'reasonable suspicion' requirements of the Police and Criminal Evidence Act 1984.

The Code of Practice may help to enforce the data protection principles, and makes some well-intentioned suggestions about how to approach the use of CCTV, but it is only a lukewarm attempt to regulate CCTV. The revised edition of 2008 is much less detailed than its predecessor. Principal reliance is on self-monitoring by the body concerned with surveillance.

---

[71] Data subjects can take proceedings in court to enforce their rights under ss 7, 10, 11 and 12 of the DPA 1998, and may claim compensation for damage and distress caused as a result of a contravention by a data controller of the requirements of the Act (s 13(1)–(3)).

Compliance with its suggestions regarding the execution of surveillance that are not dictated by the Data Protection Act 1998 is not legally required.

Neither the Data Protection Act 1998 nor the Code of Practice addresses the ethical dilemma of the collection of personal data as such and the resulting interference with anonymity. They promote transparency in the use of the collected personal data, and regulate their handling, but they impose no real limitations on surveillance. The 1998 Act imposes no effective constraint against unwarranted and pervasive implementation of public CCTV schemes, as it allows the installation of CCTV for the general purpose of crime prevention and public safety without further restrictions. The 'purpose specification' requirement might create hurdles for private CCTV operations serving private interests, but public CCTV schemes have instant legitimacy. No greater precision than 'crime prevention' or 'public safety' is required, reducing the 'purpose specification' to a mere formality.

The Code of Practice points out that local authorities should carefully consider whether to use CCTV, and take into account what benefits can be gained whether better solutions exist, and what effect surveillance has on individuals, but mentions in the same provision that the assessment need not be an extensive or a time-consuming process (see CCTV Code of Practice, ch 4). There are no standards dictating how thorough and knowledge-based this process must be. There is no obligation to undertake a proper risk assessment. (It is interesting to note that the Home Office has imposed much stricter standards for new public CCTV partnership projects seeking central funding; these should really have been included in the Code of Practice.[72])

The concept of anonymity in public space is never acknowledged or endorsed. Neither the Data Protection Act 1998 nor the Code of Practice makes a reference to anonymity or imposes specific constraints to protect it. The Code of Practice would have lent itself to highlighting anonymity interests and explaining their implications for surveillance practices, but never makes use of this opportunity. It admits that using CCTV can intrude on privacy, as it is 'capable of putting a lot of law-abiding people under surveillance and recording their movement as they go' (para 4 of the Code of Practice), but one looks in vain for an affirmative statement of the kind setting the tone of the Cambridge Code, namely 'that cameras will

---

[72] Section 4.3 of the 1999 CCTV Initiative Application Prospectus, states that the partnership must paint 'aclear and detailed picture of the crime and disorder problem to be tackled, set in its local social and physical context'. Furthermore, 'the cause of the problem and/or risk factors for offending (must) have been established, as a basis for designing the intervention'. S 4.3 also sets out the criteria for identifying a relevant crime prevention mechanism. See Scarman Centre National CCTV Evaluation Team, *National evaluation of CCTV: early findings on scheme implementation – effective practice guide*, Home Office Development and Practice Report 7.

not be used to monitor the progress of individuals in the ordinary course of lawful business' and that 'individuals will only be monitored if there is reasonable cause to suspect that an offence has been or may be committed'.[73] The Code is mute on discriminatory practices, and does not propose any restrictions on recording and reviewing. There is just a casual suggestion that if a system has been installed to deal with a specific problem, one might consider limiting recording to the time when the problem usually occurs (oddly placed in s 6, dealing with selecting and siting the cameras). The Code suggests adequate training of surveillance staff and periodic reviews of the system's effectiveness (s 10), but it is left to the operating agency to see to it.

Disclosure of images from the CCTV system must be 'consistent with the purpose for which the system was established' (s 8(2)), but it is up to the surveillance agency to make judgements about disclosure. Requests by third parties should be 'approached with care, as a wide disclosure of these may be unfair to the individuals concerned', and disclosure of images of individuals to the media for entertainment purposes would be inappropriate. However, disclosure to the media for purposes that are connected with crime prevention and public safety, as well as the release of footage for private claims (eg insurance claims), might be acceptable.

The Information Commissioner has neither the power nor the resources (he has only a small unit at his disposal and CCTV is only one aspect of his remit) to ensure the consistently high professional standards of conduct of those involved with CCTV operations.[74] He has called for compulsory powers of inspection and audit, and stronger penalties to punish flagrant breaches of data protection laws, and has suggested the introduction of mandatory privacy impact assessments.[75] He warned that the risks that arise from excessive surveillance affect both individuals and society as a whole, urging that pre-emptive action was needed to halt the slide towards a surveillance society.[76]

---

[73] Code of Practice for the Cambridge CCTV Scheme, cl 1.2

[74] Private individuals have the right to request the Information Commissioner to make an assessment as to whether data processing is likely or unlikely to comply with the DPA 1998. The Commissioner is entitled to issue an 'information notice' to a data collector to check the implementation of the data principles.

[75] See Statement of the Information Commissioner's Office, Tuesday, 1 May 2007, <www.ico.gov.uk>.

[76] The Information Commissioner presented a critical report to the 28th International Conference of Data Protection and Privacy Commissioners in London, 2–3 November 2006. See K Ball and D Murakami Wood (eds), *Report on the Surveillance Society* (London, ICO, 2006). He later urged the commissioners and their organisations to redouble their efforts to ensure that the privacy and surveillance dimensions are considered more seriously, and to seek more effective legal powers and legal sanctions. See K Ball, K Murakami Wood and C Raab, *Postscript Following the Conference of Privacy Commissioners* (London, ICO, 2007).

The Code of Practice is no substitute for a dedicated statutory regulation of CCTV systems. As a standard manual for CCTV it suffers from some glaring omissions. The Cambridge model of CCTV management and its code of practice, which has been cited repeatedly, is in many respects superior. It is more sensitive to anonymity issues, provides a detailed operational manual, incorporating physical and managerial safeguards, concerns itself properly with training standards, and has a mechanism for external performance assessment and effectiveness evaluation.[77]

One cannot rely on Article 8 ECHR to remedy the shortcomings of the current UK regulations concerning CCTV. Article 8 ECHR contains declarations of principle and may guarantee a minimum level of respect for private life, but it does not set standards of sufficient particularity to guarantee the protection of anonymity against intrusions by CCTV surveillance. It is largely the prerogative of the national legislator to determine which measures are necessary and justifiable for crime prevention, as long as they are not entirely unsuitable or plainly disproportionate, which in spite of reservations one cannot say about CCTV. The European Court of Human Rights has tended to accept the way local institutions and national courts have resolved the conflict between privacy and public safety. When the previousUK Government saw fit to implement an extensive public surveillance network for promoting public safety, it was not hindered from carrying out that policy. Nevertheless, if public CCTV were to become an active instrument of repression and discrimination—which, given the ambiguities and shortfalls of the current regulations in the UK, cannot be ruled out—there could be scope for a complaint before the Strasbourg Court based on Article 8 and other relevant provisions of the Convention, such as Article 10 (freedom of expression), Article 11 (freedom of assembly) Article 14 (prohibition of discrimination) and Article 6 (right to a fair trial). However, with the Freedom (Great Repeal) Bill, announced in the Queen's Speech in May 2010, the new liberal/conservative UK Government promised to bring forward legislation to restore freedoms and civil liberties, and to introduce new legislation to regulate the use of CCTV.

---

[77] To establish whether all CCTV installations of the Cambridge scheme respond to an empirically determined urgent need for crime prevention (see ch 3 III C (iii)) would go beyond the scope of this analysis.

Conclusion

THERE ARE MORAL reasons for broadening the concept of privacy to the public space. To maintain his dignity and autonomy, a person must be able to control access to himself and protect himself against unwanted scrutiny and judgement, irrespective of whether or not he is secluded in his private home or is abroad in public. When a person steps out in public, the scope of his control over being scrutinised may change, but he retains personal preserves that are not for sharing. For his physical and psychological integrity a person needs to be able to maintain boundaries of the self and defend them against potential intruders. Grounded in this rationale is the entitlement to anonymity, which should ensure that encounters with others in public remain at arm's length and that a person is subjected to only fleeting and impersonal appraisal. Like all privacy-related claims, anonymity is of particular value in fending off the controlling powers of the State.

It is a myth that CCTV is merely 'another pair of eyes', replicating the passing glance by which we assure ourselves that the person we encounter in the street has no hostile intentions. Surveillance by CCTV replaces informal social rituals, practised by civilians, with systematic supervision by the authorities. There is no doubt that anonymity is violated by public CCTV surveillance. The fact that the scrutiny by cameras is virtual does not prevent its being intrusive. Operators have greater powers of observation than the person in the street and their assessment exercises greater pressure, for we have more to fear from the judgement of those who have access to the State's legitimate use of force. Surveillance by CCTV is an instrument of social control with a wider scope than routine police enforcement. It exercises pressure to conform to the expectations of the authorities' standards of 'good behaviour', and could create a chilling and oppressive effect.

While public CCTV is clearly at odds with fundamental values and individual interests, there is no unequivocal answer as to whether crime prevention can provide the countervailing justification for the practice. The belief that CCTV surveillance markedly increases our security in public has yet to be confirmed. The conclusions of the two systematic empirical studies of note today have not been encouraging in that respect. In certain circumstances, CCTV might have some effect on crime, although the overall reduction may be rather small. The greatest success was achieved in surveillance of car parks. The public interest in CCTV is thus far less compelling than usually portrayed.

How much risk of intrusion into citizens' rights should policy makers be prepared to accept in the interest of trying to achieve somewhat enhanced protection against street crime? Citizens themselves rate their anonymity cheap, it seems, and are willing to trade it off for unsubstantiated promises of security. Fear of crime and terrorism is widespread, and surveillance appears to many to offer a lesser threat. For politicians there is a strong connection between the apparent provision of security and political authority. The British Labour Government was convinced that a pervasive public CCTV scheme was a 'good investment'. As we have seen, there are reasons to doubt this—not just from a purely instrumentalist point of view, ie whether it was a good use of finite law enforcement resources, but also when assessing whether the non-financial costs have been suitably weighted.

The fact is that public CCTV is often ill thought-out and an unnecessary overreaction. It also has an enormous potential for abuse. Today CCTV footage is mostly locked into routine data collection and not systematically exploited. The information generated is often less harmful than useless. But once the process of surveillance and collection of information is set in motion, and with new methods of electronic processing, facilitating the sorting and identification of people, it only needs the political will to assert the control that the accumulated knowledge allows. Taking a dystopian view, we are at the beginning of the total surveillance society, and CCTV will play the role of informer.

Complex regulatory schemes and administrative procedures are required to contain the negative potential of public CCTV surveillance schemes, and there always remains a risk of intrusive practices. My recommendation is that policy makers should opt for very selective implementation of public CCTV, within a narrow setting, targeted on particular crimes and a particular type of offender. On a reduced scale, the downsides of surveillance are of less major consequence. If anonymity is invaded only selectively and to a limited degree, the undesirable effects of unwanted scrutiny can be contained. High professional standards are easier to secure if there is only a limited number of schemes to monitor. By concentrating resources on fewer locations, greater effectiveness may possibly be achieved. Above all, it is important to remember that surveillance can never be a substitute for frontline crime-prevention work in and with the community, for the normative legitimacy of criminal prohibitions and the moral incentive to abstain from harming others.

Bibliography

Albrecht, K, 'RFID Tag—you're it' (2008) 299(3) *Scientific American, Special Issue: 'Will Technology Kill Privacy'* 48

Alldridge, P and Brants, C (eds), *Personal Autonomy, the Private Sphere and the Criminal Law—A Comparative Study* (Oxford, Hart Publishing, 2001)

Alterman, A, 'A piece of yourself: Ethical issues in biometric identification' (2003) 5(3) *Ethics and Information Technology* 139

Amelung, K, 'Zur Behandlung des Rechts am eigenen Bild' (1980) *Neue Juristische Wochenzeitschrift* 1560

—— 'Zur strafprozessualen Verwertbarkeit von Videoaufzeichnungen ohne spezialgesetzliche Ermaechtigung—BGH, NJW 1991, 2651' (1993) 3 *Juristische Schulung* 196

—— 'Zulaessigkeit laengerfristiger Videoueberwachung: Anmerkung zu BGH, Urteil v. 29.1.1998' (1998) *Neue Strafrechts Zeitung* 631

Anderson, R, Brown, I, Dowty, T et al, *Database State* (York, The Joseph Rowntree Reform Trust, 2009)

Archard, D, 'The Value of Privacy' in E Claes, RA Duff and S Gutwirth (eds), *Privacy and the Criminal Law* (Antwerp, Intersentia, 2006)

Arendt, H, *The Human Condition* (Chicago, Ill, University of Chicago Press, 1958)

Ashworth, AJ, *Human Rights, Serious Crimes and Criminal Procedure* (London, Sweet & Maxwell, 2002)

—— 'Social Control and "Anti-Social" Behaviour: The Subversion of Human Rights?' (2004) 120 *Law Quarterly Review* 163

—— *Sentencing and Criminal Justice*, 4th edn (Cambridge, Cambridge University Press, 2005)

Australian Institute of Criminology, *Closed circuit television (CCTV) as a crime prevention measure*, AI Crime Reduction Matters No 18 (Canberra, Australian Institute of Criminology, 2004)

Bagaric, M and Clarke, J, *Torture: when the unthinkable is permissible* (Albany, NY, State University of New York Press, 2007)

Ball, K and Murakami Wood, D (eds), *Report on the Surveillance Society* (London, Surveillance Studies Network, Information Commissioner's Office, 2006)

Ball, K, Murakami Wood, D and Raab, C, *Postscript following the Conference of Privacy Commissioners* (London, Surveillance Studies Network, Information Commissioner's Office, 2007)

Bennett, T (ed), *Preventing Crime and Disorder: Targeting Strategies and Responsibilities* (Cambridge, Institute of Criminology, 1996)

Birks, P (ed), *Privacy and Loyalty* (Oxford, Clarendon Press, 1997)

Bleyleveld, D, *A Bibliography on General Deterrence* (Farnborough, Saxon House, 1980)

Bottoms, AE, 'Crime prevention facing the 1990s' (1990) 1(1) *Policing and Society* 3
—— 'Incivilities, Offence and Social Order in Residential Communities' in A von Hirsch and AP Simester (eds), *Incivilities: Regulating Offensive Behaviour* (Oxford, Hart Publishing, 2006)
Bottoms, AE and Brownsword, R, 'Dangerousness and Rights' in J Hinton (ed), *Dangerousness: Problems of Assessment and Prediction* (London, Allen & Unwin, 1983)
Bottoms, AE, Hay, W and Sparks, R, 'Situational and social approaches to the prevention of disorder in long-term prisons' in T Flanagan (ed), *Long-term Imprisonment: Policy, Science and Correctional Practice* (London, Sage, 1995)
Bottoms, AE and von Hirsch, A, 'Deterrence' *Oxford Handbook of Empirical Studies* (Oxford, Oxford University Press, forthcoming 2010
Bottoms, AE and Wiles, P, 'Understanding Crime Prevention in Late Modern Society' in T Bennett (ed), *Preventing Crime and Disorder* (Cambridge: Institute of Criminology, 1996)
Brantingham, RJ and Faust, F, 'A Conceptual Model of Crime Prevention' (1976) 22(3) *Crime and Delinquency* 130
Brey, P, 'Ethical Aspects of Facial Recognition Systems in Public Places' (2004) 2(2) *Journal of Information, Communications and Ethics in Society* 97
Brown, S, 'What's the problem, girls? CCTV and the gendering of public safety' in C Norris, J Moran and G Armstrong (eds), *Surveillance, Closed Circuit Television and Social Control* (Aldershot, Ashgate Publishing, 1999)
Buellesfeld, D, *Polizeiliche Videoueberwachung oeffentlicher Strassen und Plaetze zur Kriminalitaetsvorsorge* (Stuttgart, Boorberg, 2002)
Burchell, G, Gordon, C and Miller, P (eds), *The Foucault Effect: Studies in Governmentality* (Chicago, Ill, University of Chicago Press, 1991)
Cambridge City Council, *CCTV System Annual Report 1st April 2003 to 31st March 2004*
—— *A Guide for the Management and Operation of the CCTV Control Room* (2005)
—— *CCTV Operators: Training Programme Block Syllabus* (2005)
—— *A Code of Practice for the Cambridge City Council's Public CCTV Scheme* (2006)
—— *Cambridge City Council's CCTV Scheme: An Overview* (2006)
Caryl, C, 'Why they do it?', *New York Review of Books*, 22 September 2005
Castel, R, 'From Dangerousness to Risk' in G Burchell, C Gordon and P Miller (eds), *The Foucault Effect: Studies in Governmentality* (Chicago, Ill, University of Chicago Press, 1991)
Claes, E, Duff, RA and Gutwirth, S (eds), *Privacy and the Criminal Law* (Antwerp, Intersentia, 2006)
Clancey, G, *Considerations for establishing a public space CCTV network*, Australian Institute of Criminology, Resource Manual No 08 (2009)
Clarke, RV, 'Situational crime prevention: its theoretical basis and practical scope' in M Tonry and N Morris (eds), *Crime and Justice: An Annual Review of Research*, vol 4 (Chicago, Ill, Chicago University Press, 1983)

—— 'Situational crime prevention' in M Tonry and D Farrington (eds), *Building a Safer Society: Strategic Approaches to Crime Prevention. Crime and Justice: A Review of Research* (Chicago, Ill, Chicago University Press, 1995)

Clarke, RV and Mayhew, P, *Designing out Crime* (London, HMSO, 1980)

Cohen, S, *Visions of Social Control: Crime, Punishment and Classification* (Cambridge, Polity Press, 1985)

Cohen, L and Felson, M, 'Social Change and Crime Rate Trends: a Routine Activity Approach' (1979) 44 *American Sociological Review* 588

Constant, M and Turnbull, P, *The Principles and Practice of CCTV* (Hertfordshire, Paramount Publishing, 1994)

Cowan, R, 'Fiasco and function blurs CCTV's image', *Security Insider*, Australian Security Industry Association, June/July 2008

Critchley, TA, *A History of Police in England and Wales* (London, Constable, 1978)

Crook, S, 'Ordering Risks' in D Lupton (ed), *Risk and Sociocultural Theory: New Directions and Perspectives* (Cambridge, Cambridge University Press, 1999)

Damrosch, L, *Jean-Jacques Rousseau: Restless Genius* (Boston, Mass, Houghton Mifflin, 2006)

Davis, M, *City of Quartz—Excavating the Future in Los Angeles* (Pimlico, Random House, 1998)

Davies, SG, *Big Brother: Britain's Web of Surveillance and the New Technological Order* (London, Pan Books, 1996)

—— 'CCTV: a new battleground for privacy' in C Norris and G Armstrong (eds), *Surveillance, Closed Circuit Television and Social Control* (Aldershot, Ashgate Publishing, 1998)

Dean, M, 'Risk, calculable and incalculable' in D Lupton (ed), *Risk and Sociocultural Theory: New Directions and Perspectives* (Cambridge, Cambridge University Press, 1999)

de Hert P, 'Balancing security and liberty within the European human rights framework. A critical reading of the Court's case law in the light of surveillance and criminal law enforcement strategies after 9/11' (2005) 1(1) *Utrecht Law Review* 68

—— 'Biometrics: Legal Issues and Implications', Background paper for the Institute of Prospective Technological Studies, DG JRC (Sevilla, European Commission, 2005)

de Hert, P and Gutwirth, S, 'Privacy, data protection and law enforcement. Opacity of the individual and transparency of power' in E Claes, RA Duff and S Gutwirth (eds), *Privacy and the Criminal Law* (Antwerp, Intersentia, 2006)

Ditton, J and Short, E, 'Yes it Works, No it Doesn't: Comparing the Effects of Open-Street CCTV in Two Adjacent Scottish Town Centres' in K Painter and N Tilley (eds), *Surveillance, Lighting, CCTV and Crime Prevention* (Monsey, NY, Criminal Justice Press, 1999)

Dolderer, M, 'Verfassungsfragen der "Sicherheit durch Null-Toleranz"' (2001) *Neue Verwaltungszeitung* 130

Doob, A and Webster, C, 'Sentence Severity and Crime: Accepting the Null Hypothesis' in M Tonry (ed), *Crime and Justice: A Review of Research* (Chicago, Ill, University of Chicago Press, 2003)

Duff, RA, *Punishment, Communication and Community* (Oxford, Oxford University Press, 2001)
Duff, RA and Marshall, SE, 'Benefits, Burdens and Responsibilities: Some Ethical Dimensions of Situational Crime Prevention' in A von Hirsch, D Garland and A Wakefield, *Ethical and Social Perspectives on Situational Crime Prevention* (Oxford, Hart Publishing, 2000)
Dworkin, R, *Taking Rights Seriously* (Cambridge, Mass, Harvard University Press, 1977)
—— *Freedom's Law* (Oxford, Oxford University Press, 1996)
Eck, JE, Chainey, S, Cameron, JG, Leitner, M and Wilson, RE, *Mapping Crime: Understanding Hotspots* (Washington, DC, US National Institute of Justice, 2005)
Eckblom, P, 'Towards a Discipline of Crime Prevention: a systematic approach to its nature, range and concepts' in T Bennett (ed), *Preventing Crime and Disorder: Targeting Strategies and Responsibilities* (Cambridge, Institute of Criminology, 1996)
Equality and Human Rights Commission, *Stop and think: A critical review of the use of stop and search powers in England and Wales* (www.equalityhumanrights.com, 2010)
Ewald, F, 'Insurance and Risk' in G Burchell, C Gordon and P Miller (eds), *The Foucault Effect: Studies in Governmentality* (Chicago Ill, University of Chicago Press, 1991)
Farrington, DP, 'Human Development and Criminal Careers' in M Maguire, R Morgan and R Reiner (eds), *The Oxford Handbook of Criminology*, 2nd edn (Oxford, Oxford University Press, 1997)
Farrington, DP, Langan, PA and Wikstroem, PO, 'Changes in Crime and Punishment in America, England and Sweden between the 1980 and the 1990s' (1994) 3 *Studies in crime and crime prevention* 104
Farrington, DP, Bennett, TH and Welsh, BC, 'The Cambridge Evaluation of the Effects of CCTV on Crime' in G Farrell (ed), *Imaginations: Essays in Honour of Ken Pease* (Monsey, NY, Criminal Justice Press, 2007)
Feinberg, J, 'The Nature and Value of Rights' in J Feinberg. *Rights, justice and the bounds of liberty* (Princeton, Princeton University Press, 1980)
—— *Harm to Others* (Oxford, Oxford University Press, 1984)
—— *Offence to Others* (Oxford, Oxford University Press, 1985)
Feldman, D, 'Secrecy, dignity, or autonomy? Views of privacy as a civil liberty' in D Feldman (ed), *Current Legal Problems* (Oxford, Oxford University Press, 1994)
—— 'Privacy-related Rights and their Social Value' in P Birks (ed), *Privacy and Loyalty* (Oxford, Clarendon Press, 1997)
—— *Civil Liberties and Human Rights in England and Wales* (Oxford, Oxford University Press, 2002)
Felson, M, *Crime and Everyday Life—Insights and Implications for Society* (Thousand Oaks, CA, Pine Forge Press, 1994)
Felson, M and Clarke, RV, 'The ethics of situational crime prevention' in G Newman, RV Clarke and SG Shoham (eds), *Rational Choice and Situational Crime Prevention: Theoretical Foundations* (Aldershot, Ashgate 1997)
Field, F, *Neighbours from Hell: The Politics of Behaviour* (London, Politico's, 2003)

Foucault, M, *Discipline and Punish* (London, Penguin Books, 1977)
Fried, C , 'Privacy (A moral analysis)' in FD Schoeman (ed), *Philosophical Dimensions of Privacy: An Anthology* (Cambridge, Cambridge University Press, 1984)
Gambetta, D, 'Can we Make Sense of Suicide Missions?' in D Gambetta (ed), *Making Sense of Suicide Missions* (Oxford, Oxford University Press, 2005)
Gardner, D, *Risk—the Science and Politics of Fear* (London, Virgin Books, 2008)
Garland, D, 'The culture of high-crime societies: some preconditions of recent "law and order" policies' (2000) 40(3) *British Journal of Criminology* 347
Gavison, R, 'Privacy and the limits of law' in FD Schoeman (ed), *Philosophical Dimensions of Privacy: An Anthology* (Cambridge, Cambridge University Press, 1984)
Giddens, A, *The Consequences of Modernity* (Cambridge, Polity Press, 1990)
Gill, M, 'CCTV: Is it effective?' in M Gill (ed), *The Handbook of Security* (London, Palgrave Macmillan, 2006)
Gill, M and Loveday, K, 'What Do Offenders Think About CCTV?' in M Gill (ed), *The Handbook of Security* (London, Palgrave Macmillan, 2006)
Gill, M and Spriggs, A, *Assessing the Impact of CCTV* (London, Home Office, 2005)
Gill, M, Spriggs, A, Little, R and Collins, K, 'What Do Murderers Think About the Effectiveness of CCTV?' (2006) 2(1) *Journal of Security Education* 11
Gill, M and Turbin, V, 'Evaluating "Realistic Evaluation": Evidence from a Study of CCTV' in K Painter and N Tilley (eds), *Surveillance: Lighting, CCTV and Crime Prevention* (Monsey, NY, Criminal Justice Press, 1999)
Goetz, V, 'Oeffentliche Videoueberwachung im Kontext der praeventiven Polizeiarbeit' in J-M Jehle and M Gras (eds), *Oeffentliche Videoueberwachung im Europaeischen Vergleich (Little Brothers are Watching you—A European Comparison)* (Goettingen, Universitaet Goettingen, 2003)
Goffman, E, *Asylums* (Harmondsworth, Penguin Books, 1961)
—— *Behaviour in Public Places* (New York, Free Press, 1963)
—— *Relations in Public, Microstudies of the Public Order* (London, The Penguin Press, 1971)
—— *The Presentation of Self in Everyday Life* (London, The Penguin Press, 1990)
Goldstein, H, *Problem-Oriented Policing* (New York, McGraw Hill, 1990)
Goold, B, 'Privacy Rights and Public Spaces: CCTV and the Problem of the "Unobservable Observer"', *Criminal Justice Ethics*, Winter/Spring 2002, 21
Graham-Rowe, D, 'Warning ... Strange Behaviour', (1999) *New Scientist* No 2216, 25
Graham, S, 'Towards the fifth utility? On the extension and normalisation of public CCTV' in C Norris, J Moran and G Armstrong (eds), *Surveillance, Closed Circuit TV and Social Control* (Aldershot, Ashgate Publishing, 1998)
Gras, M, *Kriminalpraevention durch Videoueberwachung* (Baden Baden, Nomos Verlagsgesellschaft, 2002)
Grounds A, 'Effects of Wrongful Convictions' in *Criminology in Cambridge* (Newsletter of the Institute of Criminology, November 2005) 3
Haggerty, KD and Ericson, RV, 'The surveillance assemblage' (2000) 51(4) *British Journal of Sociology* 605
Hart, HLA, *The Concept of Law* (Oxford, Oxford University Press, 1961)

192 Bibliography

Hefendehl, R, 'Observationen im Spannungsfeld von Praevention und Repression. Oder was von CCTV und laengerfristingen Observationen zu halten ist' (2000) 5 *Der Strafverteidiger* 270

Home Office, *Reassuring the Public: a Review of International Policing Interventions Findings 241*, November 2004

—— *Modernising Police Powers: Review of the Police and Criminal Evidence Act (PACE)*, Consultation Paper, March 2007

—— *Operation of police powers under the Terrorism Act 2000 and subsequent legislation: Arrests, outcomes and stop and searches. Great Britain 2008/09*, Statistical Bulletin No 18, 26 November 2009

House of Lords Constitution Committee, *Surveillance: Citizens and the State* (Second Report, Session 2008–09)

Hudson, B, *Justice in the Risk Society* (London, Sage, 2003)

Information Commissioner's Office, *CCTV Code of Practice* (London, ICO, 2008)

Innes, JC, *Privacy, Intimacy and Isolation* (Oxford, Oxford University Press, 1992)

Innes, M, 'Signal Crimes and Signal Disorders: Notes on Deviance as Communicative Action' (2004) 55 *British Journal of Sociology* 335

Jain, AK and Pankanti, S, 'Beyond Fingerprinting' (2008) 299(3) *Scientific America, Special Issue: Will Technology Kill Privacy* 54

Jehle, JM and Gras, M(eds) *Oeffentliche Videoueberwachung, oder Little Brothers are Watching you: A European Comparison* (Goettingen, Universitaet Goettingen, 2003) http://www.jura.uni-goettingen.de/privat/j-m.jehle/videoueberwachung

Jones, T and Newburn, T, *Private Security and Public Policing* (Oxford, Clarendon Press, 1998)

Jones, RP, *Modern Penality and Social Theory* (Cambridge, Institute of Criminology, 1997)

Kleinig, J, 'The Burdens of Situational Crime Prevention: an Ethical Commentary' in A von Hirsch, D Garland and A Wakefield (eds), *Ethical and Social Perspectives on Situational Crime Prevention* (Oxford, Hart Publishing, 2000)

Kopel, D and Krause, M, 'Face the Facts—Facial recognition technology's troubled past—and troubling future' (2006) *Reason Magazine* 2002 http://www.reason.com/archives/2002/10/01/face-the-facts

Langan, PA and Farrington, DP, *Crime and Justice in the United States and in England and Wales 1981–96* (Washington, DC, Bureau of Justice, 1999)

Laycock, G, 'Rights, Roles and Responsibility in the Prevention of Crimes' in T Bennett (ed), *Preventing Crime and Disorder: Targeting Strategies and Responsibilities* (Cambridge, Institute of Criminology, 1996)

Liberty and the University of Northumbria at Newcastle, *Digital Image as Evidence*, Evidence to the House of Lords Select Committee on Science and Technology: Sub-Committee II (2000)

Lupton, D (ed), *Risk and Sociocultural Theory: New Directions and Perspectives* (Cambridge, Cambridge University Press, 1999)

Lustgarten, L and Leith, I, *In from the Cold—National Security and Parliamentary Democracy* (Oxford, Clarendon Press, 1994)

Lyon, D, *The Electronic Eye: The Rise of Surveillance Society* (Minneapolis, MN, University of Minnesota Press, 1994)

Lyon, D (ed), *From Surveillance as Social Sorting. Privacy, Risk and Digital Discrimination* (London, Routledge, 2003)

Maguire, M, 'Restraining Big Brother? The regulation of surveillance in England and Wales' in C Norris, J Moran and G Armstrong (eds), *Surveillance, Closed Circuit Television and Social Control* (Aldershot, Ashgate Publishing, 1998)

McCahill, M and Norris, C, 'Literature Review' in *On the Threshold to Urban Panopticon? Analysing the Employment of CCTV in European Cities and Assessing its Social and Political Impacts* (University of Hull, urbaneye Working Paper No 2, 2002)

——, *CCTV in Britain* (University of Hull, urbaneye Working Paper No 3, 2002)

——, *CCTV Systems in London. Their Structures and Practices* (University of Hull, urbaneye Working Paper No 10, 2003)

MacIntyre, A, *Whose Justice? Which Rationality?* (London, Duckworth, 1988)

Mackenzie, S, Bannister, J, Flint, J, Parr, S, Mille, A and Fleetwood, J, *The Drivers of Perception of Anti-Social Behaviour*, Home Office Research Report 34 (2010)

Mendus, S (ed), *Justifying Toleration: Conceptual and Historical Perspectives* (Cambridge, Cambridge University Press, 1988)

Murphy, J, 'Cruel and Unusual Punishments' in J Murphy (ed), *Retribution, Justice, Therapy* (Dordrecht, D Riedel, 1980)

Nagel, T, 'Concealment and Exposure' (1998)27 *Philosophy and Public Affairs* 3

Nagin, DS, 'Criminal Deterrence Research at the Outset of the Twenty-First Century' (1998) 23 *Crime and Justice: A Review of Research* 51

Neumann, U, 'Das Verhaeltnismaessigkeitsprinzip als strafbegrenzendes Prinzip' in A von Hirsch, K Seelmann and W Wohlers (eds), *Mediating Principles— Begrenzungsprinzipien bei der Strafbegruendung* (Baden Baden, Nomos, 2006)

Norris, C, 'From Personal to Digital. CCTV, the panoptikon, and the technological mediation of suspicion and social control' in D Lyon (ed), From Surveillance as Social Sorting (2003)

Norris, C and Armstrong, G, *The Maximum Surveillance Society: The Rise of CCTV* (Oxford, Berg, 1999)

Norris, C, Moran, J and Armstrong, G (eds), *Surveillance, Closed Circuit Television and Social Control* (Aldershot, Ashgate Publishing, 1998)

O'Flynn, C, *What was lost* (Birmingham, Tindall Street Press, 2007)

O'Malley, P, 'Risk and responsibility' in A Barry, T Osborne and N Rose (eds), *Foucault and Political Reason: Liberalism, Neo-Liberalism and Rationalities of Government* (London, University College of London Press, 1996)

Painter, K and Tilley, N (eds), *Surveillance: Lighting, CCTV and Crime Prevention* (Monsey, NY, Criminal Justice Press, 1999)

Paul, EF, Miller, FD Jr and Paul, J (eds), *The Right to Privacy* (Cambridge, Press Syndicate of the University of Cambridge, 2000)

Phillips, C, 'A Review of CCTV Evaluations: Crime Reduction Effects and Attitudes Towards its Use' in K Painter and N Tilley (eds), *Surveillance: Lighting, CCTV and Crime Prevention* (Monsey, NY, Criminal Justice Press, 1999)

Post, R, 'The Social Foundations of Privacy: Community and Self in the Common Law Tort' (1989) 77(5) *California Law Review* 957

Pratt, TC, Cullen, FT, Blevins, KR, Daigle, LE and Madensen, TD, 'The Empirical Status of Deterrence Theory: a Meta-Analysis' in F Cullen, SP Wright and KR Blevins (eds), *Taking Stock—The Status of Criminological Theory* (New Brunswick, NJ, Transaction Publishers, 2006)

Raban, J, *Surveillance* (London, Picador, 2006)

Rayan, A, 'Private selves and public parts' in SI Benn and GF Gaus (eds), *Public and Private in Social Life* (New York, St Martin's Press, 1983)
Rawls, J, *A Theory of Justice* (Oxford, Oxford University Press, 1972)
—— 'The idea of overlapping consensus' (1987) 7 *Oxford Journal of Legal Studies* 1
Raz, J, *The Morality of Freedom* (Oxford, Oxford University Press, 1986)
Roberts, P, 'Privacy, Autonomy and Criminal Justice Rights' in P Alldridge and C Brants (eds), *Personal Autonomy, the Private Sphere and the Criminal Law—A Comparative Study* (Oxford, Hart Publishing, 2001)
Robertson, AH (ed), *Privacy and Human Rights*, Reports and Communications presented at the Third International Colloquy about the Convention on Human Rights, Brussels 1970 (Manchester, Manchester University Press, 1973)
Rosen, N, *How to Live Off-Grid, Journeys Outside the System* (London, Doubleday, 2007)
Rosenberg, A, 'Privacy as Matter of Taste and Right' in EF Paul, FD Miller Jr and J Paul (eds), *The Right to Privacy* (Cambridge, Press Syndicate of the University of Cambridge, 2000)
Sampson, RJ and Raudenbush, SW, *Disorder in Urban Neighbourhoods: Does it Lead to Crime?* (Washington, DC, National Institute of Justice, 2001)
Sandel, M, *Liberalism and the Limits of Justice*, 2nd edn (Cambridge, Cambridge University Press, 1998)
Scarman Centre National CCTV Evaluation Team – *National evaluation of CCTV: early findings on scheme implementation – effective practice guide* (Home Office Development and Practice Report 7)
Schauer, F, *Free Speech: A Philosophical Enquiry* (Cambridge, Cambridge University Press, 1982)
—— 'Can Public Figures Have Private Lives?' in EF Paul, FD Miller Jr and J Paul (eds), *The Right to Privacy* (Cambridge, Press Syndicate of the University of Cambridge, 2000)
Schoeman FD (ed), *Philosophical Dimensions of Privacy: An Anthology* (Cambridge, Cambridge University Press, 1984)
—— *Privacy and Social Freedom* (Cambridge, Cambridge University Press, 1992)
Sennett, R, *The Fall of Public Man: On the Social Psychology of Capitalism* (New York, Vintage Books, 1978)
Shapland, J and Vagg, J, *Policing by the Public* (London, Routledge, 1988)
Short, E and Ditton, J, 'Seen and now Heard; Talking to the Targets of Open Street CCTV' (1998) 38(3) *British Journal of Criminology* 404
Simester, AP and Sullivan, GR, *Criminal Law: Theory and Doctrine* (Oxford, Hart Publishing, 2001)
Simester, AP and von Hirsch, A, 'Regulating Offensive Conduct Through Two-Step Prohibitions' in A von Hirsch and AP Simister (eds), *Incivilities: Regulating Offensive Behaviour* (Oxford, Hart Publishing, 2006)
Snook, H, *Crossing the Threshold: 266 Ways the State Can Enter your Home* (London, Centre for Policy Studies, 2007)
Sontag, Susan –*Aids and its Metaphors* (Harmondsworth, Penguin 1989)
Stenson, K, 'The New Politics of Crime Control' in K Stenson and RR Sullivan (eds), *Crime, Risk and Justice. The Politics of Crime Control in Liberal Democracies* (Devon, Willan, 2001)

Stolle, P and Hefendehl, R, 'Gefaehrliche Orte oder gefaehrliche Kameras? Die Videoueberwachung im oeffentlichen Raum' (2002) 4 *Kriminologisches Journal* 257

Taylor, C, *Sources of the Self: The Making of the Modern Identity* (Cambridge, Cambridge University Press, 1989)

Thomson, JJ, 'The right to privacy' in FD Schoeman (ed), *Philosophical Dimensions of Privacy: An Anthology* (Cambridge, Cambridge University Press, 1984)

Tilley, N, 'Evaluating the effectiveness of CCTV schemes' in C Norris, J Moran and G Armstrong (eds), *Surveillance, Closed Circuit Television and Social Control* (Aldershot, Ashgate Publishing, 1998)

Toepfer, E, Hempel, L and Cameron, H, *Watching the Bear. Networks and islands of visual surveillance in Berlin* (Berlin, Berlin Institute of Social Research, urbaneye Working Paper No 8, 2003)

Tuffin, R, Morris, J and Poole, A, *An Evaluation of the Impact of the National Reassurance Policing Programme* (London, Home Office, 2006)

van Dijk, J, 'Police, Private Security and Employee Surveillance: trends and prospects, with special emphasis on the case of the Netherlands' in C Fijnaut *et al* (eds), *Changes in Society, Crime and Criminal Justice in Europe*, vol 1 (Antwerp, Kluwer, 1995)

von Hirsch, A, *Censure and Sanctions* (Oxford, Clarendon Press,1993)

—— 'The Ethics of Public Television Surveillance' in A von Hirsch, D Garland and A Wakefield (eds), *Ethical and Social Perspectives on Situational Crime Prevention* (Oxford, Hart Publishing, 2000)

von Hirsch, A and Ashworth, A, *Proportionate Sentencing—Exploring the Principles* (Oxford, Oxford University Press, 2005)

von Hirsch, A and Bottoms AE, 'Deterrence' in *Oxford Handbook of Empirical Studies* (Oxford, Oxford University Press, 2010)

von Hirsch, A, Bottoms, AE, Burney, E and Wikstroem, PO (eds), *Criminal Deterrence and Sentence Severity* (Oxford, Hart Publishing, 1999)

von Hirsch, A, Garland, D and Wakefield, A (eds), *Ethical and Social Perspectives on Situational Crime Prevention* (Oxford, Hart Publishing, 2000)

von Hirsch, A, Roberts, J and Bottoms, AE (eds), *Restorative Justice and Criminal Justice: Competing or Reconcilable Paradigms?* (Oxford, Hart Publishing, 2003)

von Hirsch, A, Seelmann, K and Wohlers, W (eds), *Mediating Principles: Begrenzungsprinzipien bei der Strafbegruendung* (Baden Baden, Nomos, 2006)

von Hirsch, A and Shearing, C, 'Exclusion in Public Space' in A von Hirsch, D Garland and A Wakefield (eds), *Ethical and Social Perspectives on Situational Crime Prevention* (Oxford, Hart Publishing, 2000)

von Hirsch, A and Simester, AP, 'Penalising Offensive Behaviour: Constitutive and Mediating Principles' in A von Hirsch and AP Simester (eds), *Incivilities: Regulating Offensive Behaviour* (Oxford, Hart Publishing, 2006)

—— (eds), *Incivilities: Regulating Offensive Behaviour* (Oxford, Hart Publishing, 2006)

Wade, G, 'Funding CCTV: the Story so far' (2001) 7(2) *CCTV Today* 28

Wakefield, A, 'Situational Crime Prevention in Mass Private Property' in A von Hirsch, D Garland and A Wakefield (eds), *Ethical and Social Perspectives on Situational Crime Prevention* (Oxford, Hart Publishing, 2000)

Weber, D, 'Instinkiv falsch. Staendig versuchen wir, Risiken zu vermeiden.Leider sind wir schlecht darin, sie richtig einzuschaetzen', *Neue Zuerch'er Zeitung*, Folio 09/2007

Weintraub, J, 'Varieties and Vicissitudes of Public Space' in P Kasinitz (ed), *Metropolis: Centre and Symbol of our Times* (Basingstoke, Macmillan, 1995)

Weir, S and Boyle, S, 'Human Rights in the UK' (1997) 68 *Political Quarterly* 128

Welsh, BC and Farrington, DP, *Crime Prevention Effects of Closed Circuit Television: A Systematic Review* (London, Home Office, 2002)

——, 'Surveillance for crime prevention in public space: Results and policy choices in Britain and America' (2004) 3 *Criminology and Public Policy* 497

——, *Effects of Closed Circuit Television Surveillance on Crime* (Campbell Systematic Reviews 2008:17)

——, 'Public Area CCTV and Crime Prevention: An Updated Systematic Review and Meta-Analysis' (2009) 26:4 *Justice Quarterly* 716

——, *Making Public Places Safer: Surveillance and Crime Prevention* (Oxford, Oxford University Press, 2009)

Westin, AF, *Privacy and Freedom* (New York, Atheneum Publishers, 1967)

Whitman, JQ, 'The Two Western Cultures of Privacy: Dignity Versus Liberty' (2004) 113 *Yale Law Journal* 1151

Wikstroem, PO, 'Causes of Crime and Crime Prevention' in T Bennett (ed), *Preventing Crime and Disorder: Targeting Strategies and Responsibilities* (Cambridge, Institute of Criminology, 1996)

Wirtz, B, 'Biometrische Verfahren. Ueberblick, Evaluierung und aktuelle Themen (1999) 23 *Datenschutz und Datensicherheit* 12

Zeckhauser, R and Viscusi, W, 'The risk management dilemma' (1996) 545(1) *Annals of the American Academy of Political and Social Science* 1144

Zedner, L, 'Too much security?' (2003) 31 *International Journal of the Sociology of Law* 155

Index

aberrant behaviour 3
abuse of position 75
access control 15, 18, 55, 66
   boundaries 20–1, 30, 30–6
   discretion, conventions of 27–8
   disempowering effect of observer's inaccessibility 69–71
   privacy 5–11
   reviewing, recording without 82, 84
account, taking altered risks into 138, 139–41
accountability 12, 24, 37, 84, 160, 171, 175
active or live monitoring systems 54, 59, 97–8, 132–5, 144–5, 164–5, 176
actuarial practices 73
administrative guidelines 174–5
agency responsible for CCTV 53, 84, 150, 160–3, 168, 172–5, 178–9
airport security checks 45, 47, 88, 115, 148
alcohol 128, 140, 157–8
algorithmic monitoring (smart cameras) 42, 43–4, 46–9, 50–1, 144
anonymity interest
   'Big Brother' effect 150
   boundary control 29–30, 113
   CCTV surveillance, justification of 38–40
   civil inattention, conventions of 25, 29, 112–15
   communitarianism 36–7, 38–9
   consequentialist approach 116
   crime prevention 93, 103–22, 149–50, 152–3
   cursory attention, claim to receive only 24
   dangerous events, suspension due to 36
   data protection 77, 181–2
   discretion, conventions of 21, 41
   disembedding, effect of 79–81
   evidence collection 152–3
   exposure to an uninvited audience 81–2
   facial recognition systems 78 *see also* facial recognition systems
   factual enjoyment 112–13
   fear of crime 124, 126
   fishing expeditions 97

   fixing of one's picture, implications of 77–9
   friction, reducing 28–9
   guardianship in public place, lack of 122–3
   home, privacy of the 115–17, 150
   hostile intent 37, 38
   Human Rights Act 1998 177
   identification of recorded individuals 78, 166–9
   individual accountability 24
   Information Commissioner's Code of Practice 181–2
   institutional guarantees 30
   intimacy 113–17
   intrusiveness of CCTV 62, 77–84
   late modern society, scope in 36–9
   legitimate expectations 30
   local authorities 41, 53
   loss of protection 115
   material expectations in public space 35
   minor crimes and incivilities 151–2
   moral concerns about restrictions 38–40
   names and identity 63
   non-acknowledgment, practice of 30
   police 53, 150
   policy principles 147–52
   presentation of self 23–4, 63–5, 78
   privacy 80–1, 93, 98–103, 159, 177, 183
   private life, justification for interference with 93, 98–103, 177, 183
   ranking of anonymity in public space 111–17
   rationale 62
   real space appraisal and CCTV surveillance, effects of 59–60
   recording 77–84, 165–6
   regulation of CCTV 159, 174–5
   responsibility for safety of public place 36
   reviewing of recordings 82–4, 165–6
   risk assessment 122
   sanitisation of CCTV surveillance 76–7
   scope in late modern society 36–8
   searches 95, 150

self-consciousness 80
small communities, migration from 24
social tolerance for intrusion 112
state, *vis-à-vis* 29–30, 115
stop and search 116–17
strangers, standing up to 123
street crime 37
sui generis implications 62
suspension 36
'three circle' theory 2–6, 17, 32–4, 95–8
training 173
value 111
victims 148
violation of anonymity interests 41–92
virtual scrutiny compared to physical scrutiny 66
witnesses 147–8
'another pair of eyes' euphemism 40–1, 59, 89, 185
anti-social behaviour 38, 90–1, 128, 129, 140, 151
anxiety, prevention measures increasing 125–6
appearance, judging by 37–8
apprehension and conviction, increase in likelihood of 87–8, 93, 127–8, 132–46, 152
Archard, David 63, 66, 79
Arendt, Hannah 12
Armstrong, G 87
Ashworth, Andrew 100, 118
assembly, freedom of 177
audio capability, cameras with 44, 129, 163
audit trails 169–70, 171
authoritarian societies 10, 13, 29
automatic number plate recognition (ANPR) 51, 157
automatic recognition of suspicious behaviour 42, 43–4, 46–7, 50–1
autonomy 7–10, 15, 17, 69, 85, 108–10, 113, 159, 185

benefits and burdens 97, 102, 106, 108, 140
Bentham's Panopticon 63, 83, 88
'Big Brother' effect 150
biometrics 42, 47, 48–9, 52, 168
Bond, David 70
Bottoms, AE 73, 118, 136–7, 142–3
boundaries of access control in public spaces 19–20, 29–36, 109
bounded rationality 139–40, 146
'broken windows' approach 129–30, 151
Brownsword, R 118
budgeting and funding 132, 160–1
Burney, E 136

Cambridge City Council 2, 119–20, 126, 161–2, 172, 183
cars, monitoring people in their 51, 157–8
cash points 97, 148
Castel, Robert 72
CCTV technology 42–53
Central London Congestion Charge Scheme 45, 47, 162
choices, offenders must be willing to alter 138, 142–4
civil inattention, conventions of 21, 25–9, 35–6, 67
civility and tact 25, 37
clothing 19–20
codes of practice
  ethics 84
  Information Commissioner 45, 56, 59–60, 170, 178–83
  regulation 175
Cohen, S 129, 145
commercial strategy, fear of crime as a 126
Common Assessment Framework (CAF) 52
communal interests 103–4, 119
communitarianism 36–7, 38–9
competing interests 93, 94–117
complaints and enquiries 162, 172, 173–4
Comprehensive Performance Assessment (CPA) 171
confidentiality 75, 172–3
conform, pressure to 28, 29, 63, 83–92, 143, 145
congestion charge 45, 47, 90, 162
consequentialism 105–6, 154
contact numbers, provision of 163
conventions
  anonymity 21
  civil inattention 21, 25–9, 35–6, 67
  discretion 21–30, 41, 70
  non-acknowledgment 21, 30
  regulatory functions 28–9
conversational preserves 19, 27
conviction, likelihood of 87–8, 93, 127–8, 132–46, 152
co-present 20, 24, 60, 65–6, 79, 81–2, 113, 115, 165
cost benefits 102, 140
cost of equipment 43, 53, 132, 160–1, 164
coverage and positioning of cameras 131, 144, 161
covert surveillance 56–7, 69, 97, 154–5, 177
crime prevention 56–9 *see also* deterrence
  anonymity interests 93, 103–23, 149–50
  anti-social behaviour 38, 90–1, 128, 129, 140, 151
  anxiety, prevention measures as increasing 125–6

autonomy 159
benefit thieves 91
civil liberties 118
clear objectives and suitable targets 144
communal interests 119
competing interests 93, 94–103
congestion charge 90
conform, pressure to 89–92
coverage and positioning of cameras 131, 144, 161
covert surveillance 57, 154–5
Crime and Disorder Reduction Partnership schemes 176
danger, requirement of 121
data protection 56
decision-making processes of potential criminals 137–44, 145–6
designing out crime 71
direct intervention 94
displacement of crime 118
distribution of cameras 144
effectiveness of CCTV 130–46, 159, 185–6
evidence collection 152–4
face recognition and data processing technologies 144
fair treatment, offenders' claim to 118
fear of crime 94, 120, 124–6, 186
guardianship, lack of 94, 122–3, 134, 145
home, protection of 111
illegal and unpleasant behaviour, distinction between 91
importance of crime prevention mission 117–30
instrumental obedience to law 154
interests served by public CCTV 117–19
legitimising role 93–146
list of objectives 119
  management and operation of control room 144
  moral reasons for desisting from crime 153–4
objectives of CCTV 119–20
persuasive force of crime prevention arguments 120–30
police, discretion of the 90
privacy
  conflicts with crime prevention, model for resolving 95–8
  legitimising role of 93, 94–103

private and family life, justification for interference with 93, 98–103
pro-active policing 120–1, 127–8
public interests 117–19, 186
punishment, increase in likelihood of 93
quality of equipment 144
rates of crime 137–8, 142
regulation of CCTV 159, 173–4
restricting options 71–2, 89–92, 133
  risk 90–1, 121–2
sanctions 91
seriousness of crime 127–30
shame 89
situational crime prevention (SCP) 71, 133–4
  stifling expression 89
suspicion, grounds for 122, 127–8
threats, conditional upon documented and significant 160
torture 104
traffic offences 90
types of crime 90–1
urgent action 121–8, 173–4
victims, rights of 117–19
Crook, Stephen 125
crowd as part of a crowd, treating members of a 22
curfews and exclusion orders, enforcing 47
cursory attention, claim to receive only 24

danger, requirement of 121
dangerous events, suspension of anonymity due to 36
data manipulation 46, 135–6, 169
data processing 42, 46, 135, 144, 176
data protection
  active monitoring 176
  anonymity 77, 181–2
  CCTV technology 45
  compensation 179
  crime prevention 56, 181
  Data Protection Act 1998 176, 178–81
  data protection principles 54, 56, 77, 178–80
  databases, data sharing with public sector 51–3
  ethics 181
  Information Commissioner's Code of Practice 178, 179–83
  night vision cameras 45
  processing, definition of 176
  public sector database projects, examples of 52
  purpose specification 56, 166, 178

reasonable suspicion requirement 180
recording 59–60
registration of CCTV schemes 178
regulation of CCTV 176, 178–83
reviewing of recordings 166
sensitive personal data 52
transparency 77
databases, data sharing with public sector 51–3
de Hert, Paul 77, 168
deceit, placebo surveillance and 155
decisional privacy 11, 14–15, 17–18
decision-making processes of potential criminals 137–44, 145–6
definition of public or open-street CCTV 41
degree of control 86–9
demonstrations, identification of persons on 167
despatching the police 69, 84–7, 131, 134, 145, 164
detection, likelihood of 87–8, 93, 127–8, 132–46, 152
deterrence
  account, taking altered risks into 138, 139–41
  alter choices, offender must be willing to 138, 142–4
  anti-social behaviour, alcohol and 140
  apprehended, belief in being 87–8, 133, 136–44
  bounded rationality 139–40, 146
  cars, monitoring people in their 157
  certainty effect 94, 136–8, 150
  change in probability of apprehension 138, 139
  crime prevention, legitimising role of 94, 120
  conform, pressure to 87
  conventionality, low stakes in 143, 145
  covert surveillance 154
  cost benefit analysis 140
  crime rates 137–8, 142
  decision-making processes of potential criminals 137–44, 145–6
  detection and conviction more likely, making 87–8, 93, 127–8, 132–46, 152
  displacement of crime 145
  drug dealers and users 128, 140, 143
  general deterrence 136, 142–3
  identified and apprehended, belief in non-negligible likelihood of being 138, 141–2, 145–6

impulsive or persistent offenders 140, 142
marginal general deterrence 136
  placebo cameras 87, 155
policy inferences 138
precautions taken by offenders 141–2
preconditions 138–44
premeditation 140
property crimes 128, 140, 145
public awareness 139
rationality 139–43, 146
sanctions, types of 143
spies and reprisals, fear of 88
street crime 133, 136–45
suicide missions 144
targets, suitability of 146
terrorism 128–9, 140, 141, 144
vandalism 128. 143
violent crimes 128, 140
warning signs 139
digital CCTV systems 46–53
dignity
  anonymity 83
  authoritarian societies 10
  autonomy 7, 9
  conform, pressure to 83
  discretion, conventions of 26
  ethical principles, privacy and 7, 8–10, 185
  exposure, indignities of 7, 70–1
  institutions, persons in 113
  intimacy 110
  intrusiveness of CCTV 62
  liberal democracies 10
  privacy 7, 8–10, 108, 185
  social policy 9–10
  waiver 9
direct marketing, RFID tags and 49
directed covert surveillance 56–7, 154–5
discipline 86–7, 89, 174
disclosure 2–5, 32–4
discretion 21–30, 41, 70, 90, 120, 172
discrimination 177, 182–3
disembedding, effect of 79–81
disempowerment 69–71
displacement of crime 118, 145
distanciation 60, 66–9
distribution of cameras 144
Doob, A 136–7
drivers
  automatic number plate recognition (ANPR) 51, 157
  cars, monitoring people in their 157–8
  congestion charge 45, 47, 90

drink driving 157–8
traffic offences 90
vehicle theft, reduction in 131
drug dealers and users 128, 140, 143
Duff, RA 97, 148, 153
dummy surveillance 43, 87, 155
Dworkin, Ronald 93, 94–5, 105–6, 111

E-borders 52
effectiveness of CCTV in crime prevention 130–46, 185–6 *see also* **deterrence**
   active intervention in crimes in progress 132, 134, 144–5
   apprehension and conviction, increase in likelihood of 132–3, 134–6, 152
   clear objectives and suitable targets 144
   coverage and positioning 131, 144
   dispatch facilities, inadequacy of 131, 145
   distribution of cameras 144
   face recognition and data processing technologies 144
   lighting, improvements in 132
   location 132
   management and operation of control room 144
   multi-agency responses 132
   police, intervention by 131, 132, 134, 145
   professional personnel 133
   quality of equipment 144
   targeted crime, wrong type of 132
   terrorism 156
   warning message, CCTV as a 134
egocentric preserves 19–21, 68
encryption 50
entertainment, action programs in places of 151–2
entertainment purposes, use for 56
Ericson, RV 78
ethics
   access control 5–9
   agent, moral authority of individual as an 8
   autonomy 7–9, 15, 38–40, 185
   civil inattention 25–9
   codes 84
   data protection 181
   demeaning, unwanted exposure as 7
   desisting from crime, moral reasons for 153–4
   dignity 7, 8–10, 185
   disempowering effect of observer's inaccessibility 70

evidence collection 153–4
exclusion of others 16
fear of negative judgment 7, 8
Information Commissioner's Code of Practice 181
liberty values 7–8
placebo cameras 166
privacy 5–10, 185
searches 95
self ownership or sovereignty 5–6
European Convention on Human Rights 100, 170–1, 177, 183 *see also* **private life, justification for interference with evidence**
   apprehension and conviction, increase in likelihood of 135–6
   audit trails 169–70
   'four eyes' principle 170
   legal representatives, examination by 170–1
   manipulation of images 135–6, 169
   masters, identification of 169
   policy principles 152–4
   quality of images 169–70
   service routines 169
   value of recordings, safeguarding the 169–70
   witnesses 147–8, 167, 172
exclusion orders, enforcing 47
exclusive preserves in spaces accessible to others 18–19, 26–7
execution of surveillance 162–83
   anonymity 42–59
   duration of storage period 170–1
   evidential value of recordings, safeguarding the 169–70
   fair practice safeguards 171–3
   identification of recorded individuals 166–9
   informing the public 162–4
   night vision cameras 163–4
   passive versus active monitoring schemes 164–5
   quality 76
   reviewing of recordings 165–6
exposure 7, 17, 70–1, 81–2
expression, freedom of 95, 105–9, 177
'Face It' software 48

facecams or smart CCTV 47
faceprints 48
facial recognition systems 47–9, 78, 135, 144, 167–8
fair practice safeguards 58, 83, 118, 171–3

fair trials 100, 105, 170–1, 177, 183
fear of crime 94, 120, 124–6, 186
Feinberg, J 5
Feldman, David 3
Felson, Marcus 122
fishing expeditions 56, 97, 135, 165
fixing of one's picture, implications of 77–9
'four eyes' principle 170
Freedom (Great Repeal) Bill 177, 183
freedom of assembly 177
Freedom of Information Act 2000 177
freedom of speech 95, 105–9, 177
freedom of the press 8
friction, reducing 28–9
function creep 168–9
funding and budgeting 132, 160–1
future offender level, attacking crime on 133

Gardner, Dan 125, 155–6
geographic profiling 127
German/Germany
  constitutional law 82
  danger, requirement for 121
  evidence, preserving 54
  hotspots of crime 58
  live surveillance 82–3
  locations, choice of 58
  public interest 39
  suspicion, reasons for 90
Giddens, A 34–5, 76, 79–80, 83, 124
Gill, Martin 141, 144
Goffman, Ervin 3, 19–24, 27, 31
Goold, Benjamin 76, 171
government employees and people seeking public office 32–3
guardianship, lack of 94, 122–3, 134, 145
Gutwirt, S 77

Haggerty, KD 78
handheld phones, use of 157–8
heat-sensitive cameras 42, 44–5, 64
help others, losing initiative to 123, 164
hierarchy of rights 95–8, 100, 107–17
highest-ranking rights, examples of 104–5
home, protection of the
  access control 15
  backstage area, as 110
  boundaries 14–15
  cars as being like homes 157
  crime prevention 95–6, 111
  hierarchy of rights 109, 110–11
  intimacy 110–11, 114, 147
  police 95–6, 111
  privacy 109, 110–11
  private versus public dichotomy 14–15

property ownership 14, 15
searches 120, 147
tapping devices 14
trespass 14
hostile intent 34–5, 37, 38, 63
hotspots of crime
  Germany 58
  identification, methods of 127
  reservation of CCTV for hotspots 149–50
Hudson, Barbara 86, 91
Human Rights Act 1998 176–7

identification of recorded individuals 78, 135, 166–9
illegal and unpleasant behaviour, distinction between 91
image processing 42
image, right to one's own 82–3
impact statements 162, 182
implementation of CCTV schemes 160–2
  budgeting and funding 160–1
  locations, selection of 160
  multi-agency cooperation 160
  periodic operational reviews 161–2
  regulation of CCTV schemes 160–2, 173–83, 186
  risk assessment 160, 161
  threats, conditional upon documented and significant 160
impulsive offenders 140, 142, 152
incident logs 161–2
incivilities 129, 151
increase in likelihood of apprehension and conviction 87–8, 93, 127–8, 132–46, 152
Information Commissioner's Code of Practice 45, 56, 59–60, 170, 178–83
informational preserves 19, 29
infra-red cameras 42, 44–5
inspections 171, 175, 182
institutional guarantees of anonymity 30
institutions, autonomy of persons in 113
intelligent cameras 42, 43–4, 46–7, 50–1
intervene to protect others, unwillingness to 123, 164
intimacy 1–2, 17, 96, 109–17, 120, 147, 157, 163
intimidation and coercion 87
intrusiveness of CCTV 21, 56–7, 62–85, 112, 154–5, 165

Jones, Richard 121
judicial controls 174, 175

Index   203

justifications of public CCTV surveillance 38–40 *see also* crime **prevention**; deterrence

late modern society, scope of anonymity in 36–9
legal representatives, examination of evidence by 170–1
legislation, regulation by 174–83
legitimate expectations 30–1, 34
legitimising role of crime prevention
  anonymity interests 93, 103–22
  civil liberties 118
  communal interests 119
  competing interests 93, 94–103
  danger, requirement of 121
  deterrence 94, 120
  direct intervention 94
  displacement of crime 118
  effectiveness of CCTV 130–46, 185–6
  fair treatment, offenders' claim to 118
  fear of crime 94, 120, 186
  guardianship, lack of 94, 122–3, 134, 145
  importance of crime prevention mission 117–30
  interests served by public CCTV 117–19
  objectives of CCTV 119–20
  persuasive force of crime prevention arguments 120–30
  privacy 93, 94–103
  private and family life, justification for interference with 93, 98–103
  pro-active policing 120–1, 127–8
  public interests 117–19, 186
  punishment, increase in likelihood of 93
  risk 121–2
  seriousness of crime 127–30
  suspicion, grounds for 122
  urgent action 121–8
  victims, rights of 117–19
left alone, right to be 107
liberalism 10, 13, 39
liberty values 7–8
lighting, improvements in 132
live monitoring systems 54, 59, 97–8, 132–5, 144–5, 164–5, 176
local authorities 41, 53, 57, 176–7, 181
location of cameras 58, 132, 160, 166
logs 161–2, 172, 180
Lyon, David 91–2

MacIntyre, A 39
maintenance logs 180

management and operation of control room 144, 160–2 *see also* **fair practice safeguards**; **personnel**
Mandrake, use in Newham of 47
manipulation of data 46, 135–6, 169
mapping crime 127, 160
margin of appreciation 101
Marshall, SE 97, 148, 153
master recordings, identification of 169
material access barriers 20–1
material expectations in public space 34–6
materiality, disclosure and 33–4
media 8, 56, 124–5, 141, 167, 182
microwave cameras 42, 45
military surveillance methods 44
minor matters, use of CCTV for 57, 129–30, 150–2, 177
mission statements 162
mobile cameras 44
mobile phones, use of 157–8
model for resolving conflicts between privacy interests and crime protection objectives 93–8
  European Convention on Human Rights model 93, 98–103
  Face and Gesture Recognition Working Group (European Commission) 50
  rights as trumps model 93, 94–5
  Schengen Information System 52
  von Hirsch model 95–8
monopoly over use of force, state's 41, 61
morality *see* ethics
multi-agency cooperation 53, 132, 160
Multi-Agency Crime Prevention Partnerships 53
multifunctional systems 43
multiplex analogue tape systems 45–6

Nagel, Thomas 3, 21
Nagin, DS 138
National Identity Register 52
national security 98, 155–6
necessity 56–7
negative judgment, fear of 7, 8
neutral concept of privacy 16–18, 31, 107
NHS detailed care record 52
night vision cameras 42, 44–5, 64, 163–4
nominative (personally identifying) data 47, 78
non-acknowledgment, practice of 21, 30
non-confrontation, rule of 28
non-judgmental, CCTV as 71–4
Norris, C 87
number plate recognition 51, 157

objectives of CCTV 119–20, 144
observer and observed, inequality of 61

obtrusive behaviour 34
occurrence logs 172
on-demand recording 45, 165
ONSET database 52
'one way mirror' 61, 64, 66
operation of control room 144, 160–2 *see also* fair practice safeguards; personnel

pan, tilt and zoom (PTZ) cameras 43–4, 50, 64, 74
Panopticon 63, 83, 88
passive monitoring *see* recording (passive or time-delayed) systems
performance assessments 171, 175
periodic operational reviews 161–2
persistent offenders 142
personal detachment 75
personal effects, possessional territory of 19
personal space 27
personally identifying data 47, 78
personnel
    backstage experts 84
    frontstage experts 84
    management and operation of control room 144, 160–2
    professionals 74–5, 133
    supervision 172–3
    training 173, 182
pervasiveness of CCTV 58, 149–52
placebo or dummy surveillance 43, 87, 155
police
    access 55
    active monitoring 54
    anonymity 53, 150
    CCTV technology 44
    Crime and Disorder Reduction Partnership schemes 176
    danger, requirement of 121
    degree of control 86–7
    despatching the police 84–7, 131, 134, 145, 164
    discretion 90
    distanciation 69
    help others, losing initiative to 164
    Home Office's Second CCTV Initiative 87
    home, protection of 111
    inadequacy of facilities 131, 145
    mobile cameras 44
    pro-active policing 120–1, 123, 127–8, 151
    problem-oriented policing 127
    propositional knowledge 68
    re-embedding of social relations 84
    resources, limited 150

    restricting options to commit crime 90
    reviewing policies 55–6
    'Ring of Steel' police initiative 56
    stop and search 116–17
    street crime, intervention in 131, 132, 134, 145
    visibility, reassurance through police 125
policy principles 55–6, 71–2, 125, 138, 147–59
political capital, using fear of crime as 125, 186
political speech 106
positioning of cameras 131, 144, 161
positive and nominative (personally identifying) data 47, 78
possessional territories 27
precautions taken by offenders 141–2
premeditation 140
presentation of self 22–4, 63–7, 78
press, freedom to 8
pressure to conform 28, 29, 63, 83–92, 143, 145
presumption of innocence 165
preventive evidence collection 152–4
privacy 5–11
    access control 5–11
    active surveillance 97–8
    agent, moral authority of individual as an 8
    anonymity 16, 80–1, 111–17, 159
    audio surveillance 163
    autonomy 7–9, 108–9, 185
    benefits and burdens, distribution of 97
    boundaries of private sphere, normative aspects of 11
    cars, monitoring people in their 157
    civil inattention, convention of 67
    claims to privacy 15–30
    communal benefits 108
    communal spaces, boundaries of private sphere in 16
    concept of privacy 2–15
    constitutive qualities 108
    crime prevention
        conflicts with privacy, model for resolving 95–8
        legitimising role of 93, 94–103
    decisional privacy 11, 14–15, 17–19
    degree of importance 109
    degree of interference 97
    demeaning, unwanted exposure as 7
    dignity 7, 8–11, 108, 185
    distanciation 60, 66–6
    encroachment of the State 11–12

ethics 5–10, 16, 185
exclusion of others 10, 16
fear of negative judgment 7, 8
freedom of speech 108–9
hierarchy of rights 95–8, 107–17
home, protection of the 109, 110–11, 115–17
identification of recorded individuals 167
impact statements 162, 182
Information Commissioner's Code of Practice 178, 181–2
informational privacy 11
instrumental qualities 108
intrusion 63–4
interference 107–9
intimacy 17–18, 96, 109–11, 113–14
left alone, right to be 107
liberty values 7–8
mundane matters 16
negative liberty, as 107
neutral concept of privacy 16–18, 31, 107
physical or emotional exposure 17
presentation of self 16, 18, 63–4
private life, justification for interference with 93, 98–103, 177, 183
private versus public dichotomy 12–15
public space, privacy interests in a 1, 15–30
regulation of CCTV 159, 173–4, 178, 181–3
reviewing, recording without 82–3
scope of privacy claim 10–12
scrutiny in public places, normative reasons for protection against
searches of private premises 95–6, 115–17, 147
self ownership or sovereignty 5–6
sensory privacy 11, 15
seriousness of crimes 96
social and working sphere 2–3
society, protection in and from 11–12
subjectivity 107
'three circle' theory 2–6, 17, 32–4, 95–8
training 173
trumps, rights as 93, 94–5
types of privacy interest 10–11
private enterprises 53, 123, 158–9
private territories in a public environment 18–22
private versus public dichotomy 12–15, 39–40
pro-active policing 120–1, 127–8

processing 42, 46, 135, 144, 176
property crimes 128, 131, 140, 145
property ownership 14, 15
proportionality 56–7, 99–101, 118
propositional knowledge 66, 68
psychosocial identity 168
PTZ (pan, tilt and zoom) cameras 43–4, 50, 64, 74
public authorities *see also* local authorities
    databases, data sharing with public sector 51–3
    government employees and people seeking public office 32–3
    private life, justification for interference with 93, 98–103
public figures, private lives of 13
public, informing the 41, 65, 139, 162–4, 179
public office, persons seeking 32–3
public order 38, 84, 129
public space, privacy interests in a 1, 15–30
public support 83
purpose specification principle 166, 178, 182

radio frequency identification (RFID) tags 49–50
rationality 126, 139–43, 146, 152
Rawls, John 25
Raz, Joseph 9
real space appraisal and CCTV surveillance, effects of 59–92, 185
reassurance, fear of crime and 125–6
reckless and intrusive behaviour 21
recording (passive or time-delayed) systems
    active monitoring 54, 164–5
    anonymity interests 77–84
    cameras with recording facilities 45
    data protection 59–60, 77
    disembedding, effect of 79–81
    duration of storage period 170–1
    evidence 152–4, 169–70
    exposure to an uninvited audience 81–2
    facial recognition software 78
    fixing of one's picture, implications of 77–9
    identification of recorded individuals 78, 166–9
    Information Commissioner
        Code of Practice 60
        registration with the 59–60
    intrinsically inappropriate measures 153
    on demand 45, 165
    passive versus active monitoring schemes 164–5

positive and nominative information 78
presentation of self 78
privacy 80–1
real space appraisal and CCTV surveillance, effects of 59–60
reviews 55–6, 63, 82–4, 97, 165–6, 171–2
self-consciousness 80
street crimes 144–5
third parties 56
tracing suspects 78
transparency 77
without reviewing, recording 82–4
record-keeping 171–2
'Red Road' 69–70
re-embedding of social relations 83–4
reflexive, monitoring as not being 61
registration of CCTV schemes 178
regulation of CCTV 159–83
  accountability 160
  administrative guidelines 174–5
  anonymity 159, 174–5
  codes of practice 175
  complaints 174
  Crime and Disorder Reduction Partnership schemes 176
  crime prevention 159, 173–4
  data protection 176, 178–83
  disciplinary procedures 174
  execution of surveillance 162–83
  Freedom (Great Repeal) Bill 177, 183
  Freedom of Information Act 2000 177
  Human Rights Act 1998 176–7, 183
  implementation of schemes 160–2, 173–83, 186
  Information Commissioner's Code of Practice 178, 179–83
  inspections 175
  judicial controls 174, 175
  legislation 174–83
  limitation, principles for 159–60
  performance assessments 175
  privacy 159, 177–8, 181–3
  private and family life, right to respect for 177, 183
  Regulation of Investigatory Powers Act 2000 177
  sanctions 174
  self-regulation 174–5
  structure of framework 173–5
  transparency 159–60
Regulation of Investigatory Practices Act 2000 56–7, 177

relevance, disclosure and 33
repressive regimes 87–8
reviewing of recordings 55–6, 63, 82–4, 97, 165–6, 171–2
reviewing, recording without 82–4
'Ring of Steel' police initiative 56
rise of the social 12
risk
  account, taking altered risks into 138, 139–41
  actuarial practices 73
  assessment 71–3, 122, 160, 161, 181
  comparative degrees of risk 127
  crime, restricting options to commit 90–1
  externalities 71–3
  fear of crime 125–6
  Information Commissioner's Code of Practice 181
  location, selection of 260
  management 71, 86, 90–1, 125–6
  periodic operational reviews 161
  rationality 126
  ritualistic risk management 126
  speculative, 90
  type-casting 149
Roberts, Paul 8–9, 17, 107
robotisation 42
role-playing 22–3
Rousseau, Jean-Jacques 5
routine activity theory 122
Ryan, Alan 3

safeguards 58, 83, 118, 171–3
sanctions 85–8, 91, 143, 174
Sandel, M 39
sanitisation of CCTV surveillance 74–7
Schauer, F 13, 16, 32–3, 111
Schengen Information System 52
Schoeman, Ferdinand 3
scrutiny 3, 17, 22–30, 33–4, 50, 79–81
searches 88–9, 95–6, 115–17, 120, 144, 147–50
seclusion 1, 10
secrecy 12, 24, 63, 65, 69, 76
self-consciousness 80
self-determination 18, 166
self-monitoring 180–1
self-ownership or sovereignty 5–6
self, presentation of 22–4, 63–7, 78
self-regulation 174–5
sensory access 66
sensory appraisal, limits of 20
sensory privacy 15
sentencing, proportionality 118
seriousness of crime 96, 128–30, 166–7
shame 89, 109

shoplifters 54, 158–9
situational boundaries 20–1, 30
situational crime prevention (SCP) 71, 133–4
skin and clothing, sheath of 19
smart cameras (algorithmic monitoring) 42, 43–4, 46–9, 50–1, 144
social and working sphere 2–3, 17, 32–4
social control 85–6, 122–3
social practices 24–6, 34–5
social relations, re-embedding 83–4
social rituals, supervision by officials of 41
social sorting 73
Sontag, Susan 125
spatial boundaries of access control in public spaces 30–1
speech, freedom of 95, 105–9, 177
spying 64–5, 88
Spriggs, Angela 144
state monopoly over use of force 41, 61
static surveillance 43
statistics
　deterrence of violent crime 140
　fall in crime rate 124, 130
　high-crime risk groups 74
　incidence of crime 161
　likelihood of punishment and crime rate, correlation between 137
　risk factors 149
　serious crimes, risk of 128
stop and search 116–17, 120
storage period 170–1, 180
street *see also* **street crime**
　discretion, conventions of 21–2
　liberalising function 115
　public location, as 16
　responsibilities towards people on the street 30
street crime 128–44
　active intervention in crimes in progress 132, 134, 144–5
　anonymity 37
　anti-social behaviour 128, 140
　apprehension and conviction, increase in likelihood of 132–3, 134–6, 152
　conventionality, low stakes in 143
　definition 128
　deterrence 133, 136–45
　dispatch facilities, inadequacy of 131, 145
　drug dealing and use 128, 140
　effectiveness of CCTV 130–46
　empirical studies, findings of 130–2
　examples 128–9
　future offender level, attacking crime on 133
　inadequate coverage 131
　lighting, improvements in 132
　likelihood of success of CCTV mechanisms 132–44
　mechanisms for combating street crime 132–44
　multi-agency responses 132
　opportunity reduction 133
　performance, factors effecting 131
　police intervention 131, 132, 134, 145
　professional personnel 133
　property crimes 128, 131, 140
　proximal situational level, attacking crime on 133
　seriousness of crime 128–9
　situational crime prevention 133–4
　targeted crime, wrong type of 132
　terrorism 128–9, 140, 141, 144
　vandalism 128, 143
　vehicle theft, lowering of 131
　violence, crimes of 128, 131, 140
　warning message, CCTV as a 134
suicide missions 144
supervision of surveillance personnel 172–3
surveillance practices 54–9
suspicion that a crime may occur
　crime-mapping 127
　data protection 180
　geographic profiling 127
　legitimising role of crime prevention 122
　probable cause 122, 127–8
　problem-oriented policing 127
　risk, comparative degrees of 127
　reasonable suspicion 58–9
　searches 96
　smart cameras 42, 43–4, 46–7, 50–1
　suspicious behaviour 42–7, 50–1
　urgent action 127–8
　wrong-doing, interference with people not suspected of 147–9, 166

tailing a person 57
talking cameras 44, 129, 163
tampering with recordings 46, 135–6, 169
tapping devices 14
targets, selection of 71–2, 132, 144, 146, 151–2
technocratic approach of CCTV 71–2
technology *see* **CCTV technology**
telephones, monitoring 69
television, residents watching CCTV on 55
temporary boundaries 30

territorial sovereignty 26
territories of the self 27, 31
terrorism
    covert surveillance 57
    deterrence 140, 141, 144
    effectiveness of CCTV 156
    national security 155–6
    policy principles 155–6
    smart cameras 50
    street crime 128–9, 140, 141, 144
    suicide missions 144
third parties' use of CCTV 56, 97
Thomson, JJ 7
'three circle' theory and right to anonymity
    anonymity conventions of public space 2, 3–4
    inner and intimate life 2, 17
    non-disclosure, entitlement to 2–5
    privacy interests 2–5, 6, 17, 95–8
    public activities, freedom from scrutiny with regard to 3, 17, 33–4
    social and working sphere 2–3, 17, 32–4
time-delayed systems *see* recording (passive or time-delayed) systems
torture 104
totalitarian, authoritarian or theocratic regimes 10, 13, 29
traffic offences 51, 58, 90, 129, 157–8
training 173, 182
transparency 59, 159–60
trouble-makers, targeting 151–2

trumps, rights as 93, 94–5
trust relations 35–6, 123
type-casting 59, 74, 148–9

unchosen others, encountering 19
United States, constitutional law in 8–9
unmanned surveillance vehicles (UAVs) 44
urgent action 28, 94, 120–8, 151, 153, 159, 173–4
use of force, state monopoly over 41, 61

vandalism 128, 143
vehicle theft, reduction in 131
victims 117–19, 148, 167
violent crimes 128, 140
virtual scrutiny compared to physical scrutiny 66–71
vision-enhancing technologies 60–1, 64, 74
von Hirsch, Andrew 1–5, 6, 10, 17, 18, 19, 21, 23, 25, 32–4, 93, 108, 118, 121, 126, 136–8, 142–3, 165

Webster, C 136–7
weight of rights 103–4, 106
Wikstroem, PO 136, 151–2
Wiles, P 73
witnesses 147–8, 167, 172
Work and Pensions Data Sharing 52
working and social sphere 2–3, 17, 32–4
wrong-doing, interference with people not suspected of 147–9

zero tolerance 130, 150–1